PRACTICAL PHONETICS
FOR STUDENTS OF
AFRICAN LANGUAGES

PRACTICAL PHONETICS FOR STUDENTS OF AFRICAN LANGUAGES

D. Westermann and Ida C. Ward

Introduction by
JOHN KELLY
University of York

KEGAN PAUL INTERNATIONAL
London and New York
IN ASSOCIATION WITH THE
INTERNATIONAL AFRICAN INSTITUTE

First published in 1930 and 1933
This edition published in 1990 by
Kegan Paul International Ltd
PO Box 256, London WC1B 3SW, England

Distributed by
John Wiley & Sons Ltd
Southern Cross Trading Estate
1 Oldlands Way, Bognor Regis,
West Sussex, PO22 9SA, England

Routledge, Chapman & Hall Inc
29 West 35th Street
New York, NY 10001, USA

The Canterbury Press Pty Ltd
Unit 2, 71 Rushdale Street
Scoresby, Victoria 3179, Australia

Printed in Great Britain by T.J. Press

British Library Cataloguing in Publication Data

Westermann, D. (Diedrich)
  Practical phonetics for students of African languages.
  1. African languages. Phonetics
  I. Title II. Ward, Ida C. (Ida Caroline) III. Kelly,
  John, *1936*–   IV. International African Institute
  496

  ISBN 0–7103–0295–9

US Library of Congress Cataloging in Publication Data
Applied for

CONTENTS

DIAGRAMS

INTRODUCTION

Reprinted in this volume are two works which deal with aspects of the study of African languages. They were both written by the same two authors and first published around sixty years ago under the auspices of the then International Institute for African Languages and Cultures (IIALC).

The IIALC was established in 1926 with its headquarters in London. At an inaugural meeting in June of that year the constitutions of a Governing Body and of an Executive Council were decided upon. The Governing Body was to be made up of representatives of all member institutions, and the Executive Council of not more than fifteen members of the Governing Body, under the Chairmanship of Lord Lugard. The member institutions included universities, learned societies, research councils, museums and missionary organisations. Two Directors were appointed, Professors D. Westermann of Berlin and M. Delafosse of Paris. On Professor Delafosse's death soon after appointment his place was taken by Professor H. Labouret, also of Paris.

The Institute's terms of reference were
- to act as a clearing-house for information
- to undertake and assist in anthropological and linguistic investigations
- to bring about a closer association of scientific knowledge and research with practical affairs

and were outlined by Lugard in an introductory article (Lugard 1928) written for the first number of the Institute's journal *Africa*.

Delegates to the 1926 meeting had heard an address from the then Minister for the Colonies which stressed the importance of education for the projected development of Africa and went on to commend matters of language to their particular attention. It was appropriate, then, that one of the first tasks undertaken was the preparation of a Memorandum on the writing of African languages. This was a matter of some urgency, given the emphasis placed by the Institute on the need for Africans to be educated in their own languages: and it was shown to be so by the number of appeals coming in to the Institute, then and later, for help with intransigent problems of orthography-making in African territories.

Westermann set about the task of producing this first Memorandum. He was at this time aged fifty-one and was Professor of African Languages and Cultures at the University of Berlin. He had lived for varying periods of time in Africa and had over seventy publications to his credit, including grammars of Ewe, Ful, Kpelle, Nama and Shilluk.

Westermann's first teaching post in Berlin he had taken up in 1903 at the invitation of Carl Meinhof, and it was under Meinhof's headship that he worked until 1909. One of Meinhof's preoccupations during his long career was with the development of a 'scientific' notation system and, alongside this, of 'practical' orthographies for African languages. As his basis for both he took the "Standard Alphabet" of Richard Lepsius (Kemp 1981), a system which he adapted in various ways. Meinhof was a member of the Institute and of the newly-formed Executive Council. In the first volume of *Africa* he presents his views on the subject of orthography-making in a paper (Meinhof 1928) submitted when the question of a Memorandum on the subject was first mooted. Together with his championing of the Lepsius system, in his own revised and extended version, he expresses his dislike of the system of the International Phonetic Association as a possible source of 'practical' orthographies: 'The newly invented letters of the Association Phonétique will,' he writes, 'except for a few happily chosen symbols, in all probability meet with the same fate as other such inventions'. He presses the point that it is a 'scientific' alphabet, whereas his own has a 'practical' application.

This comment relates to the fact that the Lepsius system, in Meinhof's modification of it, is based heavily on the Roman letter stock, together with a set of diacritical marks. It is a relatively straightforward process in such a case to move from a notation that is detailed and specific (='scientific') to one that is more abstract and general (='practical'), as this can be brought about by the omission of the diacritics. A good example of this is to be found at the beginning of the Konde section in Meinhof (1932). But it is disingenuous of Meinhof to suppose that other notation systems cannot be used in both a 'scientific' and a 'practical' mode, even if the move from the one to the other is made in some less simple way.

Westermann, who had been trained in the same tradition as Meinhof, had made extensive use of the system based on the Standard Alphabet. His work on Shilluk (Westermann 1912), for instance, sets out the vowels of the language with a at the apex of a triangle, and has a classificatory table for consonants which arranges them as follows:

	Mutes	Fricatives	Liquids	etc
Velars				
Palatals				
etc.				

Symbols included in the display are $\dot{n}$ for the velar nasal, η for the palatal nasal, $\underset{\sim}{d}$ for the voiced dental plosive and sh for the voiceless palatoalveolar fricative. All of these, together with the use of the italic fount throughout, are characteristic of the Lepsius system and recur elsewhere in Westermann's work, as in his Ewe grammar (Westermann 1907). It is not surprising, then, that a system very much like this reappears in his first attempt at a set of orthography proposals for the Institute's Memorandum. But a dramatic change was soon to take place.

In January of 1927 Westermann circulated an advance proof of his *Proposals for a Practical Orthography for African Languages*, with a request for comments. Recipients included members of the Executive Council such as Lugard and Labouret, but also Alice Werner, Arthur Lloyd James and Daniel Jones. This was in keeping with Lugard's exhortation that members of the Institute should be 'in personal touch with the scientists and experts of the world', and that their work should be founded on 'strictly scientific principles'. Alice Werner was at this time Professor of Swahili and Bantu Languages at the School of Oriental Studies in London. Lloyd James was about to take over the headship of the newly-established Department of Phonetics at the same institution. He had been one of the prime movers in the planning for an African Institute, and had a keen interest in the development of phonetically well-founded orthographies for African languages. Jones, for his part, was Professor of Phonetics in the University of London and had for some time been an office-holder of the International Phonetic Association. Like Meinhof, he had firm views on the preeminence of one particular system as the starting-point for work of the kind that the Institute wished to carry out, views he had expressed in print some years earlier (Jones and Plaatje 1916): 'Of the existing phonetic alphabets founded on the "one sound, one letter" basis the best is undoubtedly that of the International Phonetic Association'. In a later paper (Jones 1917) he presents Sechuana material in what he calls 'International Phonetic Orthography', an orthography which includes such IPA-based letters as ɟ, ɲ, ʃ, ɑ, and ɔ.

The *Proposals* that these scholars received from Westermann was a five-page pamphlet divided into three sections, namely: General Principles, Table of Sounds and Remarks. The Table of Sounds is in its layout not at all unlike that appearing in other works produced in the Meinhof tradition. All symbols are in italic fount, and include *ṯ*, *ḏ* for dental and *ṭ*, *ḍ* for retroflex plosives. The phonetic analysis leaves something to be desired: dental and retroflex *l*s are classified as 'liquids', whilst *tl*, *hl* and *tlh* are 'laterals'. The click symbols proposed are *c*, *q* and *x*.

The publication that eventually appeared under the Institute's imprint later in the year, though, bears only a superficial resemblance to the proof distributed in January. It is a sixteen-page booklet called *Memorandum I: Practical Orthography of African Languages*. A short preface is followed by two sections, Representation of Sounds and General Principles, the first of which concludes with a Table of Sounds. But the detail of this table is quite different from that in the proof. It is arranged differently, with a vertical listing of articulatory types and a right-to-left display of places of articulation moving from bilabial to laryngal. Vowels are set out with **a** at the base. Symbols now include ʃ, ʒ for the palatoalveolars and ʈ, ɖ for the retroflexes, and are printed in bold except when they are in running text. In other words, everything looks a good deal less like the Standard Alphabet and a good deal more like the system of the International Phonetic Association. Perhaps even more striking is the appearance of sections on 'Phonemes' and 'Diaphones', not found in the *Proposals*. In general matters the principle of the exclusion of diacritics and that of overall simplicity put forward by Westermann in the original document are maintained, and to these is added a principle of unitary letters for phonemes and for diaphones.

The Preface to this *Memorandum* says that 'The scheme has been drawn up in collaboration with experts in phonetics . . .', and Smith (1934) mentions Jones as one of Westermann's collaborators, though with no details as to the nature or extent of his involvement. In fact the conclusion must be drawn that Jones, who had been tireless in developing the principles of the International Phonetic Association and in advocating its applications, in effect rewrote Westermann's proposals. In so doing he introduced the IPA system together with such scientific notions as those of the phoneme and diaphone. The diaphone, in particular, is a concept closely associated with Jones, and could have come from nowhere else. Quite detailed evidence of Jones's influence on the contents of the *Memorandum* lies to hand in the presence there of favourite quotations of his from books on typography and psychology. These are brought in to justify the ban on diacritics, and reappear in Jones (1942). Two Italian examples used in the section on Phonemes also make their appearance in the third and subsequent editions of Jones's major work on English phonetics (Jones 1932).

A final pointer to Jones's close involvement is the fact that it was he, and not Westermann, who wrote a reply to Meinhof's paper in the first volume of *Africa* mentioned above. In his paper Jones (1928) is at pains to be placatory, stressing firstly the points on which Meinhof's approach and the Institute's final one are in accord: only then does he go on to discuss differences. Throughout his paper Jones refers to the 'authors' of the *Memorandum*, using a plural; and it seems safe to believe that his role in all of the Institute's orthography work was a considerable one. At a meeting of the Executive Council in November 1927 Westermann was open in his admission that 'numerous enquiries on questions of orthography had been received, and in dealing with these he had received valuable assistance from Professor Jones'.

The cumulative effect of the changes made to Westermann's original draft is to make the final product look more 'modern', 'international' and 'scientific' in the sense of taking cognisance of developments in the linguistic theory of the day. And these were exactly the qualities that the Institute had an avowed interest in seeing embodied in its work and its products.

Reception of the booklet on publication was mixed. The real practicality of the system was questioned by some commentators, such as a correspondent from Southern Sudan who pointed out that, because of the Institute's use of the 'long f' for the voiceless bilabial fricative, no systematic use of italics would be possible. He objects, too, to the anonymity of the authors and suggests that there should have been greater representation amongst the authorship of people familiar with the problems of teaching writing in the field. A reviewer in the *Geographical Journal* for March 1928 points out that Africans will still have to learn French and English in their traditional orthographies alongside their own languages in new orthographies, and identifies this as a likely source of confusion. The same reviewer fails totally to grasp the phoneme and diaphone concepts and ends by casting ridicule on the whole undertaking.

Comment from professional linguists was on the whole kinder. Lloyd James supplied a paper for *Africa* (Lloyd James 1928a) in which he completely endorses the approach set out in the *Memorandum*. And from overseas the Bantuist C. M. Doke wrote to Westermann in November of 1927 to congratulate him – 'I have not seen anything to equal it for conciseness, simplicity and general usefulness'. To those linguists who expressed misgivings on points of detail Westermann was conciliatory, as in a letter of

December 1927 to the Hausa scholar G. P. Bargery. Almost nobody liked ʃ, Bargery included. Westermann wrote 'If you prefer š instead of ʃ there is no objection whatever', and he sums up '(it) intentionally leaves a considerable number of problems undiscussed. It wants no more than to lay a foundation'.

Despite the fact that it was not an unqualified success the new orthography made rapid strides during the next few years. It was adopted for Ewe in 1927 and was introduced into Westermann's Ewe-English dictionary (Westermann 1928) and into the English translation of his Ewe grammar (Westermann 1930) 'since this script is now taught in the schools'. Westermann made a tour of West Africa in 1929, as a result of which the 'Africa' alphabet, as it was then coming to be called, was adopted for Efik, Mande and other languages. A list of these opens the second, revised and enlarged, edition of the *Memorandum*, published in 1930.

In the preparation of the second edition Westermann had the assistance of Ida Ward. Miss Ward had joined the staff of Jones's department at University College London, in 1919 at the age of thirty-nine. Tucker (1950) takes the story further: 'It was while lecturing at University College to missionaries that her interests turned towards West African languages – Kanuri, Igbo and Efik were her first fields of African research. . . She assisted in the preparation of the revised *Practical Orthography of African Languages* and translated into English from Professor Westermann's German'. Westermann himself later (Westermann 1950) implied that she had been solely responsible for the second edition.

The second edition is the one reprinted in this volume. It falls into four parts, Introduction, Representation of Sounds, General Principles, and Principles of Orthography, instead of the earlier three. But this is a specious distinction, as the 1927 version contains a section that amounts to 'principles of orthography' under 'General Principles'. In fact the two versions have a lot in common. The 1930 Introduction is entirely new, and the specimens of languages are increased from seven to twenty-two: but, apart from these differences, a lot is retained, particularly in the spirit of the endeavour. Discussions are more extensive, and those on clicks, implosives, and tone are new, and enlarge the 'foundation' of Westermann's letter to Bargery. Most of the innovations arose from the frenzy of activity and publication that there had been between the time of the first edition and this second one. All of the books and papers listed on pp.7–8 of the 1930 edition came out during those three years; and in both 1928 and 1929 Westermann had made visits to Africa to confer and advise on matters of orthography-making.

The missionary zeal of the writers of the 1930 edition extended to the inclusion of proposals for languages already provided with institutionalised orthographies. Swahili is such a case. A conference held in Dar-es-Salaam in 1925 had led to recommendations for a standardised Swahili spelling which ultimately included neither c nor ŋ. One Swahili grammar published in London at this time (Werner and Werner 1927) includes a note to say that 'The spelling used is that sanctioned by the Dar-es-Salaam Standardisation Committee of 1925'. But c and ŋ still appear in the 1930 version of the *Memorandum*, since the 'standardised' equivalents do not, of course, accord with the principles that underlie the Institute's approach.

Added complexity arose in this case from the fact that Meinhof, who was closely involved in the deliberations in East Africa on the future of Swahili spelling, himself perversely, but predictably, stuck to a Standard Alphabet type of notation for such important publications as the English version (Meinhof 1932) of his 1899 *Grundriss einer Lautlehre der Bantusprachen*.

Despite the confidence and energy of its makers, though, and despite the promotional work carried out in Africa by Westermann and later by Miss Ward, the Africa alphabet in later years encountered difficulties even in places where it had seemed at the beginning to have had happy prospects. A prescient reviewer in *West Africa* in April 1931 points out that in the case of Yoruba 'it is still possible that the old orthography, founded as it is on a fairly wide literature and vernacular press, may prove triumphant over its more scientific competitor'. And in April of 1937 the Director of Education for the Gold Coast was to write to the Institute that 'considerable opposition to the introduction of the script has been experienced, one main criticism being that it has not been widely accepted in this continent'.

A further, modified, version of the *Memorandum* was proposed at a meeting held in London in June of 1937 and chaired by Westermann. Jones, Miss Ward and Labouret attended. Before the meeting was a suggestion that ' a simplified form of the Orthography Memorandum should be prepared for use in French territories . . . and a similar Memorandum for use in English territories might also be of use. In both cases the Memorandum would be intended for the use of Africans rather than Europeans'. It was agreed that a draft, to be prepared by Miss Ward, should concern itself primarily with West Africa.

A number of drafts were in fact prepared by Miss Ward during 1938 and 1939 and were commented on by Westermann, Jones and A. N. Tucker, an erstwhile student in Jones's department and later on the staff of the Africa Department at the School of Oriental Studies. Westermann's comments on the final draft were sent from Berlin in May of 1939. Only a few months later contact between the two sides was to be abruptly broken off by the hostilities of the Second World War: and these versions of the *Memorandum* appear never to have been printed.

The 1930 edition has stayed in print, in the English version. The French and German versions never sold as well. Permission was given in 1947 for the type for the French version to be broken up; and in 1946 over 200 copies of the German version still remained in stock. An attempt by the Institute's then Director to sell them to German booksellers provoked the comment from the German side that 'The Memorandum is of not much use today and has more an historical as [sic] a practical interest'. Whatever its practical value, its historical interest is beyond dispute. The Africa alphabet, apart from its more or less successful role as a vehicle for a number of modern African languages, has appeared in a large number of reference works as a kind of honorary alphabet for African languages in general, much as the Institute intended. These standard works include several volumes of the Institute's own *Handbook* series, Ward's own pioneering works on Efik (Ward 1933) and Yoruba (Ward 1952) and such recent books as *The Languages of Ghana* (Kropp Dakubu 1988). Already in the 1930s there were plans to extend its use to other continents: and it later appears as the 'World

Alphabet' (Jones 1948). The fact that the 'World Alphabet' looks as it does is to be traced back to the discussions that took place in London in 1927 between the then Director of the IIALC and the phoneticians of University College.

The later fate of the Africa alphabet and its rivals in Africa has been discussed in detail by Tucker (Tucker 1971) and will not be recapitulated here. To do this would take us well beyond our purpose, which is to chronicle the background to the impressive and influential work done in concert by Westermann and Ward. But reference to what has been said above about the situation in Swahili will show that the much-desired unification of African orthographies was not to come about easily.

The collaboration between these two scholars, which began with their joint work on the 1930 edition of the *Memorandum*, continued until Ida Ward's death. But the sole work to carry their names as joint authors is *Practical Phonetics for Students of African Languages* (henceforth *PP*). This was published in 1933 and is the first of the two works reprinted here.

This book is striking in the way in which it addresses the aims of the Institute, which again sponsored publication. It is based on the first-hand work of two skilled and experienced investigators, who supplement their own knowledge with information from trusted sources: and it is concerned at all points with practical problems of language-learning and orthography-making. A foreword by Daniel Jones commends the book because of its potential contribution to the solving of practical difficulties.

The inspiration for the book is perhaps to be found in a paper on the phonetics of African languages by Lloyd James (Lloyd James 1928b). In it he writes:

the man who is called upon to study any of the languages of Africa would be well advised to avail himself as soon as possible of the services of skilled phoneticians, for they and they alone can put him in the way of learning both to hear and make the extraordinary sounds that he is sure to find. This is not the place for a detailed account of African vowel and consonant sounds, concerning the nature and distribution of which much research work remains to be done.

Lloyd James goes on to list the 'features of a spoken language necessary to intelligibility':

1 the sounds, vowel and consonant
2 relative length of sounds
3 relative pitch of voice in sounds
4 relative loudness of sounds

and it is interesting to see that *PP* deals with the first three of these in the order given.

The manuscript of the book was with the Institute in October of 1932 and it was published in the following September at a price of eight shillings and sixpence. The authors were offered, and accepted, a joint royalty of ten per cent rising to twelve and a half per cent after the sale of one thousand copies.

Reviews were, generally speaking, enthusiastic. Lloyd James had only praise for the book (Lloyd James 1934); and Jones only very minor criticisms (Jones 1933–35), befitting for one who had written in his Foreword that it was 'as perfect as a book of its kind can be'. More serious criticism came, again, from overseas, and from scholars less closely associated with the Institute and the two authors. Both Meyer (Meyer 1934) and Pienaar (Pienaar 1934) regretted the absence of information on instrumental investigation and of actual instrumental explorations themselves: all that *PP* contains of this kind are the kymograph traces on p. 93. Meyer also comments unfavourably on the use made of the phoneme concept, seeing its introduction as an unhappy amalgam of phonetics and linguistics. This phrase is a reminder that for many the traditional approach to phonetics on the European mainland was as a physical science not integral with the study of language. Meyer also misses discussions of sound-change. In this she is less than just, since quite a lot on sound-change is to be found in *PP*, albeit often by implication.

It is, of course, impossible to satisfy everyone. On the other side of the Atlantic Sapir (Sapir 1936) remarks that 'the concept of the phoneme . . . is not sharply enough defined nor is it carried far enough'. Other than this he comments, as other reviewers had, on African language phenomena omitted by the writers. In Sapir's case he missed particularly the mora concept and mention of the 'heavy' syllables discussed in his own work on Gweabo (Sapir 1931).

But all reviewers end by paying tribute to the book. To Sapir it is 'a truly valuable guide', to Lukas (Lukas 1934) 'outstanding'. A number of years later Trubetzkoy was to refer to it as a 'valuable handbook' (Trubetzkoy 1939), though again with reservations on points of detail.

One feature of *PP* that met with unanimous approval was the inclusion of nine 'Phonetic Summaries'. This, in Sapir's view, 'adds materially to the practical usefulness of the volume', whilst for Lukas they are 'more than usually instructive'.

PP shows many small signs of having been put together in something of a hurry. It should have been published early in June of 1933, but a revision of galleys made this impossible, and at the end of June the Index still had to be prepared. Both authors spent portions of that year abroad, Westermann in South Africa, Ward in West Africa on her first visit to the continent. To this circumstance we might perhaps ascribe the fact that (despite the galley revisions) quite a lot of minor imperfections remain in the published book. It would be out of place to catalogue all of them here, but some of the kinds of errors that appear can be mentioned. Attentive readers will find others for themselves.

There are a number of inconsistencies. Duala **mbɔti** 'garment/unripe bananas' and **koka** 'grow' are given with different syllabifications and different tone-marks on pp. 135 and 155. What are called 'labio-velar' plosives on p. 58 are 'velar labials' (and 'velar-labials') on p. 108. What is referred to as the 'Preface' on p. 27 is in fact the 'Acknowledgements'; there is no 'Preface'. A more detailed proof-reading would have captured these things, and other such details as the unnecessary heading 'Table 1' on p. 46: there are no subsequent Tables, and this one is already adequately labelled 'Fig. 13'.

There are quite a lot of misprints. The Dinka word for 'thirst' is given in two forms (pp. 45, 210), one of which is probably a misprint. The Kikuyu word for 'bush' is another example (pp. 80, 216). 'Cardinal No. 5' on p. 159 is probably a misprint for '6', as German *Gott* is referred to Cardinal Vowel No. 6, not 5, on p. 167. Kikuyu **moðɛnya** is glossed differently on pp. 80 and 215.

Curious omissions might also be the result of overhasty proof-reading. In the Yoruba Summary, for instance, the list of consonants omits **k** and **g** although both are present in Yoruba words used as examples in the same section.

A more serious defect is the cavalier approach to references, many of which are given without dates or are incomplete in other ways.

One last matter of presentation concerns the Index, where there are again errors. Under Kakwa 'velarised sounds' is entered; but the passage referred to, paragraph 332, tells us that Kakwa has no velarised sounds. **ny** and **nyy** are listed under Kinga with a reference to paragraph 186; but all the Kinga examples in the list there are of **nyy**. 'Articulation, double' is given in the Index, but there are no entries for 'primary' or 'secondary', though both are used in the text. Under 'Amharic' we have 'pharyngal fricative' and a reference to paragraph 247: but there is no mention of Amharic in this paragraph, rather of Arabic, which is not entered in the Index. These few examples suffice to show that it is to be used with caution.

Of the deficiencies listed above, none is of great substance from our present-day standpoint. The bibliography and references are of historical interest only and can be retrieved from other sources: and the errors and inconsistencies are trivial matters.

The book is to be judged rather on its worth as an introduction to the subject of its title. To the question 'How well does *PP* stand up now as a text on its chosen subject?' the answer has to be 'Remarkably well' – and that nearly sixty years after its first publication. One reason for this is that both authors had come to academic careers after periods spent in other fields, Westermann as a missionary, Ward as a schoolteacher, which required the gift of a clear and direct manner in imparting information. For the rest, it is well summed up in Lloyd James's review:

> . . . nothing but the truth, acquired by personal investigation and put to the test in the hard school of practical teaching . . . no airy theory . . . no fanciful philology, and no concession to the fanatical amateur.

And at the time of writing *PP* the authors were at the peak of their powers. Ward had not yet been to Africa, it is true, but she had done some ten years' work on a number of African languages, including that on Efik that was to bring her the degree of D.Litt.; and she had had these years of experience in a department that was at the forefront of developments in practical phonetics.

It seems reasonable to suppose that the plan of the book was contributed substantially by Miss Ward. At a later time Westermann was to write that 'her contribution was the lion's share' (Westermann 1950), and we might be justified in thinking that most of the phonetic writing is hers. Certainly there are many echoes of the formulations in her earlier *Phonetics of English* (Ward 1929). 'Plosive consonants' is a case in point. In the book on English we have 'Plosive consonants are made by the stoppage of the air at some point'; in *PP* 'A plosive consonant is formed by stopping the air passage at some point', and in both books reference is made in the section on phonemes to the same passage in Jones's earlier work (Trofimov and Jones 1923; both the date and the sequence of names are wrong in the *Phonetics of English* citation). Innumerable other repetitions of Ward's phraseology turn up, such as the 'black pin' example of p. 58 and the unusual term 'semi-rolled', both of which are in her book on Efik published in the same year as *PP*.

Indeed, the general plan of *The Phonetics of English* may have served as a basis for the groundplan of the new book, as already suggested above. The plan of *PP* is very similar to that of *The Phonetics of English*, which includes amongst its chapters

Ch 7 Organs of Speech
Ch 8 Classification of sounds: vowels and consonants
Ch 9 Phonemes
Ch 10 English vowels
Ch 11 English diphthongs
Ch 12 Nasalisation of vowels
Ch 13 Classification of consonants: English consonants in detail

These can be set against the sequence of chapters 3 to 16 in *PP*, and the overall pattern seen to be the same. The justification for the consonantal progression, which is that of other influential books on phonetics at the time, is of course that it moves from closer to more open articulatory types.

One interesting difference between the two books is the replacement of the term 'affricative' (*Phonetics of English*) by 'affricate' (*PP*), and the parallel change in the way in which the sound-type in question is viewed. *The Phonetics of English* takes the affricative to be a kind of plosive 'An affricative is a plosive consonant in which the articulatory organs are separated less quickly. . .', whilst *PP* has 'the affricate . . . can be considered as a group of two sounds, stop and fricative'.

In keeping with these two analyses the order of treatment is different: the English book deals with affricatives in the section on plosives and before fricatives have been reached, whereas *PP* deals with affricates after both plosives and fricatives have been described, as both are needed for the new definition. The same switch is made in the writings of Jones, but in his case quite a lot earlier.

A good deal of the phonetic theory in *PP* derives from that of Jones, as might be expected. But sometimes special areas, not handled by him, are being written about; and it is in one or two of these that the touch is least sure. The two most requiring comment are those that we now label air-stream mechanisms and multiple articulation. Both have to be discussed in a book on the phonetics of African languages, but in neither case is what we find particularly satisfying from our modern point of view.

Ejectives, for instance, are described in such a way as to confound them with glottalised plosives, since no notion equivalent to Pike's of an initiatory mechanism (Pike 1943) was available to Westermann and Ward: and for them the term 'ejective' covers Hausa ʔ, j amongst other things.

Implosives fare better. Here an initiatory function is recognised, though not, of course, named as such. But since no system of airstream mechanisms is recognised, ingressive varieties of **kp** are discussed alongside ɓ, ɗ as though on a par with them.

In the matter of multiple articulation, although the terms 'double', 'secondary' and 'primary' are used, they are not used systematically. The result is an unhappy muddle, helped into being by the authors' inability to keep their terms strictly within the descriptive domain. Inconsistency arises, for instance, between 'palatalisation'

> the raising of the front of the tongue *towards* [my emphasis] the hard palate as a secondary articulation added to the main articulation of a consonant' (p. 105)

and 'velarisation'

> the adding of a velar articulation (i.e. the back of the tongue *at* [my emphasis] or near the soft palate) to some other consonantal articulation (p. 107)

The difference between these two definitions is striking. Not only does the second allow any velar articulation, it admits an interpretation in terms of sequence, because of the ambivalence of its wording. The definition of palatalisation admits this much less readily. The second definition allows the writers of *PP* to give as examples of velarised consonants such words as **kutʃka** and **fodʒga** given by Doke (Doke 1931) for Zezuru. But this is clearly not velarisation in the sense of modern textbooks on phonetics. The term is being used here by Doke to refer to both a supposed historical process and the outcome of that process, namely, a range of phonetic phenomena in the varieties of Shona. Some of these phenomena are phonetic sequences, as are **tʃk** and **dʒg**. According to Doke **dʒg** is 'sometimes heard almost as **dʒᵊg**', an even more extensive phonetic sequence. This **dʒᵊg** is unitary from the phonological point of view, but not from the phonetic; and the use of the term 'velarisation' to describe it is a philological and phonological use. It is a pity that this section of *PP* is marred by the failure to draw these distinctions. To have done so, though, would have been to show a degree of analytical sophistication rather in advance of the time.

The negative or critical remarks above relate to only a small part of the book. And, in the matter of theoretical niceties, it has to be said that at that period other workers had done little better, and many far worse. It was to be left to phonetic theoreticians such as Catford (Catford 1939) and Pike to unravel some of these difficulties later.

Leaving aside these imperfections, we are still provided with an amount and range of information that is truly awesome, particularly in the context of the time. The languages drawn on cover practically the whole of Africa, the phonetic and phonological phenomena discussed are highly varied, and include tempo features, grammatical correlates, and such things as would be dealt with later under the heads of 'juncture', 'sandhi' and 'phonotactics'. Comparative information is often brought in, as is (*pace* Meyer's review) some historical speculation and reconstruction. Wisely, the authors refer consistently to general categories, such as, say, back unrounded vowels, quite separately from tokens of these categories. Thus, when they are unable to exemplify back unrounded vowels from any language known to them their introduction of the category still equips the student with the theoretical and descriptive framework to deal with such vowels readily should he or she come across them, as Ward herself did a few years later (Ward 1937–39). It is noteworthy that Westermann and Ward never claim that this or that phonetic type doesn't exist in African languages: the claim is simply that they have not found it. Under 'syllables', for instance, the wording is carefully put so as to allow for the existence of syllabic fricatives such as those of Lendu (Tucker 1967) or Fang (Kelly 1974), even though the authors of *PP* have no experience of them. This broad-minded approach contrasts with an unhealthy overgeneralisation that defaces a good deal of what had been written about African languages in the earlier years of the century.

By dealing with so many things that they do have first-hand experience of Westermann and Ward bestow on their book an authenticity and an immediacy that are quite out of the ordinary run, and that are only enhanced by the modesty of the claims that the authors make for their expertise. Some things they admit to knowing little about, thereby giving added authority to what they do claim to have experienced.

Perhaps the best way to arrive at an assessment of the quality of the work in *PP* is to put it side by side with extracts from comparable publications of roughly the same period. Here are some pieces of phonetic description:

> *W, B,* and *V* are common ways of pronouncing a single peculiar sound, distinct from them all, and widely used in Bantu. . . It is in fact a *W* pronounced with an approximation to *B* on the one hand, or to *V* on the other.

This is Madan (Madan 1911), and it is not helpful as a characterisation of a voiced bilabial fricative or frictionless continuant. Nor can any of the following, from Crabtree (1922), be recommended to students of African languages:

> 'd' in African phonetics is only a slightly stressed 'l', not a distinct consonant
> a very brief consideration shows that by protruding the lips a point is soon reached where it is impossible to produce 'g' or 'k'
> velar nasal is merely a stressing of nasalised 'g'

And matters have not improved a quarter of a century later. The following are from Homburger (1949):

> . . . many syllables begin with a double consonant noted *kp, gb* . . . Some authors say there is double simultaneous occlusion: but the ears hear the consonant when the air escapes, so we are sceptical as to the absolute synchronisation of the guttural and labial elements
> All languages distinguish *a, e, ê, i, o, õ, u*
> All Negro-African languages use the four nasals *m, n, ñ, ṅ*
> Plosive gutturals are much used in dialects, but the semi-plosive *x, ġ* (like Scotch *ch* and Spanish *j*) are not common and always dialectal

These extracts show the remnants of a long tradition of imprecision and ignorance in the study of the sounds and sound-systems of African languages. They also give a hint of the perennial dark confusion that existed in the minds of investigators about the difference between sounds and their systems. The presentation of **d** as 'a kind of **l**' arises from such phonological patternings as that exhibited by Swahili *ulimi* 'tongue'/*ndimi* 'tongues'. But this relationship is, of course, without prejudice for the phonetic analysis of **d**, and to try to base the latter on the former is to end up producing phonetic gibberish. These kinds of horrors *PP* spares us. It tells us quite a lot about relationships and patternings, but the phonetic analysis is done independently of these, not derived from them: an unhappy exception is the case discussed above of 'velarisation'. The phonetic analysis in *PP* is based on the best teaching available at the time and on a wealth of practical experience of both impressionistic and instrumental work. The book stands out as a monument of good practice and, since the rudiments of good practice endure, has to it a modern feel that belies its date of publication. It can, then, still be recommended as a very worthwhile textbook to students of African languages or of phonetics and linguistics in the colleges and universities.

By 1946 the print run of some twelve hundred copies was exhausted, and the publisher proposed to the Institute that the book should be allowed to go out of print. Daryll Forde, the then Director, solicited Miss Ward's opinion. The reply came that 'Professor Ward is very anxious that this book should not go out of print. . . She would like to revise it, but doesn't know when she could find the time to do it'. The publisher, though, settled the matter by declining to reset the book unless the Institute would share the costs. This proposal, set out in a letter of December of 1947, was followed by one of two days later to say 'If the corrections were withdrawn I should be prepared to reprint this book by photo-lithography and to publish it at 12/6 without any financial help'. The letter ends 'I think Dr Ward limited her corrections partly because the book is wanted very urgently by colonial service students and partly because we hoped they could be incorporated in such a way that the book could still be reprinted photographically. But they were too numerous for that'. The Secretary of the Institute replied a week later 'I saw Professor Ward yesterday and she has agreed to confine her corrections in this book to those which can be listed on one page as corrigenda. She also wishes a number of pages at the end of the book to be omitted'.

The result of this agreement was that when the second edition of *PP* appeared in 1948 it was virtually identical with the first – as far as it went. The lack of revision meant that the references were now very much out of date and that some of the information on them was simply wrong, such as the note on p. 141 that Beach's work on Hottentot was 'not yet published'. It had appeared in 1938!

A more serious drawback than this, though, was the removal of the Phonetic Summaries, which was a disaster in a number of ways.

Firstly, none of the references to them scattered through the body of the text was removed. They were still to be found on pp. 27, 73, 77, and 80 of the second edition, and elsewhere, and appeared in the Index under Ganda and Kikuyu.

Secondly, the removal of the Summaries deprived the book of what was for many linguists a chief centre of interest. A number of phonologists working in the field of general theory had used *PP* as a sourcebook, just as much later Chomsky and Halle (1968) used such books as Ladefoged (1964). Two of these were Jones and Trubetzkoy. There are several references to the Westermann and Ward work in Jones's work on the phoneme (Jones 1950) and in Trubetzkoy's treatise on phonological theory (Trubetzkoy 1939). In both cases all of these references are to the Summaries: and it is to the detriment of the book that they were removed.

It is not easy to discern a convincing reason for this alteration to the second edition. Ward writes in the revised Acknowledgements (which is presumably the 'one page' of corrigenda) that 'more extensive and more accurate information on most of the languages dealt with has appeared'. But had it? Armstrong's Kikuyu (Armstrong 1940) and Welmers's Fanti (Welmers 1946) are the two works on relevant languages that spring to mind as having come out during the fifteen years in question: but nothing of great moment had appeared on any of the other languages. The use of the word 'accurate' by Ward suggests that some of what was contained in the Summaries was inaccurate. Now this was true in one case, namely the Zulu. But this was true in the first place: it did not become so between 1933 and 1948. We will explore this a little further.

The ways the Summaries were made varied and their value is, correspondingly, variable. In some cases work was apparently carried out expressly for the purpose of making the Summary. Yoruba seems to be a case of this; the claim is made explicitly on p. 171. The Ewe we must take to be Westermann's first-hand work, and it presents what appears to be his first published piece on the Ge variety of Ewe, spoken mainly in Togo.

In the case of the Zulu it appears that a digest was made of the work of another scholar. So, although the Zulu Summary is said to be 'contributed by Dr C. M. Doke', it differs in small ways from Doke's material (Doke 1926), ways that suggest that it might have been the work of another hand. All the examples used are in Doke's book, as are such terms as 'plain' (for a category of consonant) repeated in *PP* on p. 197. But the examples are frequently simplified. Doke gives ìsɪhá:m̥mbɪ (five syllables) for 'visitor'; this is altered in two ways, by the removal of a syllable and by changes in the vowel symbols. In a similar way Doke's transcriptions u:ɬɔ́:ɓɔ and ìzɪntɬɔ́:ɓɔ 'species' are replaced by simplified (and, for the second and plural form, erroneous) versions. Doke's form in 'tortoise' is simplified to **mpf'**: and his comment on ꞓ that 'in current Zulu orthography this fricative is not distinguished from the unvoiced form. Boyaert and Samuelson use *hh* to signify it . . .' is misconstrued into the statement that **hh** is used 'in current orthography'. There is nothing at all in the Zulu Summary, then, that cannot be had in a more detailed and correct version in Doke's original. And there is nothing explicit in *PP* to explain the principles of simplifying transcriptions.

The other Summaries are in a much better case, for they give an appreciable amount of detailed and reliable information, some of it subtly observed and much of it made available here for the first time. An example of this is the Fante Summary. The observations made there on **p** and **k** (p. 176) are in complete accordance with those made by myself in recent work with a Fante speaker carried out before the *PP* Summary was consulted. And work of a more restricted compass on Kikuyu has also produced results in line with those contributed to *PP* by Armstrong.

Were doubts about the quality of the Zulu Summary behind the decision to withdraw all of them in 1948? I can find in the literature only one other possible contributory factor – and this is that Trubetzkoy, in just one of his references to *PP*, is critical of an aspect of the tonal analysis of Fante. Might oversensitivity to criticism from a distinguished co-worker have had a part to play too? These must remain for the moment matters for speculation.

The book was never properly revised. The second edition contains the names of African countries as they were in the early thirties and recommends Linguaphone records that became unavailable long ago. The number of anachronisms has, inevitably, increased with time. So we read on p. 159 that Ward's book on Yoruba is 'in the press'; the book came out in 1952.

This second edition went through a number of reprints. Its continued existence in print was always, though, the result of pressure from the Institute: letters from the publisher regularly suggest that it should be allowed to go out of print. In response to one of these, written in 1974, the then Director, David Dalby, urged that it be reprinted on the grounds that it was 'a classic of its kind'. This is undeniable. And in some ways it is a classic of its time, too, as it shows us exactly where phonetic scholarship had got to in 1933 in the hands – and minds – of two serious and sensitive professionals.

But beyond this there is an air of timelessness about the book – of a world created and lived in – that is its most compelling quality. It is this quality, the mark of a classic, that has led us to reissue the original, 1933, edition here.

Ida Ward died in 1949. She joined the School of Oriental Studies in 1932 and in 1937 became the first Head of the new Department of the Languages and Cultures of Africa. In 1944 the title of Professor of West African Languages was bestowed on her. She retired in 1947. Throughout her career she maintained a close involvement with the work of the International African Institute, as its name became, being a member of the Governing Body from 1936 on, and Chairman of the Linguistic Advisory Committee from 1944 until the time of her death.

Writing to the Institute from Germany on receipt of the news of Ward's death, Westermann commented 'Professor Ward leaves a real gap in the whole range of African linguistic studies for nobody can do the work she has been doing'.

He himself was still in an academic post at this time. He retired in 1950 from his Chairs in Phonetics and African Studies and from the headship of the Berlin Phonetic Institute. He carried on, though, with the editorship of the *Zeitschrift für Phonetik* until his death, and his association with the International African Institute too he sustained up to the end of his life. Westermann, described by Daryll Forde as 'the outstanding figure in the development of African linguistic studies in this century', died in 1956.

JOHN KELLY

References

Armstrong, L. E. (1940): *The Phonetic and Tonal Structure of Kikuyu*, Oxford.
Catford, J. C. (1939): 'On the classification of stop consonants', *Le Maitre phonetique* 65, 2–5.
Chomsky, N. & M. Halle (1968): *The Sound Pattern of English*, New York.
Crabtree, W. A. (1922): *Primitive Speech. Pt I. A Study in African Phonetics*, London.
Doke, C. M. (1926): *The Phonetics of the Zulu Language*, Johannesburg.
—— (1931): *A Comparative Study in Shona Phonetics*, Johannesburg.
Homburger, L. (1949): *The Negro-African Languages*, London.
Jones, D. (1917): 'The phonetic structure of the Sechuana language', *Transactions of the Philological Society* 1917–20, 99–106.
—— (1928): 'Principles of practical orthography for African languages', *Africa* 1, 237–239.
—— (1932): *An Outline of English Phonetics* (3rd ed.), Cambridge.
—— (1933–35): Review of *PP*, *BSOAS* 7, 1020–1021.
—— (1942): *The Problem of a National Script for India*, Hertford.
—— (1948): *Differences between Spoken and Written Language*, London.
—— (1950): *The Phoneme, its Nature and Use*, Cambridge.
Jones, D. & S. T. Plaatje (1916): *A Sechuana Reader*, London.
Kelly, J. (1974): 'Close vowels in Fang', *BSOAS* 37, 119–123.

Kemp, J. A. (ed.) (1981): *Standard Alphabet* (of R. Lepsius), Amsterdam.

Kropp Dakubu, M. E. (1988): *The Languages of Ghana*, London.

Ladefoged, P. (1964): *A Phonetic Study of West African Languages*, Cambridge.

Lloyd James, A. (1928a): 'The practical orthography of African languages', *Africa* 1, 125–129.

—— (1928b): 'Phonetics and African languages', *Africa* 1, 358–371.

—— (1934): Review of *PP*, *Africa* 7, 112–113.

Lugard, F. D. (1928): 'The International Institute of African Languages and Cultures', *Africa* 1, 1–12.

Lukas, J. (1934): Review of *PP*, *MSOS* 27, 4–5.

Madan, A. C. (1911): *Living Speech in Central and South Africa*, Oxford.

Meinhof, C. (1928): 'Principles of practical orthography for African languages', *Africa* 1, 228–236.

—— (1932): *Introduction to the Phonology of the Bantu Languages* (trans. N. J. van Warmelo), Berlin.

Meyer, E. (1934): Review of *PP*, *ZES* 24, 311–313.

Pienaar, P. de V. (1934): Review of *PP*, *Bantu Studies* 8, 119–120.

Pike, K. L. (1943): *Phonetics*, Ann Arbor.

Sapir, E. (1931): 'Notes on the Gweabo language of Liberia', *Language* 7, 30–41.

—— (1936): Review of *PP*, *American Anthropologist* 38, 121–122.

Smith, E. (1934): *The Story of the Institute*, IIALC Memorandum XII, London.

Trofimov, M. & D. Jones (1923): *The Pronunciation of Russian*, Cambridge.

Trubetzkoy, N. (1939): *Grundzüge der Phonologie*, Göttingen.

Tucker, A. N. (1950): 'I. C. Ward', *BSOAS* 13, 542–547.

—— (1967): *The Eastern Sudanic Languages*, London.

—— (1971): 'Orthographic systems and conventions in Sub-Saharan Africa', *Current Trends in Linguistics* 7, 618–653.

Ward, I. C. (1929): *The Phonetics of English*, Cambridge.

—— (1933): *The Phonetic and Tonal Structure of Efik*, Cambridge.

—— (1937–39): 'The phonetic structure of Bamum', *BSOAS* 9, 423–438.

—— (1952): *Introduction to the Yoruba Language*, Cambridge.

Welmers, W. E. (1946): *A Descriptive Grammar of Fanti*, (Supplement to *Language* 22).

Werner, A. & M. H. (1927): *A First Swahili Book*, London.

Westermann, D. (1907): *Grammatik der Ewe-Sprache*, Berlin.

—— (1912): *The Shilluk People, their Language and Folklore*, Berlin.

—— (1928): *Ewe-English Dictionary*, Berlin.

—— (1930): *A Study of the Ewe Language* (trans. A. L. Bickford-Smith), Oxford.

—— (1950): 'Professor Ida Ward – an appreciation', *Africa* 20, 2–4.

FOREWORD

By DANIEL JONES, *Professor of Phonetics at*
University College, London

'THE importance of phonetics as the indispensable foundation of all study of language—whether that study be purely theoretical, or practical as well—is now generally admitted. . . . And now that philologists are directing their attention more and more to the study of living dialects and savage languages, many of which have to be written down for the first time, the absolute necessity of a thorough practical as well as theoretical mastery of phonetics becomes more and more evident.' These words were written by Henry Sweet in 1877.[1] He may have been somewhat premature in using the expression 'generally admitted', though at the time his view had the support of many linguists, particularly in England, Germany, and the Scandinavian countries. At the present day, however, his words hold good.

The main trend of the development of phonetic science during the last fifty years has been to emphasize more and more the utility of phonetics in relation to practical language problems. People are coming to realize that phonetics is not a difficult science of merely academic interest, but that it is a science with far-reaching practical applications and with bearings on everyday life. In particular, it is now recognized that the main uses of phonetics are to help people to learn to speak languages better, and to provide the only sure basis for constructing simple orthographies for languages hitherto·unwritten and for improving orthographies which are at present defective.

It is gratifying to find that the International Institute of African Languages and Cultures has consistently kept in mind these facts, and has given to phonetic investigations an important place in its programme of activities. The Institute, which was established in 1926, soon found that there was a need for

[1] *Handbook of Phonetics,* preface.

a manual of practical phonetics specially adapted to the needs of those studying African languages, and it is through the encouragement of the Institute that the present book has been produced. It is, I think, as perfect as a book of its kind can be. It is the result of a particularly happy collaboration between the leading exponent of practical African linguistics and one of our most eminent phoneticians; so readers may feel assured that the work is both technically sound and written with full knowledge of the practical educational problems which call for solution.

It is not necessary for me to enlarge upon the value of the book as an aid to language study. Readers will immediately see that for themselves. I should, however, like to emphasize the authors' recommendations regarding oral instruction. It is important to realize that the object of a book like the present one is to tell people how to listen to speech-sounds and how to perform speech-movements. Phonetic theory is not an end in itself, but it shows the method of acquiring certain oral accomplishments. These accomplishments are attained by means of *practical exercises*—ear-training and mouth-training. The proper performance of these exercises requires the aid of a teacher. Through a book on phonetics one can get a general idea of the sounds of a language, but it is not possible to make those sounds with absolute perfection without hearing them from a native. This book will instruct the learner *how to listen* to the native and *how to imitate* his sounds with success; but the learner himself must see to it that he carries out the instructions. He will then find that the task of learning to make the 'difficult' African sounds becomes relatively easy, and that he need no longer content himself with rough approximations to the native pronunciation.

The authors' treatment of questions of orthography deserves particular notice. Every one is agreed that the current spellings of native languages should be simple and as easy as possible for the native to learn. It is therefore incumbent on those who devise orthographies for native languages to find out what sound-distinctions are important *from the point of view of the native* and what distinctions may from his standpoint be disregarded. The field-worker who has no knowledge of phonetics is liable to fall into error in regard to both these matters. He may on the one hand, through lack of ear-training, fail to show necessary distinctions between words; or he may on the other hand mark unnecessary distinctions because they happen to be 'significant' in some European language. These pitfalls are avoided by the phonetically trained worker. The simple theory of 'phonemes' (Chap. V) furnishes him with a sure means of constructing for any language an orthography which will represent it unambiguously and with the minimum number of letters. This book will show him the lines on which he should work.

It is to be hoped that this book will be studied not only by European investigators, but also by Africans. For the successful solution of many of the questions of orthography we must look to the collaboration of educated Africans, and it is important that those Africans who interest themselves in linguistic matters should have phonetic training.

Lastly, I would say that although this book is primarily a practical manual for students of African languages, it must not be thought that it is devoid of scientific interest. The book will be found invaluable to students of general linguistics, since the languages dealt with present features differing greatly from anything found in Europe. Many of the phenomena touched upon here have been dealt with in greater detail in various specialized works, of which Miss Ward's *Phonetic and Tonal Structure of Efik*[1] is a masterly example.

DANIEL JONES.

DEPARTMENT OF PHONETICS,
  UNIVERSITY COLLEGE,
    LONDON, W.C. 1.
      March 1933.

[1] Heffer & Co., 1933.

ACKNOWLEDGEMENTS

Our thanks are due to

MISS L. E. ARMSTRONG for the Phonetic Summary of
Ganda and the Notes on Kikuyu.

DR. DOKE, for the Phonetic Summary of Zulu.

PROF. H. LABOURET, for assistance with the summary
of Bambara and Malinke.

DR. H. J. MELZIAN, for notes on the tones of Duala
and Yaunde.

MR. STEPHEN JONES (Phonetics Laboratory, University College, London), for assistance in making
the kymograph tracings on p. 93.

DR. A. N. TUCKER, for the Phonetic Summaries of
Nuer and Dinka, and for notes on Bari and Suto.

MESSRS. HEFFER AND SONS, Cambridge, for permission
to use diagrams from *The Phonetics of English*, by
I. C. Ward.

Where examples are taken from books, the source is
given in footnotes.

SYMBOLS USED IN THE BOOK

I. Cardinal Vowel Symbols.

i, e, ɛ, a, ɑ, ɔ, o, u

See Chap. IV for explanation of these symbols. They are used also with special values for the vowel sounds of various languages mentioned in the book, and are illustrated as they occur.

II. Additional Vowel Symbols used (in examples from European languages and in some African languages).

ɪ as in pit; Germ. bitte
æ ,, man
ʊ ,, put; Germ. Butter
ʌ ,, much
ə: ,, bird
ə ,, above, china; Germ. bitte

Centralized vowels are shown thus: ä. (See Ch. VII: also summaries of Nuer and Dinka.)

Nasalized vowels are shown thus: ã. (See Ch. VIII.)

Long vowels are shown in the examples from African languages by doubling the letter: aa.

III. Diphthongs.

Diphthongs are shown by two vowel letters. (See Ch. IX.)

IV. Consonant Symbols.

(a) *Used in European languages.*

[Many are identical in African languages: see Chapters on the different kinds of consonants.]

p	as in	put		ny	as in	Fr. agneau, It. cam-
b	,,	bad				pagna
t	,,	too		ŋ	,,	sing, Germ. singen
d	,,	do		l	,,	long
k	,,	come		ly	,,	It. famiglia
g	,,	go		r	,,	run
m	,,	make		f	,,	fit
n	,,	no		v	,,	very

θ	as in	thin		h	as in	have
ð	,,	then		ts	,,	Germ. Zimmer
s	,,	see		dz	,,	It. mezzo
z	,,	zeal		tʃ	,,	church
ʃ	,,	shut, Fr. chambre,		dʒ	,,	jump
		Germ. Schule		w	,,	went
ʒ	,,	measure, Fr. jouer		y	,,	yes
ç	,,	Germ. ich		'	(glottal stop).	(See Ch. XI,
x	,,	Germ. ach			§§ 166–8.)	

(b) *Additional Consonant Symbols used in African Languages.*

ʈ, ɖ Retroflex **t** and **d**. (See Ch. XI, § 152.)

th, dh Aspirated **t** and **d**. (See Ch. XI, §§ 139–45.)

th, dh Used for dental **t** and **d** in Nuer and Dinka. (See Ch. XI, § 153.)

ty, dy Palatal plosives. (See Ch. XI, §§ 155–8.)

c, j Used for palatal plosives in some languages. (See Ch. XI, § 158.) Used also for the affricates **tʃ** and **dʒ**. (See Ch. XV, § 256.)

kp, gb Labio-velar plosives. (See Ch. XI, §§ 160–4.)

ɳ Retroflex **n**. (See Ch. XII, § 176.)

ɬ Breathed or voiceless **l**. (See Ch. XIII, §§ 205–6.)

lʒ Fricative **l**. (See Ch. XIII, § 203.)

ɾ Flapped **r**. (See Ch. XIII, § 218.)

ɟ, ʋ Bi-labial fricatives. (See Ch. XIV, §§ 223–7.)

ɣ Voiced velar fricative. (See Ch. XIV, §§ 243–4.)

ɓ, ɗ Implosive **b** and **d**. (See Ch. XVII, § 276–289.)

For the methods of representing ejectives and clicks, see Chs. XVIII and XIX.

V. The Marking of Tones.

The method of marking tones in this book is explained fully in Ch. XXIV, § 419.

CHAPTER I

THE DIFFICULTIES OF LEARNING A NEW LANGUAGE

1. It is a well-known fact that one may make a comprehensive study of the grammar, construction, idiom, and literature of a language from books without knowing much about the pronunciation of it. If, however, one wants to be able to understand the speaker of that language, or to be able to converse with him, either for pleasure or in the course of business, it is necessary to learn something about the way it is spoken. Formerly it was thought that in order to do this, one had only to live for a considerable time in the country where the language was spoken or have plenty of opportunities of talking with native speakers of the language. This, no doubt, gave a certain facility in the use of the language, but has proved, except with specially gifted people who are somewhat rare, to be of little value in obtaining a correct pronunciation. Every one knows foreigners who have lived in England for years and who have still a marked foreign accent, and the accent of the majority of Englishmen speaking a foreign language is proverbially bad.

2. Languages differ from each other not only in grammar, idiom, and vocabulary, but in the production of the sounds which make up the language, in the way sounds are linked together to make words and sentences, in the distribution of breath force over words and syllables, and in the way the voice goes up and down in speaking, i.e. in intonation. The learner of a new language, unless he is exceptionally gifted or unless he has a special training, transfers into the new language all the speech habits of his mother tongue. The new habits do not 'come naturally': he does not 'pick up' a correct pronunciation, but has to be taught it.

3. A great advance was made in language teaching when it was discovered that pronunciation, like any other branch of language study, could be and should be taught scientifically, that it is possible to find out the exact nature of every speech sound used in any language, to investigate how the sounds are distributed, and to present these and other scientifically ascertained facts in such a way as to make it easier for the student to acquire a good pronunciation. That is to say, the modern student now makes use of phonetics—the scientific study of the spoken language—to supplement his powers of imitation.

4. There are people who are satisfied if they can 'get on' in a language, i.e. if they can just manage to make themselves understood, and who care little about the niceties of a good pronunciation. This may be all very well if they *are* understood. But the possibilities of being misunderstood are far more numerous than such a student is aware of, particularly in the less known languages of Africa and the East. Many stories are told of traders, administrators, and missionaries not only being misunderstood but made ridiculous or even worse by a lack of realization of the difficulties of the spoken language. The mistakes they make depend upon differences in pronunciation which are possibly extremely slight to the European and which he therefore fails to recognize, but which to the native speaker are of the utmost importance, since they distinguish words. An example from European languages may serve to illustrate this point. A German may find it difficult to distinguish the vowel sounds in the English words *hat* and *hut*, since the two sounds bear some acoustic resemblance and neither occurs in his own language, but to English ears the difference is not difficult to hear since the vowels alone distinguish the two words from each other. Similarly, the Englishman may not easily recognize the difference between the German *musste* and *müsste*, because the sound of **ü** does not occur in English. In Ewe two **d**-sounds are found, one made with the tip of the tongue on the teeth-ridge and one with the tip pressed on the front of the hard palate. To European ears these two **d**-sounds are very similar because no European language possesses the two varieties of **d**, but to the Ewe speaker they are as different as **d** and **g̣** are to the European, mainly because they distinguish words, e.g. **edɔ,** *illness*; **eɖɔ,** *fishing net*[1] (the same tone in both). Examples of this kind of thing could be quoted in large numbers.

5. Up to comparatively recent years, African languages have been written down mainly by travellers, missionaries, or administrators whose accuracy in recognizing the sounds they

---

[1] For these sounds, see Ch. XI, p. 54.

were dealing with and skill in describing them has been varied. The results are necessarily of varying value. That this should have been so is hardly to be wondered at, since the scientific approach to the study of pronunciation is of comparatively recent date and the task of the untrained or semi-trained linguistic observer was overwhelming. What has been generally done by a large number of these observers has been to try to describe the language they were working on in terms of their mother tongue with occasional references to the better known European languages. Where this has been impossible, i.e. where the sounds to be described are widely removed from those within the knowledge of the writer, he has often contented himself by saying, 'This sound cannot be described', or 'Must be acquired from a native'. The science of phonetics makes it possible to analyse and describe with great accuracy the sounds of any language. It is no belittling of the pioneer work which has been done in writing down African languages to advise modern investigators to make use of the more scientific method supplied by the study of phonetics.

6. The difficulties of learning an African language have often been increased by wrong methods of setting about the business. The student—missionary, trader, or administrator —has generally either learnt something of the language in Europe before going out, from a European who has been in Africa, or he has been sent out with no preliminary study. In the first case, he has probably been taught by some one with an imperfect knowledge of the language who has passed on his own mistakes to the new learner, especially in pronunciation and intonation: in the second case, he is plunged headlong, with no preparation, into new and strange surroundings and flounders in the new language, which in every particular is so unlike anything he has met before. Moreover, his language learning is often subsidiary to other work and he has to use his spare time for it. In either case, the result is discouragement, loss of time, and a lessening of efficiency. This may have been unavoidable in the past, but at the present time there is no such excuse for these haphazard methods. It should now be possible to save time, energy, and spirit by tackling the problem in the right way before going out at all.

7. The student of to-day must first of all face the fact that many African languages are difficult, that their sounds are

different from anything he has met before, that parts of the grammar and idiom are unlike that of any European language, and finally that a considerable amount of work will be needed to overcome these difficulties. Moreover, if he undertakes work of any kind among Africans, it is a duty to learn to speak their language well, and to make himself as proficient as possible: it is a waste of opportunity to remain one of those who stumble along with a few phrases badly pronounced, expecting the native to do the rest.

8. The study of an African language should be begun at home. The first step is a training in phonetics and linguistics, which will give a thorough grounding in the sounds and tones of the new language and in methods of language study. Where good grammars exist, the grammar can be studied in outline, but the student should only learn to speak the language if a native is available.

9. The question of a native teacher is a difficult one. Because a man can speak his own language, it does not mean that he can therefore teach it: many of the natives available are not fitted by nature or by education to teach their language; they are totally incapable of explaining any linguistic phenomena. The ideal at home is a European who knows the grammar thoroughly, with a native assistant for the conversational part of the work. The native in a combination of this kind need not be an educated man, though of course, such a one is more valuable if he can be found. Where such an arrangement is not possible, a trained linguistic expert with some knowledge of one or more African languages, together with a native speaker, can do a great deal, even if the expert has no first-hand knowledge of the language itself. He can direct the lines of investigation into the language and suggest methods of work which will put the student in the way of constructing his own grammatical rules and enable him to make the best use of the native speaker. If the student has to go out without any previous work on the language and has to make what use he can of an untrained native, he should learn beforehand how to proceed. A course of lectures and practical demonstrations on the methods of language study together with a good grounding in phonetics and tone work is an indispensable preliminary to any one embarking on the study of an African language. It is with the purpose of providing in as simple a form and in as

short space as possible the material necessary for the study of
phonetics and tonetics that this work has been prepared.

Difficulties of the Spoken Language and how to overcome them.

10. The student is rarely aware of the difficulties which
confront him in the study of the spoken language, and if the
nature of them is explained and means are suggested for
meeting each type of difficulty, he is in a better position to
overcome them.

11. The first difficulty is one of ear. People are gifted in
varying degrees with what is known as an 'ear for speech
sounds'. An ear for music is not necessarily an ear for speech
sounds, though it often accompanies it and is of great use in
dealing with a tone language or with the intonation of a non-
tone language. A good linguistic ear means the power to
discriminate between sounds, the power to hear even small
differences, to call up at will sounds previously heard, to compare sounds mentally. The untrained student of a new language
hears in terms of his mother tongue, but if he has a good ear
he can soon learn to compare the new sounds he hears with
those with which he is already familiar and to note similarities
and differences. If he is to make any success of speaking a
language well, he must have his ear trained to recognize the
new sounds.

12. Training can improve any ear, good, bad, or indifferent:
a good ear can be made very good by training; an indifferent
ear can be improved. But systematic training is necessary.
Ear training is the basis of all work on the spoken language.
It is evident that unless a student can distinguish the sounds
of the language he is learning, he stands little chance of ever
being able to imitate them. The best form of ear training is
carried on by means of what is called 'meaningless dictation'.
The teacher dictates invented words or sequences of sounds or
words of a language not known to the learner, which the student
writes down in an unambiguous fashion by means of a phonetic
alphabet. The teacher can see from what the student has
written if he has heard correctly or not what was dictated. As
the words convey no meaning, the student is able to concentrate
on sounds alone without the distraction of meaning or in fact
any association that real words might bring. Moreover, if he

has not heard correctly, i.e. if he has written down something which the teacher did not say, the latter can repeat alternately the right and the wrong sequences of sounds, thus helping to develop his acoustic perception. Such exercises graded in difficulty and devised to suit the particular language the student is working at are of the utmost value at the outset of any linguistic study.

13. The second difficulty is that of *making* the speech sounds of the new language. In every language there are sounds which are peculiar to that language and which are different from those of the mother tongue, and the student has to learn to make them. This involves using the speech organs in a new and unaccustomed fashion and, since new habits are to be set up, training is necessary. Such training is best carried out under the direction of a teacher who is a phonetician. The teacher can explain to the student how the sound is made ; he can make it for him to imitate and can correct his faulty imitation and tell him how to improve it. The student can obtain considerable help from books or from lectures on phonetic theory: in this way, he can learn how sounds are articulated by the organs of speech, what relation they bear to each other and to the sounds he is familiar with ; he can also be given hints on how to produce the sounds. But books cannot tell him if he is making the sounds correctly, and it must be remembered that a theoretical knowledge of how sounds are formed is valueless without the power of recognizing them and making them, and for this, oral instruction is necessary. Phonetics is essentially a practical science.

14. The third difficulty is that of knowing when to use the sounds, i.e. the correct *distribution* of the sounds of a given language. This is a matter of memory, but the learning of the appropriate sequences of sounds in a word, phrase, or sentence is considerably facilitated by means of a phonetic transcription, i.e. an unambiguous method of indicating pronunciation in writing.[1] In this book, the recommendations of the International Institute of African Languages and Cultures towards a phonetic orthography for African languages are strongly supported. By means of such an orthography, the correct sound-order is easily learnt.

15. The fourth difficulty is concerned with the recognition

[1] See Chapters II and V.

and acquisition of the correct length of sounds, the distribution of stress, and the intonation of the language. Of these elements of speech, length and stress can be indicated in prepared texts and can be acquired by observation and the careful reading of such texts. Intonation is a somewhat different matter: in tone languages such as are a number of African languages, a careful study of the tone analysis, where such analyses have been made, should be undertaken, and exercises on the special tone-usages systematically practised. This important part of an African language is treated fully in Chapter XXIV, where hints for work in intonation are given.

16. The fifth difficulty is that of fluency, i.e. saying the sentences of the new language with sufficient ease and speed. The student must first learn to make the sounds without too much effort in isolation: unless the individual sounds can be produced with ease, there is little chance of their being used correctly and naturally in connected speech. When the student can do this, he should practise them in groups and syllables (particularly the difficult combinations) graded in difficulty. This kind of exercise is essential, as it and it alone will give practice not only in saying the new sounds, but in making those movements of tongue, lips, &c., necessary to the smooth passing from one sound to another in quick succession. When the student can say all the sounds of the language with fair ease in all kinds of combinations, he is likely to attain fluency in speaking it. Then he should practise saying the longer sequences of sounds which make up continuous speech, and in doing so, he is urged strongly to observe the grouping of words and to practise in short natural sense groups, slowing up in the first place the whole group in such a way that the relation of important to unimportant words and syllables is retained and the rhythm is not destroyed. Then he can gradually speed up the whole until he achieves a speed and fluency reasonably near that of the native speaker of the language.

CHAPTER II

PHONETIC ALPHABETS AND PHONETIC ORTHOGRAPHY

17. The science of phonetics is concerned with the analysis and recording of the elements which go to make up speech. For the *recording* of speech sounds, an unambiguous method of writing them is necessary and such a means is found in a phonetic alphabet. A phonetic alphabet is one in which each phoneme of a language has one letter and one only: so that all words distinguished in pronunciation shall be distinguished also in writing. Thus an unambiguous alphabet needs as many letters as there are phonemes in the language.[1]

18. The use of a phonetic alphabet as an adjunct to the study of the pronunciation of a language is nowadays sufficiently well known and needs no stressing here. It should be remembered, however, that a phonetic alphabet does not teach a correct pronunciation, but merely shows what sequences of sounds occur in a given language. It should also be remembered that when a phonetic alphabet is being considered for more than one language, the same symbols may be used to represent sounds in the different languages which do not exactly correspond to each other, since it would be impossible to have separate letters for all the varieties of sounds occurring in a number of languages. Thus the letter **a** may represent two or more varieties of **a**-sound in different languages, and the consonant letter **t** may stand for a dental articulation in one language and an alveolar articulation in another (as it does in French and English, for example).

19. There have been three systems of recording phonetically the sounds of a language, viz.:

(*a*) What may be called the *diacritic* method, in which the ordinary letters of the Latin alphabet have been supplemented by diacritic marks placed over or under certain of the letters to indicate sounds for which the Latin alphabet is inadequate. The best known examples of this are the 'Standard Alphabet' of Lepsius, and its improved form by Meinhof, and the 'An-

---

[1] See Chapter V. It is sometimes useful, however, especially in the teaching of pronunciation, to adopt a narrower system by adding other letters to represent subsidiary members of the phonemes. See p. 29.

thropos' alphabet devised by P. W. Schmidt. These are the only alphabets that have been used to any considerable extent in the writing down of African languages, and their scientific value is well known.

(b) The 'New Letter' method, in which new letters have been designed to supplement the Latin alphabet and to represent those sounds for which it is inadequate. The best known example of this type is the alphabet of the International Phonetic Association. Diacritic marks are not entirely dispensed with in this system, but are reserved for the most part to represent length, stress, and pitch.

(c) Alphabets consisting of entirely new forms, such as Bell's Organic Alphabet used in his Visible Speech. This has not been used for the writing down of African languages and can, for the purposes of this book, be neglected.

20. Until recent years, phonetic alphabets have been used mainly for recording sounds for scientific purposes in books describing the pronunciation of a language for foreigners, and they have been applied to a much less extent in making an orthography for the use of native speakers of a language. The orthographies of most European languages are by no means phonetic: this is the result of the history of their development. There is no reason, however, why orthographies chosen at the present day for African languages should not be constructed on a phonetic basis. This aim was behind the movement for the reform of the orthographies of African languages which was inaugurated by the International Institute of African Languages and Cultures, when it issued its Memorandum on the *Practical Orthography of African Languages*. The suggestions set out in this pamphet show the phonetic principles upon which orthographies should be constructed and how the confusion and inconsistencies which have resulted from the somewhat haphazard methods of individual investigators may be avoided and rectified. The system followed is the 'New Letter' method, and the suggested alphabets have been based on the alphabet of the International Phonetic Association with certain modifications. The reasons for the choice of this rather than the diacritic method are clearly set out in the Memorandum, with which every student of African languages should be familiar. [1]

21. In the present book the alphabet used is that which

[1] First Edition, 1926. Second Edition, revised and enlarged, 1930.

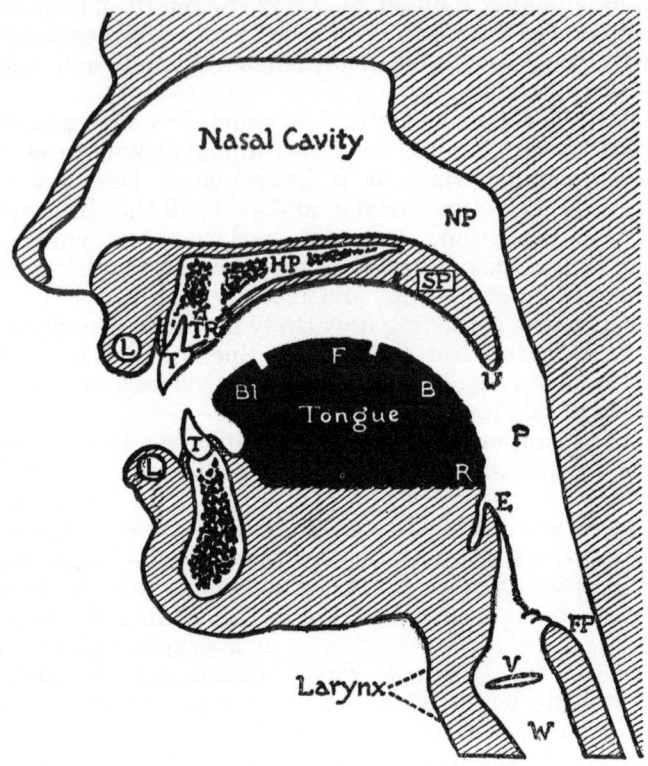

FIG. 1. Organs of Speech.

Key to Fig. 1.

L.L. Lips.
T.T. Teeth.
T.R. Teeth ridge or gums: convex part of the roof of the mouth, immediately behind the teeth.
H.P. Hard palate: concave part of the roof of the mouth.
S.P. Soft palate: membranous curtain.
U.   Uvula: pendulous end of the soft palate.
N.P. Nasal pharynx: space between the soft palate and the back wall of the throat.
P.   Pharynx: space between the back of the tongue and the back wall of the throat.
Bl.   Blade of tongue, including tip: that part which lies opposite the teeth ridge when the tongue is in a position of rest.
F.   Front of tongue: that part which lies opposite the hard palate when the tongue is in a position of rest.

has been adopted for the reformed orthographies of those languages in which decisions have been reached, and for the rest, the suggestions of the Memorandum have been followed.[1] For those readers who are familiar with the I.P.A., the symbols of this system are given as footnotes where they differ from the recommendations of the Memorandum.

CHAPTER III

THE ORGANS OF SPEECH

22. The student who is concerned with the pronunciation of a language should know something of the mechanism of speech. A detailed study of the physiology and anatomy of the speech organs is not necessary, but the student should have a clear idea of what the organs are by which speech is produced and the functions of these organs.

23. The accompanying diagram (p. 10) shows all that is absolutely necessary, i.e. the main organs of speech and their names; further details for those whom this aspect of the subject interests can be found in standard text-books on anatomy and physiology.

24. The student is advised to make himself familiar with the terms used to describe the mechanism of speech and as far as possible to investigate his own speech organs and to try to realize how these are used in making the sounds of his own language. He will, in this way, become conscious of movements and positions which have hitherto been unconscious, and this consciousness will lead to control of the speech organs which

---

[1] There is a movement afoot to make this a 'World Orthography'.

Key to Fig. 1—cont.

B.   Back of tongue: that part which lies opposite the soft palate when the tongue is in a position of rest.
R.   Root of tongue.
E.   Epiglottis.
F.P. Gullet or food passage.
V.   Vocal cords or lips: membranes stretched from front to back across the larynx.
W.   Windpipe.
La.   Larynx: that part of the windpipe in which the vocal cords are situated.
      Glottis: space between the vocal cords.

will be of great assistance in his attempts to make the unusual sounds of the language he is studying.

25. Most speech sounds are formed by the outgoing breath from the lungs. This breath stream is modified at various points and in various ways by the different organs of speech to produce articulate sounds. The first organ of speech which the breath meets is the vocal cords.

Vocal Cords.

26. The vocal cords are membranes similar to a pair of thin elastic lips stretched across the larynx from back to front. They are fastened close together at the front, but at the back each is joined to one of the arytenoid cartilages. These cartilages can move away from each other or come close together: in this way the vocal cords can either be opened in a V-shape or closed along the whole of their length. The opening which can be made between them is called the *glottis*. In Plate I[1] the vocal cords are seen in four positions.

Function of the Vocal Cords in Speech.

27. The main function performed by the vocal cords is that of producing *voice*. Voice is produced when the cords are held loosely together and the air, forcing its way between them, opens and shuts them rhythmically. These rhythmic movements set the air in vibration and thus give rise to a musical note. The pitch of the note is determined by the tightening or slackening of the cords. The loudness of the note is determined by the extent of the movements of the cords, and this is influenced by the force of the breath used. The vibration can be felt on the outside of the throat (on the Adam's apple). As far as articulate speech is concerned, this musical note is a feature of certain speech sounds and not of others. All vowels are voiced and a large number of the consonants, such as **v, z, m, n, l, r, g, d,** have this accompaniment of voice. These consonants are said to be *voiced*. Pl. I, Fig. 2 (*b*), shows the vocal cords in the position for voice.

28. When the vocal cords are not in vibration, they may be open as in Pl. I, Fig. 2 (*a*). In this position they allow the air to

---

[1] These drawings were made by Mr. A. K. Maxwell from the vocal cords of Mr. Stephen Jones of the Phonetics Laboratory, University College, London. Diagram taken from *The Phonetics of English*, by I. C. Ward (Heffer & Co., Cambridge).

PLATE I

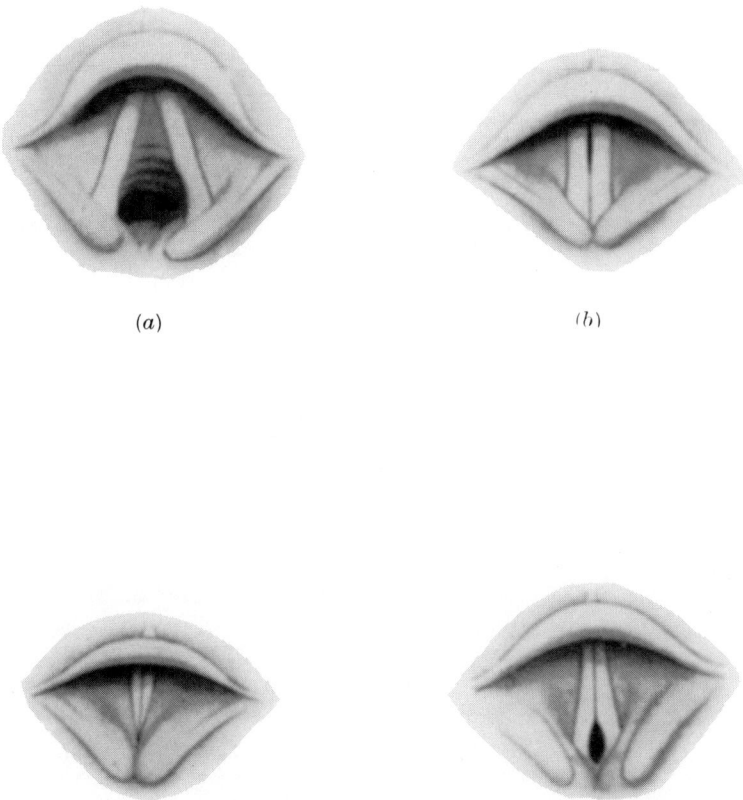

(a)

(b)

(c)

(d)

FIG. 2. Drawings of the Vocal Chords.

pass through freely and do not impede it in any way. They are in such a position for quiet breathing and for the production of a certain number of consonants such as **t, p, s, ʃ, h.** Consonants made with the vocal cords in this position are said to be *breathed* or *voiceless*.[1]

29. A further speech action performed by the vocal cords is illustrated in Pl. I, Fig. 2 (*c*). Here the cords are made to touch along their whole length and held momentarily in this position: the breath is stopped behind them (*glottal closure* or *glottal stop*) and when they are opened, i.e. when the stop is released, the compressed air escapes with a slight explosion (*glottal plosive*). The sound which is heard on the release of the stop resembles a slight cough and is an essential speech sound of many languages.[2] In German, for example, words like *abirren* are pronounced with a glottal stop before the vowel of the first two syllables (**'ap'irən**); in English, though not an essential sound, it occurs in the pronunciation of most people in emphatic words beginning with a vowel, such as *awful* (**'əfl**), and it is used in many dialects to replace a plosive consonant, e.g. the Cockney says **le'ə** for *letter*, and in many parts of the country **tei'wʌn** is heard for *take one*.[3] The glottal stop is an essential sound in certain of the African languages (see Ch. XI, p. 60), and in many languages the action of glottal closure can accompany sounds articulated by other organs of speech, such action being an essential part of their formation. For detailed description of these sounds, see Ch. XI, §§ 167–8 and Ch. XVIII, p. 96.

30. Pl. I, Fig. 2 (*d*), shows the vocal cords in the position for whisper. Here they are closed along part of their length and have a triangular opening at one end. Whisper, however, need not be considered in the discussion of normal speech.

Exercises for the Control of the Vocal Cords.

31. The vibration of the vocal cords cannot be controlled consciously by the muscles that move them. This is done by ear. We 'think' the note we want and the vocal cords obey the thought and vibrate at the necessary speed to produce that

---

[1] The term 'breathed' is usually applied to all consonants except plosives: for the latter the term 'voiceless' is better, since the stop of a plosive when no breath is issuing can hardly be said to be breathed.

[2] I.P.A. ʔ. In many languages it has no letter to represent it.

[3] For further examples of its use in English, see books on English phonetics.

note. The student, however, can make himself conscious of the presence or absence of voice in the production of speech sounds and can learn to control the vocal cords in such a way that he can add voice to or take voice from any sounds he wants to. He can also learn to make the glottal stop and know when to use it and when to avoid its use.

32. It is not always easy to voice fully certain consonants. In English and German, for instance, the so-called voiced consonants **b, d, g, z, ʒ, v, ð** are not fully voiced in initial and final positions (in German, these voiced consonants do not occur finally). In French, on the other hand, all the voiced consonants in all positions are fully voiced, i.e. the vocal cords vibrate during the whole of the time of articulation of the consonant. In many African languages fully voiced consonants are essential, consequently English and German students must learn to control the vocal cords so that they can voice a consonant fully where this is necessary.

(*a*) The pupil should pronounce the vowel in the word *bird* (ə:), and while saying this bring the bottom lip against the top teeth, making ə:v. The voice should continue throughout; if the pupil thinks of the *vowel* all the time, the voice will go on through the consonant as well. If necessary he should sing it. The contact of the lip and teeth may be light at first, but should gradually become stronger.

(*b*) Similar exercises can be performed with **z, ʒ, ð.** When the pupil can carry the voice into the consonant and throughout the consonant, he should practise the consonant alone without the preceding vowel.

(*c*) The exercise of alternating voiced and breathed consonants is of great value:

sz sz sz   ʃʒ ʃʒ ʃʒ
fv fv fv

Each of these pairs should be repeated several times without a break.

(*d*) When the vocal cords are sufficiently under control to do these familiar pairs of sounds, the same exercise should be practised with other pairs of consonants, of which the voiced one only occurs in the mother tongue, e.g. the pupil should say **l,** and then say it without voice; this gives *breathed* or *voiceless* l (ɬ), the sound of Welsh ll. These two should then be alternated and repeated a number of times. Similar exercises can be made with the nasal consonants: alternate voiced and breathed **n, m, ŋ.**[1]

(e) For fully voicing the plosive consonants, begin with the vowel **ə:** again. Bring the lips lightly together (making bilabial **ʋ**; see p. 77). Gradually tighten the contact of the lips, keeping the idea of the vowel going all the time: feel the vibration on the outside of the throat; in time this should

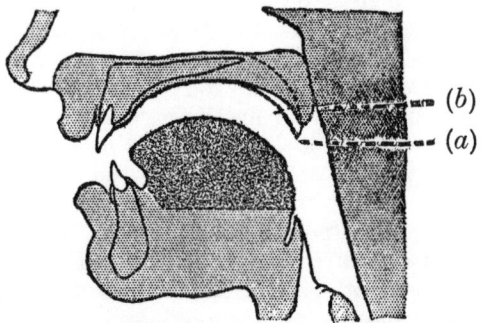

(b)
(a)

FIG. 3. Soft Palate raised and lowered.

result in **b** pronounced with voice running through it the whole time. When this is achieved, it should not be difficult to obtain the same sensation during the production of **d** and **g**.

The Soft Palate or Velum.

33. The roof of the mouth consists of teeth-ridge or gums, i.e. the convex part immediately behind the upper front teeth, the hard palate or concave bony dome of the mouth, and the soft palate, a kind of membranous curtain which hangs down at the back of the mouth. The pendulous end of it is the uvula. The soft palate is one of the movable organs of speech, and it can take up two positions:

(a) During quiet breathing it is lowered and the air can pass behind it through the nose.

(b) During speech it is raised to touch the back wall of the pharynx (Fig. 3 (b)) for all sounds except the nasal consonants

---

[1] Breathed **l, m, n, ŋ** are represented in I.P.A. as **l̥, m̥, n̥, ŋ̊**. No symbol has been suggested by the African Institute for the breathed nasals. For the description and occurrence of these, see Ch. XII, §§ 187–8.

and for nasalized vowels (e.g. French ã, ɔ̃, ɛ̃, œ̃), when it is lowered to the position shown in Fig. 3 (*a*) to allow the air to pass through the nose. Thus the function of the soft palate is to open and close the passage to the nose, to open it for nasal or nasalized sounds and to close it for non-nasal or oral sounds.

Exercises for the Control of the Soft Palate.

34. Many African languages contain nasalized vowels, and as it may be necessary for the student to use his soft palate in a way which is not natural to his mother tongue, it is well for him to learn to control its movements consciously. Exercises are suggested here for acquiring such control.

(*a*) The student should look into his mouth and say a very far back variety of **a**, something like the English a in *father*, with considerable vigour, stretching the muscles at the back of the throat. The palate should rise. Compare the two drawings of the mouth shown on Plate II (Figs. 4*a* and *b*). If the palate does not rise sufficiently in saying **a**, use a tongue spatula (or the handle of a spoon) and depress the back of the tongue with this and watch the movement of the palate. The student should continue this exercise until he can raise the palate at will.

(*b*) A further aid will be found in yawning. Open the mouth wide, keeping the tip of the tongue pressed against the bottom teeth: then yawn vigorously. The palate will rise. Relax the muscles thus stretched and the palate drops. A repetition of these two movements will help towards the control of the soft palate.

(*c*) Say the word *mutton* (**mʌtn**) with considerable force. There must be no vowel between the **t** and **n**. The explosion which can be felt and heard is made as the air compressed below that place escapes through the nose. A repetition of **tntntn** will help the student to realize the movement of the palate and in time to control it. (He must be quite sure that he is using **tn** and not the glottal stop +**n**.) Similarly **dndndn** (as in *sudden* (**sʌdn**)), **kŋkŋkŋ** (as in one pronunciation of *bacon* (**beikŋ**)), **ɡŋɡŋɡŋ** without moving the tongue in each group, and **pmpmpm** (as in *happen* pronounced **hæpm**), **bmbmbm** (as in *ribbon* pronounced **rɪbm**) without moving the lips, will give additional practice. The student should aim

PLATE II

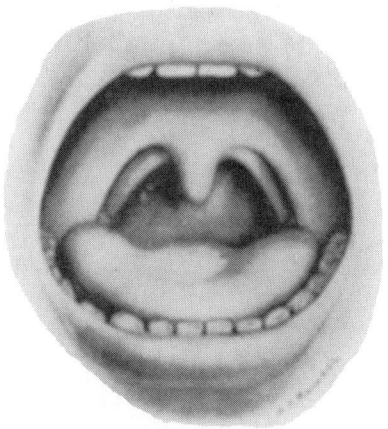

FIG. 4 (*a*) Open Mouth.

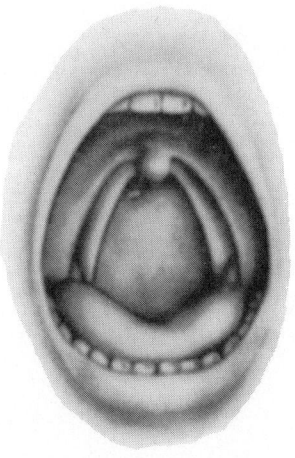

FIG. 4 (*b*) Open Mouth with Palate raised.

at feeling the position of the palate *before* the explosion is heard, i.e. when it is touching the back wall of the pharynx. A German student can use the pronunciation of the last syllable of *reiten* (**raitn**), *leiden* (**laidn**), *Rippen* (**rɪpm**), *haben* (**habm**), *gucken* (**gʊkŋ**), *legen* (**legŋ**) (without a break between the plosive and the nasal) to make exercises of this kind.

(*d*) A more difficult exercise is to alternate oral and nasal vowels, e.g. **aãaãaã, ɛɛ̃ɛɛ̃ɛɛ̃**. This should be done without any appreciable movement of the tongue, and care must be taken not to add the nasal consonant **ŋ** to the vowel.

The Tongue.

35. The tongue is, perhaps, the most important of all the organs of speech in the formation of speech sounds. For the purpose of describing its actions in the articulation of vowels and consonants, it is well to consider it as divided into three parts, although it has no such physiological divisions as the roof of the mouth. The *blade* (with the tip) is that part which normally lies opposite the teeth-ridge when the tongue is in a position of rest: it is that part which is free and can be projected beyond the teeth. The *front* is that part of the main body of the tongue which lies opposite the hard palate, and the *back* that part which lies opposite the soft palate. Farther back still is the *root* of the tongue.

36. The movements of the tongue enter into the formation of all vowels and of many of the consonants. Many consonants are articulated by the tongue touching or approaching some part of the roof of the mouth; and the movements of the tongue so alter the shape of the resonance chamber of the mouth as to give rise to vowel sounds of different quality. These movements are described in the chapters on vowels and consonants.

37. The student is advised to make himself aware of the action of the tongue in the formation of the sounds of his own language, to try to realize exactly what part of the tongue is used, what position the tongue takes up and how it moves. In this way, he will become conscious of the manner in which speech sounds are formed, and if he compares his own sensations with diagrams and descriptions given in books, he will gradually acquire the power of analysing exactly the articulation of the sounds he makes himself and those he hears.

Exercises are suggested here for the realization of the movement of the tongue and for acquiring control over it.

For Vowel Practice.

38. (*a*) Open the mouth and say as many vowels as can conveniently be pronounced with open mouth, watching in a looking-glass the movements of the tongue and the parts concerned in their formation.

(*b*) Pronounce the vowel **i** (as in *see*); while continuing the sound, round the lips without moving the tongue. This will give rise to a new vowel, similar to the sound of French **u** (as in *rue*) or German **ü** (as in *müde*). A useful exercise can now be made by alternating these two sounds: the English student will at first find it difficult to keep the tongue still, and he will want to pronounce his familiar **u** sound (as in *soon*) instead of the new one. If he finds it difficult to obtain this new sound, he can reach it another way, by first rounding the lips as if for **u** and while keeping them in this position, trying to say **i**. Similar exercises can be made from other vowels: pronounce the vowel **e**; while continuing this sound round the lips as if for **o**: and another new sound, similar to the French **eu** as in *peu* or to the German **ö** as in *Höhle* is the result.

The Lips.

39. The movements of the lips and their contribution to the formation of speech sounds are not difficult to realize as they can be seen. The lips are organs which articulate certain consonants like **p, b, m, w,** &c., and their action can be added to the formation of other consonant and vowel sounds. They can take up four positions:

(*a*) They can be wide open, allowing the air to pass freely through, as in the sounds **a, h.**

(*b*) They can be in contact, as for **p, b.**

(*c*) They can be brought close together so that the air pushes its way through, making a frictional sound. This is the sound made in blowing out a match. It is a sound found in many African languages and known as bi-labial **f** (ʃ): with the addition of voice we have bi-labial **v** (ʋ).[1]

(*d*) They can be made to vibrate. This is a sound young

---

[1] See Ch. XIV.

babies are fond of making: it is used in some countries to stop a horse.

40. In addition to this the lips come into play in the formation of vowel sounds. Such action is described in Chapter IV on vowel sounds.

Exercises for the Control of the Lips.

41. (*a*) The student should practise in front of a mirror the four positions described above.

(*b*) For the sake of practice, he should make exaggerated movements in rounding and pushing out the lips and in spreading them. Alternate the following pairs of vowels with vigorous movements of lip and jaw.

u i u i u i	a u a u a u	u e u e u e
e o e o e o	i a i a i a	a i a i a i
ɛ u ɛ u ɛ u	ə i ə i ə i	i ɛ i ɛ i ɛ

(*c*) To keep the lips still, while the tongue moves, the student should say the sound **u** (as in *soon*), and while keeping the lips in this rounded position, he should try to say the sound **i** (as in *eat*). The result will be the vowel he has already obtained in another way, i.e. the French **u** and German **ü** sound (as a tongue exercise). The two vowels can now be alternated. Similar exercises can be made from other vowel sounds. If the student pronounces **o** and with lips in this position he tries to say **e,** he will pronounce the sound of French **eu** in *peu* (as has already been done as a tongue exercise).

42. These exercises and those suggested in § 38 can be considered as exercises for both lips and tongue. In the one case, the lips must be held still and the tongue must move, and in the other, the tongue is still and the lips move.

CHAPTER IV

CLASSIFICATION OF SOUNDS: VOWELS AND CONSONANTS: CLASSIFICATION OF VOWELS

43. In describing the sounds of African languages it is necessary to start with a clear idea of the two recognized groups of sounds, *vowels* and *consonants*, and their formation and classification. A *vowel* is a voiced sound in which the air has a free passage through the mouth or through the mouth and nose. The air is not impeded in any way. All other sounds are consonants. A *consonant* is a sound, voiced or voiceless, in which the air passage is either stopped entirely at some point, or narrowed so as to give rise to audible friction.[1] Thus for the sounds **a, i, u, ɔ,** &c., the movements of the tongue do not prevent the air from issuing freely from the mouth, while for **s, z, f, v,** &c., the air has to push its way through a narrow opening and friction is heard, and for **p, b, k, g,** &c., the air passage is momentarily stopped. The first are vowels and the others are consonants. The old idea that a consonant cannot be made without a vowel is not true : it is quite possible to say many consonants alone, e.g. a dubious assent is often given by means of the consonant **m** ; a noisy child is told to be quiet with **ʃ,** and there are numerous examples of words in many languages consisting of consonants alone, e.g. *and* is reduced to **n** in the phrase *bread and butter* (**bred n bʌtə**), *from* is pronounced **frm** in a sentence like *I come from the North* (**ai kʌm frm ðə nɔɔθ**). In German the word *ihn* is pronounced **n** in quick speech in a sentence such as *Ich kann ihn nicht sehen* (**iç kan n niçt zeən**). In Shilḥ (a Berber dialect) the verb *to give* consists of two voiceless consonants **fk** : *you give* is made up of four voiceless consonants **tfkt.** An interesting example was found in one dialect of Ibo, where the word for *parcel* or *packet* was pronounced **ŋgŋgŋ** (tones [˙ . .])—five consonants and no vowel!

Classification of Vowels.

44. The difference between one vowel and another is due to the difference in the shape of the resonance chamber of the mouth, and this in turn is due mainly to the movement of tongue and lips. It is usual, therefore, in describing vowel sounds to classify them according to the part the tongue plays in their formation. A subsidiary classification is made according to lip movements.

45. The student is recommended to find out the part of the tongue which is used in the formation of the familiar vowels of his own language, and consciously to realize how that part

---

[1] This is not a very satisfactory definition, since no friction is heard in the pronunciation of the nasal consonants and of **l**: moreover, several of the so-called voiced consonants are almost frictionless. See Ch. XIV, p. 77.

of the tongue is used. He should say as many vowels as he can with his mouth wide open and watch the movements of the tongue. This will help him in the recognition and acquisition of the unfamiliar vowels of the language which he is studying. For the English vowels **i, e, æ** it is the front of the tongue which is concerned; for **ɑ, ɔ, u** it is the back of the tongue; for **ə** it is part of the front and part of the back, i.e. the central part of the tongue. Note that the blade and tip play little part in the formation of vowels. For the English vowels **i** and **u** the tongue is raised high in the mouth; for **ɑ** it is low; for **ɔ, ə, ɛ** it is in an intermediate position between high and low.

46. Vowels are classified, therefore, according to the part of the tongue used, into *front, back,* and *central,* and according to the degree of raising of the tongue, into *close* (tongue raised high), *open* (tongue low down in the mouth), and *half-close* and *half-open* (two intermediate positions). Using these terms, it is easy to classify roughly the vowel sounds of any language, to say, for instance, that the English, French, and German **i** (as in *see, lire, die*) is a close front vowel, that **u** (as in *root, trou, gut*) is a close back vowel, that French and German **a** (as in *table, Mann*) is a front open vowel, English **æ** (as in *man*) is half-open ; that English and German **ə** (as in *ought, Kopf*) is a half-open back vowel, &c. Such a classification, however, does not allow for anything but a rough description of a vowel, nor does it permit, without somewhat clumsy explanations, of distinguishing *different kinds* of close front vowels, of half-open back vowels, &c.—differences which must be accurately noted for any kind of scientific work in the comparative study of languages.

47. Until comparatively recent years, it has been customary to describe the vowel sounds of a new language in terms of the mother tongue of the writer, with occasional references to the better known European languages. Such comparison, however, is bound to be lacking in accuracy. The vowel sounds of one language do not in every case exactly correspond to those of another language. Moreover, it is a well-known fact that no two people speak exactly alike, that there are dialectal and individual differences of pronunciation—some of them marked. A comparison, therefore, with the vowels of the mother tongue, though it may serve as a rough estimate of the new vowels, cannot by any means be exact, for two reasons: first, it is impossible to describe the sounds of one language in terms of another, and secondly, if this were possible, the reader would be likely to interpret them differently from what the writer meant.

48. A means of accurate comparison of vowel sounds has been provided by the *Cardinal Vowel Scheme*, devised by Professor D. Jones. The Cardinal Vowels are a series of vowel sounds chosen irrespective of any language, to serve as a scale or measure with which the vowels of any particular language can be compared. They have well-defined tongue positions and definite acoustic qualities : X-ray photographs have been taken of the tongue positions of most of them, and the vowels have been recorded on a gramophone record.[1]

49. The original choice of the cardinal vowels was made as follows. The highest possible front vowel was made : this gave cardinal **i,** the tongue position of which is physiologically determined, since no higher or more forward tongue position could be made without passing the vowel limit, i.e. the limit beyond which friction would occur and thus a consonant be produced. The vowel limit is shown on the diagram on p. 23 by the line - - - - - ; cardinal **i** by the line ——.

50. The next position was the most open back vowel possible : this again is physiologically fixed ; the tongue is as low in the mouth as possible and drawn as far back as it can be ; such a position gives cardinal **ɑ** (shown on the diagram by the line ·········).

51. The next two, a close back vowel (cardinal **u**), and an open front vowel (cardinal **a**), cannot be physiologically fixed like **i** and **ɑ,** but for practical purposes they can be considered as the closest back and the most open front vowel respectively. (Cardinal **u** is shown by the line ·········· ; cardinal **a** by the line ··········.)

52. These four tongue positions give us the four outside limits, as it were, of possible vowel sounds.

53. Two intermediate front and two intermediate back positions have been chosen, at equal distances between the close and open limits, viz. a half-close and a half-open front vowel and a half-close and a half-open back vowel. These are represented by the letters **e, ɛ, o, ɔ.**

[1] His Master's Voice Gramophone Co., Record No. B 804. Price 3*s*. 0*d*.

54. The whole eight vowels make an acoustic sequence such that the intervals between any neighbouring pair are equal. The vowels are numbered for convenience in reference:

1 2 3 4 5 6 7 8
i e ɛ a ɑ ɔ o u

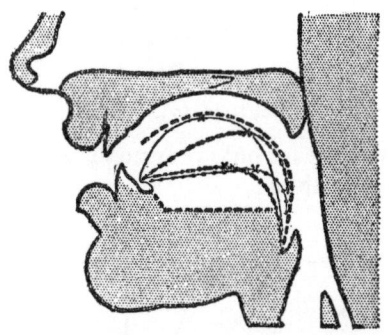

Fɪɢ. 5. Cardinal Vowel Figure (4 vowels).

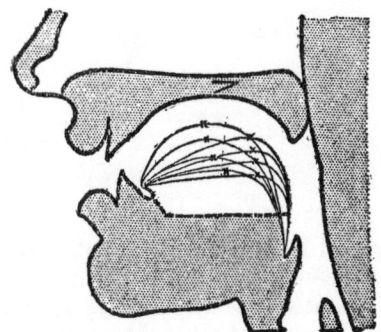

Fɪɢ. 6. Tongue Positions of the Eight Primary Cardinal Vowels.

55. The vowels of any language can be related to these cardinal vowels and their exact tongue position and acoustic quality fixed. Thus a means is provided for an accurate and scientific description of vowels which has hitherto been wanting.

56. In order to facilitate the 'placing' of new vowel sounds the drawings of the tongue positions given above have been conventionalized into a *vowel diagram*. If the highest point of the tongue is marked by a dot in each case, and the dots joined, the figure resembles this shape:

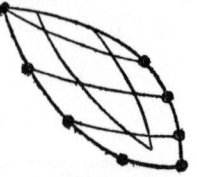

FIG. 7 (a).

This figure, however, is not practical, and has been conventionalized further thus:

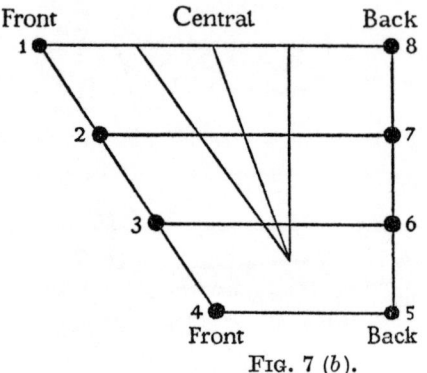

FIG. 7 (b).

Cardinal Vowel Diagrams.

It may be interpreted in this way. A dot placed on the front line of the figure represents a vowel with the front part of the tongue raised: its relation to any of the four cardinal points on the front line indicates the height to which the tongue is raised. Similarly a dot placed on the back line indicates a vowel in which the back of the tongue is used, and its relation to any of the four back cardinal vowels again shows the height to which it is raised. A dot placed in the central triangle indicates that the middle of the tongue is used, i.e. part of the front and part of the back. The neutral vowels of English, French, and German (ə) have positions—all of them different —within this central triangle. A dot placed between the front line and the central triangle indicates that although the front of the tongue is used the point of raising is not as far forward as possible but somewhat retracted. Thus for the English and German vowels in *bit* and *bitte* the point of raising is a little retracted from the most forward position. A dot placed between the back line and the central triangle shows that though the back of the tongue is used, the point of raising is not as far back as possible, but somewhat advanced. Thus for the English and German vowels in *put* and *Kunst*, the point of raising of the tongue is advanced from the farthest back position.

57. It is evident that for the 'placing' of new vowels, i.e. the comparison of new vowels with the cardinal vowels, two things are necessary. First, the student must know the cardinal vowels thoroughly; he must have a clear impression of their acoustic quality, i.e. he must be able to recognize and make them without difficulty. Secondly, he must have practice in relating other vowels to them. When he can do these two things, he is in a position to 'plot out' the vowels of any language he is dealing with and describe them with great accuracy. Such work, of course, should be done by the phonetic investigator: he should record the vowels of as many languages as possible in this way. The student of particular languages will have to interpret these analyses, and a knowledge of the cardinal vowels for this purpose is essential.

58. It should be noted that vowel sounds are learnt best through the impression they make on the ear. A student who knows theoretically the tongue positions of vowel sounds he is trying to learn does not for this reason necessarily make them correctly. Such knowledge, however, is extremely useful in that it may show him the relationship between the new vowels he is learning and those with which he is already familiar, and this will help him to make the necessary adjustments of tongue, lips, &c. to approach more nearly to the vowels he wants, and to assist his acoustic impressions.

59. The vowels of average English, French, and German speakers respectively are set out on p. 26.[1] These not only show the relation of the vowels of each language to the cardinal vowels, but a comparison of the three figures shows the relationship between the vowels of the three languages. Thus

---

[1] The symbols used in these figures are those of the International Phonetic Association. **y** as in Fr. *rue*, Germ. *Hüte*, **ʏ** as in German *Hütte*, **ø** as in Fr. *peu*, Germ. *Höhle*, **œ** as in Fr. *sœur*, Germ. *Götter*.

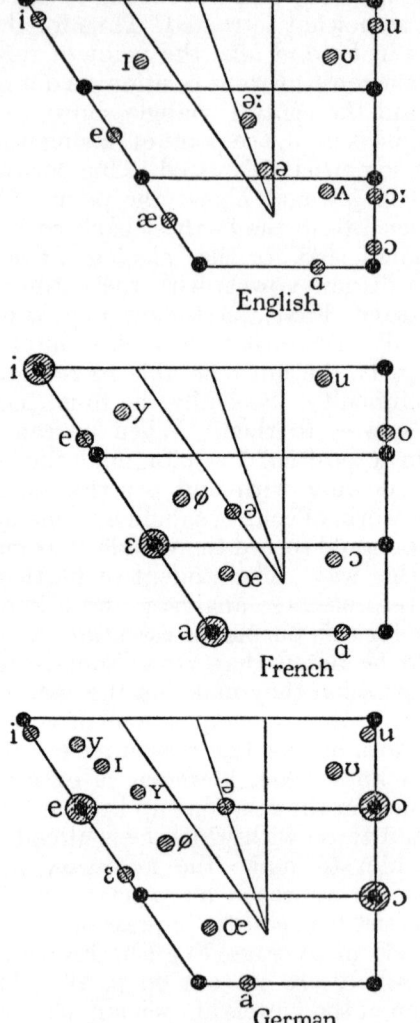

FIG. 8. Vowels of English, French, and German.

PLATE III

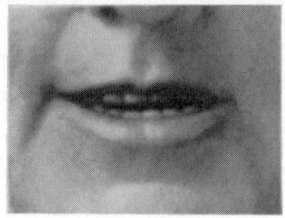

(a) Spread.

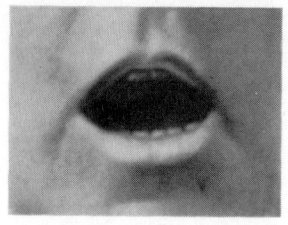

(b) Neutrally open.

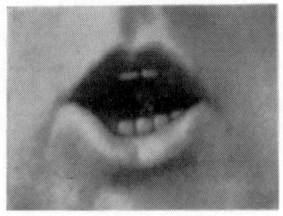

(c) Open rounding.

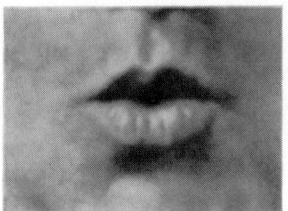

(d) Close rounding.

FIG. 9. Photographs of Lip Positions.

valuable assistance is given in acquiring the vowels of any of these languages in that the points of similarity and difference can be seen almost at a glance. A comparison of the vowels of a foreign language with those of the mother tongue will also show what mistakes a student is likely to make in the learning of the foreign vowels and what he must try to avoid. The vowels of these European languages are set out here for two reasons: first, to illustrate the value of the cardinal vowel scheme in the comparative study of languages; and secondly, to serve as a further help in comparing and contrasting the vowel sounds of any African language with those of the mother tongue of the European learner.

60. The student is advised to learn the cardinal vowels, preferably from a teacher who knows them, but if this is impossible, from the gramophone record which has been made of them, and to practise placing any vowels he hears—his own, those of other speakers of his mother tongue, and those of any language or dialect he may be familiar with. In this way he will gradually acquire the power of accurately identifying the vowels of any language he wishes to learn or investigate.

61. In this book the vowels of a number of African languages have been recorded on the cardinal figure. These will be found in the phonetic summaries at the end of the book. They have all been heard by the writers of the book or by investigators of whose accuracy the writers are convinced. Acknowledgements are made to these investigators in the preface and the languages on which they have supplied notes are stated.

62. Lip movements also affect the quality of vowels and must be taken into consideration in the classification of them. There are four main positions of the lips in the formation of vowel sounds, viz. *spread, neutrally open*, with *open-rounding*, and with *close-rounding*. Photographs of these positions are given on Plate III (Fig. 9).

63. It is generally found that front vowels have spread or neutrally open lips, the closer ones having well spread lips, and the degree of spreading lessening to the open position where the lips are neutrally open, i.e. neither spread nor rounded. Back vowels generally have some degree of lip-rounding, from close-rounding in the close vowels through degrees of open-rounding as the tongue position gets lower, until often the most open back vowels have neither spread nor rounded, but neutrally open lips.

64. The eight primary cardinal vowels have the usual lip positions, viz. **i** has spread lips, **e** spread but slightly more open, **ε** less spread, nearing the neutral position, **a** neutrally open lips. Of the back vowels, **ɑ** has neutrally open lips, **ɔ** has open-rounding, **o** closer rounding, and **u** very close-rounding.

65. These positions are generally considered the normal position of the lips for vowels of the types described. But in many languages there are vowels the lip positions of which are not normal, e.g. with front vowels lip-rounding is found, with back vowels lip-spreading. Such a reversal of the normal lip positions gives an entirely different vowel quality. If the cardinal vowels are pronounced with this change, i.e. front vowels with lip-rounding, back vowels with lip-spreading, a further set of subsidiary cardinal vowels are heard. As such vowels occur only seldom in African languages, the symbols used for them are not given here. Further remarks on these vowels will be found in Ch. VII.

CHAPTER V

PHONEMES

66. Two pitfalls lie before the investigator who wishes to record in writing a language which has not previously been written or which has been written inaccurately. He is likely either to record too many minute differences of pronunciation and so multiply symbols unnecessarily, or he may group together sounds under one letter which to him seem similar, but which to the native speaker are distinct sounds differentiating words. The standpoint of the native speaker of the language is the standard of what should be written down: the distinctions which are necessary to him, however difficult or slight these may appear to the European, must be made; those which from his point of view are not essential should be neglected in orthography. A knowledge of the theory of phonemes and skill in discovering the phoneme usages of the language he is dealing with is the only method of avoiding these dangers.

67. A phone or speech-sound proper is the result of one position of the organs of speech: if another position is taken up, however slight the difference may be, what is heard is another sound or phone. It follows, therefore, that the speech sounds of a language are far more numerous than is usually supposed, but it is not necessary to write each variety of sound which a speaker uses with a separate letter. The sounds can be grouped into families or phonemes, each group, for certain purposes, being considered as an entity and needing only one letter to represent its various members. The nature of the relationship between the members of a group, and why each particular one is used, can be understood more easily through illustration than by explanation.

68. In English the k-sounds used in *keep* and *calm* are different: the first is articulated farther forward on the roof of the mouth than the second. The same is true of the k-sounds in the German *Kies* and *Kuh*. The two l-sounds in *little* in southern English have not the same formation, the first is the 'clear' l and the second the 'dark' l (see Ch. XIII, p. 68): prolong the two l's and the different acoustic qualities will be easily perceived.[1] The final l in French words like *peuple* (preceded by a voiceless consonant) is, in the pronunciation of most French people, voiceless: l in all other positions is voiced. The k's and l's in these examples are different speech sounds, but they can be regarded respectively as one phoneme and written with one letter in the languages in which these varieties occur.

69. The use of each particular member of the group depends generally on the nature of the surrounding sounds or upon its position in a word or phrase. A phoneme may be defined as a group of sounds consisting of one main member together with others which take its place in certain sound-groups.[2] Thus the forward k in English and German (and in many other languages) is always used before front vowels, and the more retracted one before back vowels: in southern English, clear l is used before vowels and dark l finally and before consonants; in French the voiceless l occurs finally after a voiceless consonant, but in no other position. The native speaker of a language is generally unaware of the existence of the varieties of sounds he uses in such cases, since he always uses the one variety in one place and another in another place, and he thinks of them as one sound.[3]

---

[1] In French and German there is only one variety of l, viz. 'clear' l.
[2] From *The Pronunciation of Russian*, by Trofimov and D. Jones.
[3] The varieties of a sound in a phoneme group must not be confused

70. It is necessary, however, for the learner of a language to be aware of the difference between a phone or speech sound and a phoneme, since the phoneme usages of one language may not correspond to those of another. For example, clear and dark l, belonging to one phoneme in English, belong to separate phonemes (and distinguish words) in Russian; voiceless l which in French belongs to the same phoneme as voiced l, belongs to a different phoneme in Welsh. The student, unless these differences of usage are pointed out to him, is likely to transfer into the new language the phoneme habits of his own and the results may lead to misunderstanding. The test of whether two sounds belong to one phoneme or not is that of significance: if they distinguish words, they belong to separate phonemes. The difference between one member of a phoneme and another member of the same phoneme will never distinguish words. It follows, then, that the investigator or the learner of a language must be able to distinguish one phoneme from another both by ear and in speaking. Moreover, if the language is to be written down unambiguously, it must have a separate letter for each phoneme, otherwise words which are distinguished by pronunciation will not be distinguished in writing. The use of the subsidiary members of a phoneme in their right places is of secondary importance for understanding, though important in securing a good accent: the wrong use of the members of a phoneme would not lead to misunderstanding, but to a 'foreign' accent, since the native speaker would never use pronunciations of this kind.

71. OTHER EXAMPLES

English.

(*a*) The vowel sounds in words like *pity* (**piti**) are generally not alike, the second, in the pronunciation of many people, being more open than the first: but they belong to the same phoneme.

(*b*) The point of contact for the **t** sounds in *eighth* (**eitθ**—tip of the tongue on the teeth), *sits* (**sits**—tip of tongue on the teeth-ridge), *which* (**witʃ**—made with the blade of the tongue), and *try* (**trai**—made with the curled-up tongue-tip) are not the same, the difference in articulation being due to that of the following consonant.

with variant pronunciations from one person to another or with dialectal variants. A group of variant pronunciations may be termed a diaphone.

German.

The fricative consonants in *ich* and *auch* (the one articulated near the hard, the other near the soft palate) may be considered as members of the same phoneme, since the first is always used initially and after front vowels and consonants and the second after back vowels.[1]

French.

The vowel é in an unstressed position has a lower tongue position than when it is stressed. This ' e-*moyen* ' which lies between é and è can be considered as belonging to the é phoneme.

Italian.

A written **n** followed by **f** or **v** is pronounced as a labio-dental nasal, i.e. bottom lip against the top teeth, e.g. in *confondere* the first **n** is not alveolar but labio-dental. Similarly, a written **n** before **k** or **g** is pronounced **ŋ** : e.g. *in casa* is pronounced **iŋ kasa;** the labio-dental and velar nasal consonants in these cases can be considered as belonging to the **n** phoneme. They need no special letter to represent them, since they always occur in these positions and in no other. **n** and **ŋ**, however, belong to separate phonemes in English and German.

72. Examples from African Languages

Chuana.

The fronted **k** (which is almost **ky**) occurs before front vowels and is a member of the **k**-phoneme, the back **k** being used before back vowels.

Zulu.

The vowels **e** and **ɛ**, **o** and **ɔ** belong to one phoneme respectively in Zulu, **e** and **o** being used according to a scheme of vowel harmony when a close vowel (**i** or **u**) follows in the next syllable, and **ɛ** and **ɔ** when a more open vowel occurs in the next syllable : e.g.

leli, lolu this
lɛlɔ, lɔlɔ that

[1] The diminutive termination -*chen* for this purpose is by a convention considered as a separate word and the *ch* is initial.

In very many African languages **e** and **ɛ**, **o** and **ɔ** belong to separate phonemes, e.g. in Ewe, Gã, Yoruba.

Efik.

The letter **i** has two sounds, one similar to the sound of **ee** in English *see*, the other between the **i** of *bit* and the neutral vowel **ə**. These two sounds belong to one phoneme, the first being used before vowels, initially and finally, and the second in a closed syllable, i.e. followed by a consonant: e.g. **di, itoro, sio** have the close **i**; **dip, sim** have the short, lowered and retracted **i**.

Ibo. (Arochuku Dialect.)

The letter **r** has two sounds, the one a kind of flapped sound something between **l** and **r** which is used with the vowels **i** and **e** (e.g. **siri, sere**) and the other the normal rolled **r** which is used with other vowels (e.g. **sara, sɔrɔ**). Both sounds belong to one phoneme and can be represented by one letter. (See Ch. XIII, p. 75.)

Ewe.

In most Ewe dialects the **s** before the vowel **i** is palatalized, i.e. it represents a sound intermediate between **s** and **ʃ**: before all other vowels the normal **s** occurs; thus **s** and the palatalized **s** belong to the same phoneme. (See Ch. XIV, p. 82.)

Twi.

The semi-vowel **w** is used before back vowels, while a palatalized **w** (i.e. made with the front of the tongue raised towards the hard palate—like the initial sound in French *huit*) is used before front vowels. These two sounds belong to the same phoneme and need only one letter to represent them. (See Ch. XVI, p. 91.) They belong to different phonemes in French, e.g. *Louis* and *lui* are distinguished by this difference.

Fante.

The velar nasal **ŋ** occurs only before velar consonants (**k, g, w**), and before **h**: it can be considered as belonging to the **n** phoneme.

73. Frequent references will be found to phonemes in subsequent chapters: the examples here should suffice to illustrate the theory of phonemes and enable students to apply it to

the particular languages they are studying. In the new orthographies decided upon for certain African languages, the principle of one letter per phoneme[1] has been generally followed
as far as present-day knowledge allows. It may, of course, be
found that further investigations will reveal other phonemic
differences: if so, these should be incorporated into the orthography.

CHAPTER VI

VOWELS OF AFRICAN LANGUAGES

74. Many African languages have a seven-vowel system: a
few have more than seven, others have five or six only. Some
languages may have vowels of a less normal type, such as
central vowels, front rounded vowels, or back unrounded
vowels. For information about these and the languages in
which they have been found, see next chapter.

75. The cardinal vowel system as a method of vowel classification and comparison has been explained and illustrated
in Chapter V. In this book, the vowels of those languages
which have been analysed and of which records are given have
been 'placed' in relation to the cardinal vowels. On pp. 26, 39
the English, French, and German vowels are shown on the
cardinal figure. These diagrams should be referred to when
examples from these languages are given in illustration. While
it is impossible to describe and place all African vowels, a few
notes on the general types found and hints as to their pronunciation are given here.

76. i. Every language contains a vowel of the **i**-type (Card.
No. 1); this can be more or less close: in African languages it
is usually closer than the English **i** in *see*, resembling the **i** in
French *si*, and in German *sie*. The English vowel in *see* is often
diphthongized, i.e. a gliding sound is made by the tongue
moving from a low **i** position to a closer one. Such diphthongization should be avoided in African languages.

---

[1] It is sometimes useful for the learner to use a narrower transcription
and mark in some special way some of the subsidiary members of the
phonemes: this is especially the case if the phoneme usages vary considerably from those of the learner's mother tongue. But it should be
remembered that this is a device to assist the foreign learner and has
nothing to do with an orthography for the native reader.

77. e and ε. A large number of African languages contain two e-sounds, the one close as in the French *bébé*, and the German *fehlen* (belonging to the Cardinal No. 2 class), and the other open as in the French *très* and the German *Bett* (Card. No. 3 class). Where these two vowels occur distinguishing words they should always be distinguished in pronunciation and in writing. The English vowel in *bed* lies between the two: it is generally nearer to the more open sound; the vowel in *bad* is more open still. English people are apt to associate the close **e** with the diphthong **ei** (as in *make*): in many books on African languages, the close **e** is described as 'the sound of long **e** in *make*'. This is not correct for the majority of English speakers, and the pronunciation of a diphthong for close **e** is always wrong. Scottish and northern English speakers can generally say a pure **e** without difficulty: other English students are advised to listen to the gramophone record of the cardinal vowels and try to imitate the **e** and **ε**. The tongue and lips should not move during the production of the sound. Another method of obtaining a pure **e** is to pronounce the vowel in *bit* with considerable vigour and lengthen it: this approaches to an **e** and the student can work from it to obtain a better one. In those languages where only one e-sound is found, it is generally between the Cardinal No. 2 and No. 3, and resembles the English vowel in *bed* (as in Efik **ekpe**, *leopard*).

78. Note that in some languages, e.g. Zulu, the two sounds **e** and **ε** belong to one phoneme and are used according to definite rules which can be learned. In such cases, only one letter is needed to represent the two sounds in orthography. (See Ch. V on Phonemes, and Ch. XXIII on Vowel Harmony: also summary of Zulu, p. 197.)

79. a. Most African languages have only one **a** vowel. This is an open sound: in some languages it lies nearer to the front **a** (Card. No. 4) and in others it is nearer to the back **a** (Card. No. 5). A vowel in a preceding or following syllable may sometimes affect the quality of the **a**, a front vowel, **i** or **e**, bringing the **a** forward, and a back vowel, **u** or **ɔ**, making it nearer to the back position. The **a** of African languages often resembles the Italian **a** in *famiglia* and the German **a** in *Vater*: it is rarely like the English **a** in *man*. English people who find it difficult to imitate should say the diphthong **ai** (as in *right*) and try to isolate the first element: in the pronunciation of most people, this would give a good African **a**. The tendency of English people is to use three sounds for the letter **a**, all of them depending on English usage. Thus when they hear it short, they are tempted to use the vowel in *sat* (**æ**): when long, to use the **a** in *father* (**ɑ:**): and when unstressed, especially in initial and final positions, they use the neutral vowel **ə** as in *about* and *sofa* (**əbaut, soufə**). In most African languages the quality of the **a** is not changed in an unstressed position and a final **a** is pronounced **a** and not **ə**. In some languages it is found that a short **a** sometimes resembles the English sound in *but*. (See the description of the Fante vowel on p. 173.)

80. **o** and **ɔ**. A large number of African languages contain what strikes the ear as two **o**-sounds. Like **e** and **ɛ**, one is close and the other open: the exact quality of **o** and **ɔ** must be discovered for each particular language. **ɔ** is generally near to Card. No. 6, similar to the German vowel in *Gott*, not quite so open as the English vowel in *not*, but somewhat like that in *caught*. Note that the English vowel in *caught* is usually long and that in *Gott* is short: the African **ɔ** can generally be long or short without changing its quality. When it is long it strikes the English ear as the **ɔ** in *caught* and when short as the vowel in *not*.

81. The exact quality of the **o** in an African language must be found out: it is often close with well-rounded lips (Card. No. 7 type), something like the **o** in the French *beau* and in the German *rot*. This sound does not occur in English (except in northern English and in Scottish), and English people replace it by two sounds, both depending on English usage. When it is long, the Englishman uses the diphthong **ou** (as in *note*). It has been wrongly described as 'the sound of long **o** in *note*'. Such a pronunciation is always wrong. When it is short, he hears it as the short **u** in *put*. This sound is the nearest equivalent in English to short **o** and the two sounds bear some considerable resemblance to each other. To a certain extent the German student also falls into the second error (but not the first), because close **o** in German is always considered as long and a short **o** strikes him as the short **u** in *Mutter*. But both the English and German short **u** have a more forward position and less lip-rounding than the African **o**, and the two should be differentiated.

82. The English student who finds it difficult to pronounce a pure o is advised to listen for a long time to the cardinal vowel record of o and ɔ and to practise with well-rounded lips and without moving lips or tongue during the production of the sound. If this is not sufficient he can use the similarity between English short u and a close o to obtain the latter. He should pronounce the vowel in *put* with considerable vigour and lengthen it: this gives a kind of o sound, from which it is possible to work and which is in any case better than a diphthong.

83. u. All languages contain a u sound of some kind (Card. No. 8 type). In African languages the u is generally close, resembling the vowel in German *Buch*. The English u is usually lower than this, while the French u, as in *nous*, has a somewhat advanced tongue position. The u of African languages can be long or short without changing its quality. This sound is not difficult to acquire: those English people who use a slight diphthong in words like *too* should avoid this diphthongization, i.e. they should not make a gliding sound but should keep the tongue still during the production of the sound.

84. The front vowels i, e, ɛ as described above are pronounced with spread lips, while ɔ, o, u are pronounced with lip-rounding, the degree of lip-rounding being closer for u than for ɔ; a has neither lip-rounding nor spreading. These are the normal positions of the lips; front vowels with lip-rounding and back vowels with lip-spreading are less normal: these are described in the next chapter.

85. There is generally a parallelism between front and back vowels: if a language has two e sounds (e and ɛ) it usually has two o sounds (o and ɔ). (Efik, however, has two o sounds and only one e.)

86. Many West African languages contain a sound which lies between close i and close e, i.e. a vowel resembling the English i in *bit* and the German i in *bist*. It is often very difficult to distinguish this sound from e. Similarly, in the back group of sounds, a vowel between u and o often occurs: this resembles the English vowel in *put* and the German vowel in *Kunst*. It is often very difficult to distinguish from o. If symbols are required for these sounds, ɪ and ʊ can be used.

These two sounds occur in Bari as the 'lax' forms of i and u respectively; they distinguish words as the following examples show: **ġir**, *to wipe a plate*; **ġɪr**, *to cicatrise*; **kur**, *to borrow*; **kʊr**, *to till*. Where these are significant sounds, they should be distinguished in pronunciation and in orthography. Much practice is required to recognize and make this difference. In Fante, in which they occur, they have not been distinguished in the new orthography, presumably because the words containing the vowels intermediate between **i** and **e** and between **u** and **o** are not numerous and are not likely to be confused with those which have the sounds **e** and **o**. In the phonetic summary of Fante at the end of this book, the distinctions have been made.

87. In the Suto-Chuana group of languages, there are also two varieties of close **e** and two of close **o**. Dr. Tucker writes the opener in each case **ę** or **ǫ**. They are described in his book on the *Comparative Phonetics of the Suto-Chuana Group of Bantu Languages*. See also Professor D. Jones and S. T. Plaatje, *A Sechuana Reader*, for their use in this language.

88. Ibo has eight vowels, some of which are difficult to distinguish. The front series consists of **i**, a very close **e** (above Card. No. 2, more forward than the English and German short **i**), **ɛ** (a little higher than Card. No. 3), and **a** : **i** and **e** are difficult to distinguish. The back series consists of **u**, a very close **o** (closer than Card. No. 7), a more open **o** with an advanced tongue position, and **ə**. **u** and **o** are extremely difficult to distinguish, and sometimes **o** and the centralized variety of **o**. In the orthography adopted for this language, the symbol **ɵ** has been used for the closer of the two **o**-sounds. (See Ch. XXIII on Vowel Harmony in this language.)

89. One characteristic of many West African languages should be noted. There is often an interchange between front and back vowels, **i** in one language or dialect being used and **u** in another; **e** and **o** in the same way are interchanged.

90. EXAMPLES

Ibo.

ane and **ano** animal, meat

Edo.

ewili and **owuli** palm oil
ki   ,,   **ku** to take
lie   ,,   **lue** to make

Ewe.

blikɔ	and **blukɔ** darkness	:	**avivɔ** and **avuvɔ** cold
mimi	,, **mumu** mute	:	**blisi** ,, **blusi** cotton cloth
de	,, **do** to put into	:	**ɗe** ,, **ɗo** to reach

Bambara.

nima and **numa** living   : **fila** and **fula** leaf

Malinke.

sisɛ	and **susɛ** fowl	:	**mita** and **muta** to hold
jeli	,, **joli** ulcer		

Bari (**i, ɪ, u,** and **ʊ** only).

kulu   and **kilu** those
ŋurɔ   ,, **ŋɪrɔ** child

In each interchange of this kind between front and back
vowels, the two vowels are similar in the height to which the
tongue is raised: thus **i** and **u** are both close vowels, **e** and **o**
both half-close vowels. This interchange is sometimes (but
not always) due to the influence of vowels in neighbouring
syllables. See Chap. XXIII, on Vowel Harmony.

91. The attention of the student is drawn to the fact that
a vowel in a close syllable (i.e. followed by a consonant) often
varies slightly from one (belonging to the same phoneme) in an
open syllable. This variation sometimes leads to misinterpretation of African vowels. Variations of length also affect the ear
as variations in quality, particularly when the usages in length
in the African language vary from those of the mother tongue:
and this again makes misinterpretation easy. For example, the
Efik **o** in an open syllable is easily recognized as **o** and is not
likely to be taken for anything else: but **o** in a close syllable is
very short and strikes the ear as a kind of **u**: thus the verbs
kut, *to see,* and **kot,** *to call,* have been confused: the final vowel
in **uto** is easily recognized as **o,** but in **utom,** *work,* it is very
u-like. Considerable work must be done by the phonetic investigator in determining the phoneme usages of the vowels of the
language he is working on.

CHAPTER VII

LESS USUAL VOWELS

I. Central Vowels.

92. In the preceding chapter the usual front and back vowels which occur in most African languages have been described. In addition to these, there occur in some languages vowels which are known as *central vowels*: in their production

Central Vowel Area

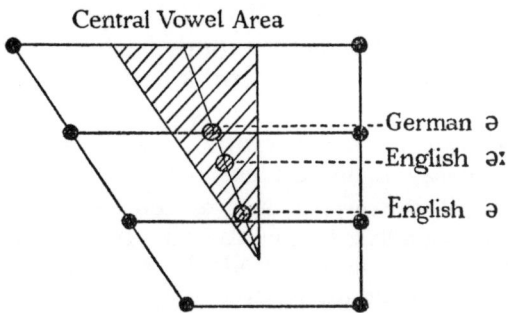

--German ə
--English əː
--English ə

FIG. 10. Central Vowels.

the part of the tongue used is neither the front nor the back, but a part of the front and part of the back, i.e. the centre of the tongue. In English there are two central vowels, viz. the ə: in *bird* and the neutral[1] vowel in *about, china* (ə); in German the **e** in *bitte* is a central vowel (but different from the English ones) and in French a central vowel ə with some lip-rounding (as in *le*) also exists.

93. There can be numerous varieties of central vowels: some are nearer to the front series and therefore resemble **i, e, ɛ** somewhat, while others are nearer to the back series and resemble the back vowels. In the cardinal vowel figure central vowels are placed within the central triangle.

94. The quality of central and centralized vowels is always somewhat obscure and difficult to distinguish. It is not usual to find many central vowels in one language. When only one occurs, the letter ə is recommended for it (see Memorandum

[1] Used in an unstressed position.

on Orthography); where several occur the use of diacritic marks over the letter is suggested: e.g. in Nuer, besides o, ə, a, there are ö, ɔ̈, ä.

95. EXAMPLES

Temne. ə is frequent in Temne: **bəp**, *meet*; **afəm**, *persons*; **ɡbəf**, *to bark*; **ɡbək**, *to cut.*

Ewe (Aŋlɔ dialect). The sound corresponding to e in other dialects is very often pronounced ə: **ɡəɖəə**, *much*; **xəxəmə**, *world.*

Kru. **səla** or **səra** house

Nuer. **rök** molar (cf. pl. **rok**)   **yööth** women's cloth
     cök feet   **mök** buffaloes (cf. **mək** buffalo
                                  sing.)

Dinka. **kwïn** porridge, pl. **kwɪɪn**   **ebën** all (cf. **ben** again)
     bär long (cf. **bar** orphan)

Bari. The central vowel **ö** may be considered as the 'tense' vowel corresponding to the 'lax' **a**. It is found sometimes as the 'umlaut' form of **a** (**ködini**, *tree*, pl. **kadɛn**), and very occasionally as an alternative for **e** (e.g. **deru** or **döru**, *grass*); but it is generally an independent vowel: **bön**, *to shake*; **löri**, *drum.*

Amharic. In Amharic there are two central vowels, viz. **ë** and **ɛ̈**: **s'ëhai**, *sun*; **t'ëmt'ëmo**, *wrapped.*

Kanuri.[1] **firtə** root   **kəladotu** to poison   **ʃəntəra** a kick
Kaidikanem.[2] **dəna** power   **dəli** wilderness

96. Central vowels occur also in Yaunde. See P. Hermann Nekes and L. W. Planert, *Lehrbuch der Jaunde-Sprache*, Berlin, 1911, pp. 3 ff., and M. Heepe, *Jaunde-Texte*, Hamburg, 1919, p. 152. They are also found in other languages spoken in the Cameroons, e.g. Bali, Bamum.

II. Rounded Front Vowels.

97. Normal front vowels are pronounced with spread lips, while back vowels generally have a certain amount of lip-rounding. It is possible, however, to pronounce front vowels with

---

[1] A. von Duisberg, *Grundriss der Kanuri-sprache in Bornu*, Berlin, 1913.
[2] J. Lukas, *Die Sprache der Kaidikanembu*, Berlin, 1931.

lip-rounding and back vowels with lip-spreading. Say the front vowel i, and while continuing the sound, round the lips without moving the tongue: the resulting sound is a front rounded vowel. Another way of obtaining this sound is to round the lips as if for u and then try to say i without any movement of the lips. A sound similar to this occurs in French *rue* and in German *Hüte*.[1] This is a close front rounded vowel. The German vowel in *Hütte* is also a front rounded vowel with a somewhat lower tongue position and is always short. A half-close front rounded vowel can be made by adding lip-rounding to e: such a vowel also occurs in French *peu* and in German *Höhle*:[2] and again a half-open front rounded vowel is made by adding lip-rounding to ε as in French *seul* and German *Hölle*.[3]

98. Front rounded vowels are not common in African languages. In the Mandingo languages a close front rounded vowel is found (similar to the French u in *rue*). No new symbol has been suggested for it: it is written in the orthography as ü. The word for *at night* in Bambara is pronounced **süfε**; *to sleep* is **sinəγə, sünəγə**, or **sunəγə**. This vowel was also found in Kru after the palatal plosive *dy*, and the palatal nasal *ny* (e.g. **dyuro**, *doctor*; **nyuno**, *sleep*).

III. Back Unrounded Vowels.

99. Back vowels are usually pronounced with lip-rounding, but in some languages there occur back vowels with spread lips: these are somewhat unusual and are difficult to imitate. A close unrounded u is produced by pronouncing u and then stretching the lips while the tongue remains in the u-position, and an unrounded o is produced by holding the o tongue-position and spreading the lips, and an unrounded ə by taking away the lip-rounding from ə. The English vowel in *but* is similar to the unrounded ə, but a little centralized, i.e. advanced from the full back position.

100. The present writers have not found any examples of back unrounded vowels in African languages.

[1] I.P.A. y.   [2] I.P.A. ø.   [3] I.P.A. œ.

CHAPTER VIII

NASALIZED VOWELS

101. A vowel has been defined as a voiced sound in which the air has a free passage through the mouth or through the mouth and nose. When the air escapes wholly through the mouth, the soft palate is raised to touch the back wall of the throat, i.e. the nose passage is closed; the vowel then is *oral*.

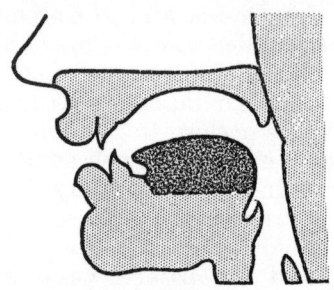 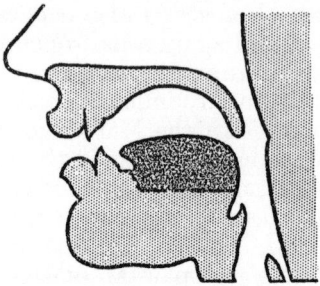

FIG. 11. (*a*) The vowel **a** (oral). (*b*) The vowel **a** (nasalized).

When the air escapes through both nose and mouth, the soft palate is lowered to allow some of the air to go through the nose. In this case, the vowel is *nasalized*, i.e. nasal resonance is added to the resonance of the mouth cavity.

102. Nasal vowels are shown by the sign ˜ placed over the vowel letter, thus: ĩ, ẽ, ɛ̃, ã, ɔ̃, ũ, &c.

103. Nasal vowels occur in French: in the words *un bon pain blanc*, the vowels are all nasalized (œ̃ bɔ̃ pɛ̃ blã). In Swabia ã and ĩ are sometimes used instead of the **an** and **in** of North Germany: *du kannst* is pronounced **du kãã∫t**, *unangenehm* as **ũãknɛ̃**.

104. All vowels can be nasalized, and the student of African languages is advised to practise the nasalizing of as many vowels as he can. He must be careful not to add the nasal consonant ŋ to the back vowels: there should be no contact of the tongue with any part of the roof of the mouth.

105. Nasal vowels occur in many African languages. In the neighbourhood of nasal consonants, the vowels are normally nasalized: this nasalization is due to the influence of the consonant, i.e. the soft palate begins to be lowered during the production of the vowel, in readiness for the nasal consonant, or the nasality continues into the vowel following a nasal consonant. In such cases, it is not usually necessary to mark the vowel nasal, as all vowels in this position will be nasal and such nasality is not significant. But nasalization of vowels which is not dependent on an adjoining nasal consonant is significant in a number of African languages, and this must be shown in the pronunciation and in the orthography.

106. EXAMPLES

Ewe.	dɔ	belly	dɔ̃	be weak
	duu	in heaps	dũũ	staring
	akpa	division	akpã	trap
	ma	not	mã[1]	to divide

Twi.	nsa	hand	nsã	palm wine
	sa	cut	sã	tie, connect
	se	say	sẽ	hang about

Gã.	ʃia	sand	ʃiã	house
	ka	stick to	kã	lie
	kpa	to remove	kpã	thread

Yoruba.	eri	evidence	erĩ	laughter
	ha	scrape	hã	itch

CHAPTER IX

DIPHTHONGS

107. A diphthong is a gliding sound in which the tongue starts in the position of one vowel and immediately leaves it to glide towards another vowel position by the most direct route, without any diminution and subsequent reinforcement of the

---

[1] Note that there are degrees of nasalization: in this pair of words, for example, the a of **ma** will be slightly nasalized owing to the proximity of the **m**, but in **mã** the nasalization will be much stronger; in the first case, the nasalization is accidental, as it were, and in the second, it is deliberate.

breath force. A diphthong strikes the ear as one syllable: it is made with one impulse of the breath.

108. Diphthongs are of two kinds, viz. falling and rising. A *falling diphthong* has its greatest prominence at the beginning: it is a decrescendo diphthong, >. The English diphthongs **ei** in *make*, **ou** in *home*, **ai** in *time*, &c., and the German **ai** in *Heim*, **au** in *Haus*, &c., are falling diphthongs. A *rising diphthong* has its greater prominence at the end: it is a crescendo diphthong, <. The French diphthong in *trois* (**trwa**) is a rising diphthong.

109. In a falling diphthong it is possible to state with considerable accuracy where the tongue starts and the direction in which it glides, but not exactly how far it goes: in a rising diphthong, which may also be considered as a semi-vowel+a vowel, it is not possible to say exactly where the tongue starts, but the end of the movement can be distinguished.

110. Falling diphthongs can be made by the tongue starting from *any* vowel position and moving towards any other position. It is customary to write them with two vowel letters, the first representing the starting-point of the glide and the second the *direction* in which the tongue moves: e.g. for the English diphthong **ai** in *time*, the tongue starts from near to the Cardinal 4 position and glides towards (but does not reach) the **i** position. If the movement of the tongue is considerable, as in this English diphthong, it is said to be *wide*: if the tongue does not move very far as for the **ei** in *make*, the diphthong is said to be *narrow*.

111. Rising diphthongs usually start from a close or half-close position and glide to a more open one: they can be represented by the semi-vowels **w** and **y**+a vowel, e.g. **wa, we, yi, yɔ, yɛ,** &c.

112. Falling diphthongs can be represented on the cardinal vowel figure by a dot showing the starting-point and an arrow showing the direction in which the tongue moves: in this way the exact quality of the diphthong can be realized and accurate comparisons can be made.

113. The number of diphthongs in an African language is, as a rule, not very large, though most languages have a few. It is not possible here to give details of all the diphthongs occurring in African languages: in the summaries at the end of the book, the diphthongs of each language recorded are noted. In Nuer and Dinka a very large number of significant diphthongs

occur: some of these are shown on the figure below to illustrate
how diphthongs can be indicated and compared.

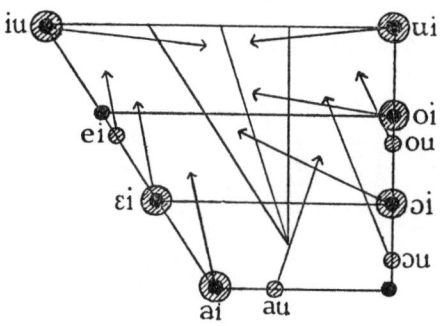

FIG. 12. Diphthongs.

114. EXAMPLES (from Dinka).

wei to breathe   **wɛi** to fall   **lai** wild game
liəi soft   **loi** to work   **lui** work
kiu to roar   **dau** string   **rəu** hippopotamus
rou two, thirst

CHAPTER X

CONSONANTS: CLASSIFICATION AND DESCRIPTION (GENERAL)

115. A consonant has been described as a sound in which
the air passage is either stopped entirely at some point, or
narrowed so as to give rise to audible friction. Consonants are
classified according to the *manner* in which they are formed,
i.e. according to the state of the air passage, and according to
the *organs* which articulate them. By this double classification
consonants can be conveniently shown on a table, the manner
of articulation being indicated down the side and the place of
articulation along the top.

116. A table showing the consonants occurring in English,
French, German, and Italian (and also in many African languages) is given here to illustrate the formation of consonants
in general and the terms used in describing them. Other

consonants used in African languages are dealt with in subsequent chapters.

TABLE I

Consonant Sounds occurring in English, French, German, Italian (and African Languages).

	Bi-labial.	Labio-Dental.	Dental.	Alveolar.	Palato-Alveolar.	Palatal.	Velar.	Uvular.	Glottal.
Plosive	p, b		t, d	t, d			k, g		'
Affricate			ts, dz		tʃ, dʒ				
Nasal	m			n		ny	ŋ		
Lateral				l		ly			
Rolled				r¹				r¹	
Fricative		f, v	θ, ð	s, z, r¹	ʃ, ʒ	ç	x	r¹	h
Semi-vowel	w, ɥ					y (ɥ)	(w)		

(Sounds enclosed in brackets indicate a secondary articulation.)

FIG. 13.

EXPLANATION OF TERMS

(with examples from European languages)

Manner of Articulation.

117. The terms down the side are explained briefly in the following paragraphs: a fuller description is given as each class of consonant is described in detail.

118. *Plosive* consonants are those formed by the stopping of the air passage at some point; when the stop is released a slight explosion is heard as the air escapes, e.g. the **p, b, t, d, k, g** of most languages.

119. *Affricates* are consonants formed like plosives by the stopping of the air passage; the stop, however, is released

¹ The same symbol is used here for four kinds of **r**: for these see later, pp. 72f.

slowly so that no explosion is heard, but a fricative consonant (see below) follows the stop, e.g. **ts** (as in the German *Zimmer*, and English *hats*), **tʃ** (as in English *church*, and in German *futsch*), **dz** (as in Italian *mezzo*). These are sometimes considered as groups of two consonants.

120. *Nasal* consonants are formed when the mouth passage is closed at some point, but the soft palate is lowered to let the air pass through the nose, e.g. **m, n** of all languages, **ŋ** (as in English *sing*, and German *singen*), **ny** (as in French *montagne*, and Italian *bisogna*).

121. *Lateral* consonants are formed when the mouth passage is stopped in the middle, the air escaping along the sides of the tongue, e.g. **l** in most languages and **ǵl (ly)** in Italian *famiglia*.

122. *Rolled* consonants are formed by a succession of taps of some elastic organ against some other organ, e.g. the rolled **r** which is made by the vibration of the tip of the tongue against the teeth-ridge, as in Scottish, Russian, Spanish, and the French rolled uvular **r** which is formed by the uvula making taps against the back of the tongue.

123. *Fricative* consonants are formed by a narrowing of the air passage at some point so that audible friction is heard, e.g. **s, z, f, v,** &c., of most languages.

124. *Semi-vowels* are gliding sounds made by the tongue starting from the position of a close (or half-close) vowel and immediately moving towards a more open vowel, e.g. **w** and **y** (as in English *won, yes*, German *Jude*), and the sound at the beginning of French *huit*.

Place of Articulation.

125. The terms across the top of the table are explained below. The student should consult the diagram of the organs of speech on p. 10.

126. *Bi-labial* consonants are those which are articulated by the two lips, e.g. **p, b, w.**

127. *Labio-dental* consonants are those which are articulated by the lower lip against the top teeth, e.g. **f, v.**

128. *Dental* consonants are those which are articulated by the tip of the tongue against or near the upper front teeth, or between the teeth, e.g. French and Italian **t** and **d**, English **θ** and **ð** (as in *thick, then*).

129. *Alveolar* consonants are those which are articulated by the tip or blade of the tongue against or near the upper gums or alveoli, e.g. English and German **t, d,** and **s.**

130. *Palato-alveolar* consonants are articulated by the blade of the tongue against the back part of the upper front gums and the front part of the palate, e.g. English, French, and German ʃ (as in *sheep, chambre, Schaf*), and English and French ʒ (as in *measure, jamais*).

131. *Palatal* consonants are articulated by the front of the tongue against or near the hard palate, e.g. French **ny** (as in *agneau*), Italian **ny** (as in *Bologna*), **ly** (as in *figlio*), German ç (as in *ich*), English **y** (as in *yes*).

132. *Velar* consonants are articulated by the back of the tongue against or near the soft palate, e.g. **k, g,** German **x** (as in *ach*).

133. *Uvular* consonants are articulated by the back of the tongue against or near the uvula, e.g. French and German uvular **r.**

134. *Glottal* consonants are articulated in the glottis, e.g. **h,** the glottal stop.

Voiced and Breathed or Voiceless Consonants.

135. All consonants can be produced with or without voice, i.e. with the vocal cords in vibration, when they are said to be *voiced*, or with the vocal cords open, when they are said to be *breathed* or *voiceless*. (See diagram, Plate I, fig. 2.) In the foregoing table, where consonants occur in pairs, the first is voiceless and the second voiced. Thus **p** is voiceless and **b** its voiced counterpart, **s** is voiceless, **z** voiced, &c. (see Ch. III, on the action of the vocal cords). It will be seen that the nasal, the lateral, and the rolled consonants are given singly: these are all voiced; it is quite possible to make these consonants without voice, and the student is advised to practise unvoicing them as a good exercise, but as they occur only rarely as speech sounds, they have not been inserted in the table.

136. The main difference between a voiced and a breathed consonant lies in the presence or absence of voice, the rest of the articulation being the same. There is, however, one further difference which should be noted. It is generally found that voiced consonants are pronounced with less breath force than the breathed ones, and that the articulation is less vigorous. Take a deep breath and pronounce **s**; then do the same with **z**:

it will be found that z can be held on longer. Pronounce **f**, holding the hand in front of the mouth, then **v** : for **f** the breath stream is felt to be stronger.

137. The so-called voiced consonants are not fully voiced in all languages, e.g. in English and German the initial voiced plosives and fricatives are not fully voiced, i.e. the vocal cords do not vibrate during the whole time of their articulation. Similarly English final voiced plosives and fricatives are not fully voiced, the voice stopping before the end of their articulation. (Final plosives and fricatives are all voiceless in German.) In French, on the other hand, initial and final voiced consonants are fully voiced during the whole time of their production. The exercises suggested on p. 14 for the control of the vocal cords should be practised especially by English and Germans, so that they may be able to voice fully the consonants of African languages where such voicing is necessary.

CHAPTER XI

PLOSIVE CONSONANTS

138. A plosive consonant is formed by stopping the air passage at some point; it consists of three parts: (a) the stop, (b) the release of the stop, and (c) some subsequent sound which follows the release (the off-glide).[1]

Aspiration and Non-aspiration of Voiceless Plosives.

139. Voiceless plosives before a vowel can be pronounced in two different ways: (1) on the release of the stop a small puff of breath can be heard before the beginning of the vowel, i.e. the off-glide is a kind of **h**, or (2) no puff of breath is heard, but the vowel itself constitutes the off-glide. In the first case the plosive is said to be aspirated, in the second unaspirated.

---

[1] The release of a stop can be either *explosive*, i.e. the air escaping outwards, or *implosive*, i.e. the air going inwards, through suction. In most languages, sounds of a plosive nature are *explosive*. In some African languages, however, implosive consonants are also found: these are described in Ch. XVII. To distinguish the two different kinds of plosion, the terms *explosive* and *implosive* may be used. The term *plosive*, however, is retained here for the normal explosives, since it is the common one in use in most books on phonetics. In the table of consonants on p. 112 the two are differentiated.

In English and German the voiceless plosives (**p, t, k**), when they begin a syllable bearing stress, are aspirated (in German more than in English); in French and Italian, on the other hand, the voiceless plosives are unaspirated. Compare the pronunciation of English *park* with French *parc*, English *too* with French *tout*, German *Tee* and English *tea* with French *thé*, English *key* and German *Kies* with French *qui*. In unstressed positions in English and German, the voiceless plosives are much less aspirated. Compare the two **p**'s in *paper*, in German *Puppe*; the two **t**'s in *tatters*, in *tea* and *eating*, in German *Tüte*; the two **k**'s in *kicking*, in *keep* and *baker*, in German *Kuckuck*.

140. In investigating the pronunciation of any African language, the aspiration or non-aspiration of the voiceless plosives should be noted, and if they differ in this respect from the sounds of the mother tongue, these differences should be learnt. In Kru, for example, **p, t,** and **k** are aspirated somewhat as in German; **puɛ**, *ten*, sounds like **pʰuɛ, tu,** *tree*, sounds like **tʰu**.

141. Aspiration and non-aspiration of plosives is significant in some languages, i.e. differences in meaning may depend upon differences in this element of the consonant. When this happens, the aspiration is usually greater (i.e. there is a more noticeable **h** sound) than it is in English or German, where it is not significant. In such cases, it is recommended that the aspirated consonants should be written as digraphs, **ph, th, kh**.

142. EXAMPLES

Swahili.

Unaspirated		*Aspirated*	
tembo	palm wine	**thembo**	elephant
paa	roof of a house	**phaa**	gazelle
kata	ladle	**khata**	head pad
kaa	coal	**khaa**	crab

Suto-Chuana group of languages.

pola	to thrash	**phola**	to jump off (same tones)
pelo	heart	**phiri**	hyena
nɔtɔ	hammer	**motho**	person
tonna	huge	**thunya**	to explode
kae	where ?	**khunoŋ**	red

143. Considerable confusion has been caused by investigators of African languages (of Bantu languages in particular) who have not realized the three possible kinds of plosive consonants, viz. aspirated, unaspirated, and voiced. Familiar with their own type of plosives only—voiced and voiceless—they have failed to recognize the two kinds of voiceless consonants, viz. aspirated and unaspirated. The following words in Suto will illustrate the three types and their significance:

Voiced	*Voiceless, unaspirated*	*Voiceless, aspirated*
diba encircle	**tiba** to stamp	**thiba** to stop up
dila to smear with cow dung	**tila** avoid	**thili** udder
dula sit	**tula** crack (a nut)	**thula** to butt

144. *Further examples* of aspirated and unaspirated consonants from Suto.[1]

tabə	jumping	**thabə**	joy
tata	forbid	**thata**	hard, strong
kula	purify	**khula**	to stop for a time (rain)
kudu	very (adv.)	**khudu**	tortoise
kiba	to plug	**khiba**	skin apron
pəta	to take a by-way	**phəta**	kill
pala	be too heavy	**phala**	antelope (kind of)
pela	quick	**phela**	live
penya	bind	**phenya**	to look round
peta	squeeze	**phetha**	finish

145. In the Ndau group of languages, aspirated and unaspirated plosives occur: the unaspirated plosives, however, are

---

[1] *Note.*—Aspirated **p** and **f** (or **ʃ**) are acoustically somewhat similar. It is sometimes found that words beginning with **ph** in one dialect have **f** (or **ʃ**) in a neighbouring dialect. In Suto, however, **f**, **p**, and **ph** all exist, distinguishing words:

feta pass by	**peta** squeeze	**pheta** finish
fola cool down	**pola** thrash	**phola** jump off

In addition, Pedi has **v**, **p**, and **ph** as distinguishing sounds:

vəta trust	**pəta** to take a by-way	**phəta** kill
vala count	**pala** be too heavy	**phala** kind of antelope
vela bubble	**pela** quick	**phela** live

ejective, i.e. pronounced with simultaneous closure of the glottis. (See Ch. XVIII.)

k'amba be a magician   **khamba**   leopard
p'anda perhaps   **phanda** to scratch

Incomplete Plosives.

146. It has been stated that a plosive consists of three parts, viz. stop, release, and off-glide. In some cases, however, a plosive occurs in which not all these parts are produced, i.e. when the stop is made but no sudden release and no off-glide. Such a pronunciation, consisting of stop only, is called an *incomplete plosive*. This may occur finally as in Efik **mbup,** an exclamation of disgust, where the lips are kept together and no explosion is heard.

147. EXAMPLES

Somali. **rrɔɔp** rain   **ʕarrap** tongue
Dinka. The voiceless explosives at the end of a sentence or breath group may be exploded or not exploded:

     aca kap I took it.

When the **p** is unexploded, the sentence appears to be more emphatic than when it is exploded.

[Alternative pronunciations *aca kap^h* and *aca kaf*.]

148. In English an incomplete plosive is heard when one plosive follows another: the first stop is not released until the second is made, e.g. in the word *stopped* (**stɔpt**), the **p** stop is held until the tongue is in position for **t,** and no explosion of **p** takes place. Similarly in *doctor, actor*, the **k** stop is held until the **t** is formed. Where one plosive ends one word and the second begins the next word, the same thing takes place, e.g. *last post, stop talking, black tie, back door*. Where the two plosives are homorganic a long stop is made, e.g. *last time, black cap, bad dog, black gang, big gun, last day*. Mention is made of unexploded plosives here in order to draw the student's attention to his own habits of speech and to enable him to observe in the new African language what happens in similar cases. In Efik, for instance, one part of the verb is formed by adding the suffix **de**; where the root of the verb ends in a plosive consonant, this is usually fully exploded before the **de** is pronounced, e.g. **ədək^hde** (not like *dark day* in English).

149. Different Kinds of Plosives.

Plosives in European Languages (and in African Languages).

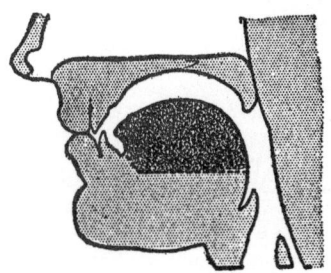

FIG. 14. Bi-labial, **p** and **b**.

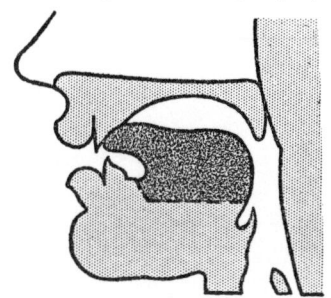

FIG. 15. Dental, **t** and **d**.

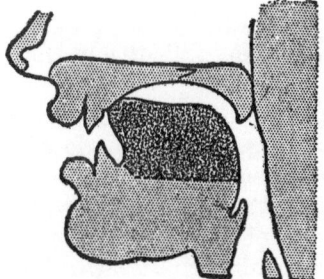

FIG. 16. Alveolar, **t** and **d**.

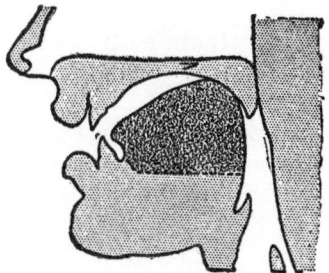

FIG. 17. Velar, **k** and **g**.

Other Plosives in African Languages (and not in the better known European languages).

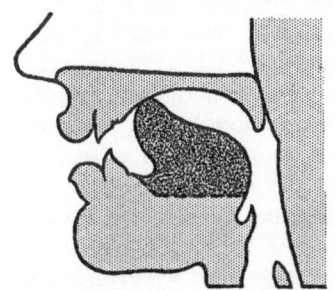

FIG. 18. Retroflex **t** and **d** (**ṭ**, **ḍ**).

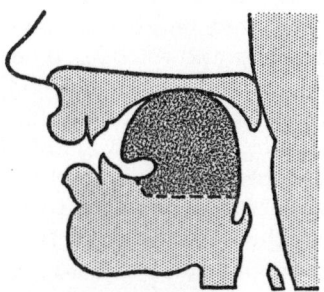

FIG. 19. Palatal, **ty, dy**.

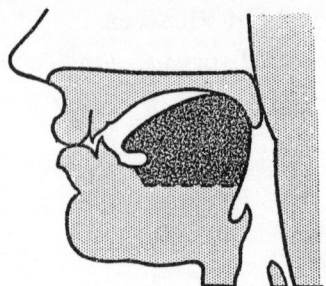

Fig. 20. Labio-velar, **kp, gb.**

Short Description of these Consonants, with Examples from African languages.

150. p and **b** are bi-labial plosives, made by stopping the breath stream with the two lips. There is no difficulty in these sounds.

151. t and **d.** It will be seen from the diagrams that there are three kinds of **t** and **d**, viz. *dental* (Fig. 15), i.e. made with the tip of the tongue on the teeth, *alveolar* (Fig. 16), i.e. made with the tongue pressed against the teeth-ridge, and *retroflex* (Fig. 18) (ṭ, ḍ), i.e. made with the tip of the tongue pressed against the front of the hard palate (behind the teeth-ridge). In most languages only *one* variety of **t** and **d** occurs: the student should observe which it is, and if it is different from his own he should practise it. In some languages two varieties occur as separate phonemes distinguishing words, and in such cases the student must learn to hear the difference between them and be able to make them both. In Ewe, for instance, alveolar and retroflex **d** occur (but only one **t** which is alveolar). As the retroflex **d** (special letter ḍ) is not articulated very far back, it is not very difficult to acquire, though some practice will be needed to enable the student to pass with ease from another sound to ḍ, and from ḍ to the next sound. It will also require practice to *hear* the difference between **d** and ḍ. In the combinations **tr** and **dr**, where **r** is rolled, there is a tendency for **t** or **d** to become dental, e.g. Ewe **ewetri,** *moon*, **adrẽ,** *seven.* In Ewe, retroflex **d** is not followed by **r**.

152. EXAMPLES *of two kinds of* **d,** *one alveolar or dental and the other retroflex.*

Ewe.

	Alveolar		*Retroflex*
de	to reach	ɖe	to take away
de	to put into	ɖe	toward
da	snake	ɖa	hair
du	town	ɖu	powder

Kreish (Gbaya).

ada	word	ɖaɖa	tamarind
bede	another	ɡaɖe	to rest

The non-retroflex **d** is dental, not alveolar in this case.

Somali.[1]

dap	five	ɖap	truth
daarɔ	houses	ɖaarɔ	swear

Herero has dental and retroflex **t** and **d** (also **n**, see Ch. XII).[2]

ta	to die	ʈa	to fit
teka	to reach	ʈeŋge	begins
tika	to accompany	ʈakamisa	holds fast
		hiɳɖi	sends
		ombaɳɖa	cloak

The voiced plosives belong to the same phonemes as the voiceless ones, the former occur only after nasals, and the latter do not occur at all in those positions.

EXAMPLES *of two kinds of* **t** *and* **d,** *one dental and the other alveolar.*

153. In Shilluk, Dinka, and Nuer, two kinds of **t** and **d** occur, the one being dental and the other alveolar. Dental **t** and **d** in these languages resemble the English th-sound in *thin* and *their* (usual phonetic symbols θ, ð), with a stop in front of them, i.e. **tθ, dð** (rather like the pronunciation of **th** in *eighth*, of **t** and **th** in *not thick* and of **d** and **th** in *read them*). Thus the dental **t** and **d** are somewhat affricated (see Ch. XVI), and it is this characteristic which helps materially to distinguish

---

[1] There is some other element besides retroflexion which distinguishes these two *d's*.

[2] We are indebted to Miss Amy Starke of Capetown for this information. She contributes a Herero text to *Le Maître Phonétique* of July–Sept. 1932. Meinhof marks dental and alveolar **t, d,** and **n** in Herero: and says that 't' is evidently retroflex.

them from alveolar **t** and **d.** The digraphs **th** and **dh** have been decided upon[1] to represent them in orthography: these signs usually indicate aspirated plosives, but as no aspirated plosives occur in Shilluk, Dinka, or Nuer, they have been adopted for this other purpose in these languages.

Dinka.

	Alveolar			*Dental*	
tok	one		**thok**	mouth
ket	song		**keth**	gall
duk	forms neg. imper.		**dhuk**	return
dier	pig		**dhier**	mosquito

Nuer.

tor	swamp		**thor**	to mix
buot	tree (kind of)		**buoth**	goat
dai dai	warm		**dhai**	sightless

154. k and ̧g are the velar plosives made with the back of the tongue against the soft palate (see Fig. 17), occurring in European languages. There is no difficulty in these sounds, and therefore no need to illustrate them.

155. ty and dy are palatal plosives. The stop is made by the front of the tongue against the hard palate, the tip being down behind the bottom teeth (see Fig. 19). Because of the nature of these sounds, there are certain difficulties in the understanding of their formation, particularly in combination with other sounds.

(*a*) *The off-glide.* When the tongue goes from the palatal position to that of an open or half-open vowel, it goes through the position of the semi-vowel **y** (see Fig. 38, Ch. XVI, p. 90); thus **ty, dy** sound like a combination of **t**+**y** and **d**+**y**.[2] But the consonant is one, and the glide is an essential part of the sound—a dependent glide. When a close or half-close vowel follows (**i, e, o, u**), because of the smaller distance the tongue has to travel, the **y**-glide is not so noticeable and the consonants often sound like the affricates **tʃ** and **dʒ** as in *church, jump.* (See Ch. XV, p. 87.)

(*b*) *The on-glide.* When an open vowel precedes **ty** and **dy**, it sounds like a diphthong, e.g. **maty** in Nuer sounds like *maity*. This is because the tongue in travelling from **a** to **ty** must go

---

[1] At the Rejaf Conference in 1928.

[2] The writing of these with the digraphs **ty, dy** possibly encourages this idea.

through the **i** position. But again, this is an essential glide
dependent upon the palatal position, and should not be written.
156. **ty** and **dy** occur very frequently in African languages:
they are not often found in final positions, however. In Nuer
and Dinka, where they do occur finally, the letters **c** and **j** have
been adopted for the orthography.[1]

157. EXAMPLES

Ewe (Gɛ̃ dialect).

	edyi	he will	**tyi**	money
	ŋwetyi	ŋwetyi speckled	**tyã**	to select
	edyro	he wishes	**dyi**	heart
Noho.	**dyom**	ten		
Kru.	**dyuruti**	children	**dyɛi**	finger
	dyuɡbe	boy		
Malinke.	**dyiri**	tree	**dyi**	water
Mossi.	**tyuɡu**	moon		
Chuana.	**dya**	to eat (Alternative pronunciation with **y**.)		
	dyo	this		
Nuer.	**jec**	to stand	**juɔl**	tail
	lɔc	heart	**jal**	traveller
Dinka.	**cam**	to eat	**jam**	to talk
	rac	bad	**joŋ**	dog

158. Although **ty** and **dy** are usually single sounds, not
groups of two sounds, in some African languages these single
sounds can occur in addition to a combination of **t** and **d**
followed by the semi-vowel **y**. Where **ty, dy** are pure palatal
plosives, the contact is made by the front of the tongue against
the hard palate (see Fig. 19), and the **y**-glide is dependent upon
this essential position. Where, however, the groups **t+y** and
d+y consist respectively of two sounds, the **t** and **d** are
articulated like the normal **t**, i.e. the tip of the tongue is against
the teeth-ridge and the tongue *goes out of its way* to make the
y-glide: in this case the **y** is longer and more noticeable. [This
happens in English *tune* (**tyuun**), *due* (**dyuu**).] In the languages
in which both these occur, the distinction may be significant:
where it is, it should be shown in the orthography. The groups
tyy and **dyy** have been suggested to show the combined
sounds. If **c** and **j** are chosen to represent the single palatal

[1] To the Englishman **ty** and **dy** finally would always suggest the last
syllable in *pity, tidy*—and not one sound.

sounds, **ty** and **dy** will serve for the combination of the two sounds. This has been done in Shilluk and Nuer.

159. EXAMPLES

Shilluk.	**camo**	to eat	**tyɛlo**	foot
	ceth	to walk	**tyɛto**	to carry
	cɛt	very	**dyɛlo**	sheep
	jamo	to talk	**dyɛr**	middle
	jaago	chief		
Nuer.	**cat**	to slip	**tyath**	to smash
	jal	to travel	**dyɛl**	antelope (kind of)
	jen	he, she; it	**dyel**	craftsman

160. kp and **gb** are labio-velar plosives, i.e. a double stop is made, the lips being together and the back of the tongue touching the soft palate (in the **k, g** position) at the same time (Fig. 20). The following points should be noticed about these sounds which occur in some form or other in a large number of African languages:

(*a*) The native considers **kp** and **gb** respectively as one sound, not as a combination of two.

(*b*) The two articulations must be simultaneous, i.e. when the sound occurs between two vowels there must be no on-glide to the **k** heard before the lips come together for the **p** position, i.e. it must be **a–kpan** not **ak–pan** (not like English *black pin*), **a–gba** not **ag–ba** (as in English *big boy*).

(*c*) The two stops must be released simultaneously.

(*d*) There is no aspiration in **kp.**

(*e*) The glottis often rises during the formation of the stop. [This can be seen on the outside of the throat.]

161. In some languages (Efik, for example, which contains only **kp** and no **gb**) the release is more in the nature of a **b** than a **p**. In most dialects of Ibo the sounds written **kp** and **gb** are implosive. (See Ch. XVII.)

162. Europeans experience some difficulty in pronouncing these sounds; they do not hear the **k** and **g** articulations easily and are inclined to pronounce only **p** and **b**: thus Efik **kpukpru,** *all*, is often pronounced as **pupru.** To the Europeans the **p** element seems the more important, but for the native, if anything, the **k** predominates. This is borne out by the fact that where **kp** or **gb** are weakened it is the labial element which disappears and the velar element remains, sometimes reduced to **x,** or **ɣ.**

163. kp and ɡb are most difficult to hear and imitate in initial positions: in intervocalic positions, the on-glide from the vowel makes it easier to hear the k and ɡ. Students should practise it in this position first, saying, for example, *black pin*, *big boy*, and holding on the k and ɡ stops, then trying to say blæ–kpin, bi–ɡbəi (making the first syllable end with a vowel, and beginning with a new impulse of breath on the kp and ɡb). Germans can use the word *Hackbau* in the same way, dividing it thus *Ha-ckbau*.

164. EXAMPLES

Kru.	ɡbe	dog	dyuɡbe	boy	kpə back
	ə mu daɡba	he is going a journey			kpɛ power
	semɡbati	daybreak			ɛkpati it falls

Ewe (Gɛ̃ dialect).

	ekpe	stone	eɡbə goat	tuɡbɛdyɛ	girl
	akpa	division	akpaku	calabash
	ekpe	it is heavy	kpə	to see
	aɡbe	life	aɡba	load
	aɡbã	dish	eɡbe	to-day
	ɡbəɡbə	breath	ɡbeɡbe	refusal
Gã.	okplɔ̃	table	kpã	thread
	kpawo	seven	ɡblã̃ʃihĩlɛ	marriage
	ɡbomo	person	ɡbla	to draw
Zande.[1]	kporo	village	ɡbua	for nothing
	kpoto	chief	ɡbe	to pull
Banda.[2]	kpukpu	a feast of beer	ɡbaku	prohibit
	kpoto	dense	ɡbala	falsehood
Efik (kp only).			
	kpa	die	okpo	corpse
	ekpri	little	akpa	river
Yoruba.	akpa	he kills	ɡboɡbo	all
	kpɔ̃	carry on the back	aɡbo	old man
Kreish.	kpu	ten	ɡboɡbo	skin
	ndakpa	people	Gbaya	Kreish
Kakwa.	kpen	birds	ɡbaɡbe	wild cat

Bari. The western Bari dialects (e.g. Pöjulu, Kakwa, Kuku) have ɡb in addition to 'b:[3] e.g. 'bəja, *to weed*; ɡbəja, *to dance*.

---

[1] E. C. Gore, *Zande Grammar*, London.
[2] Ch. Tisserant, *Dictionnaire Banda-Français*, Paris, 1931.
[3] See Ch. XVII for the description of this sound.

165. A plosive can be made by the back of the tongue touching the uvula. This is the *qaf* of Arabic (phonetic symbol **q**). It sounds like a very far back **k**. It occurs in Somali, e.g. **aqal**, *house*; **qət**, *dig*; **qiiq**, *smoke*.

166. Glottal Plosive.

The glottal stop is a plosive consonant made by bringing the vocal cords together momentarily and then releasing them: a slight explosion is heard. In an exaggerated form it is heard as a slight cough. It is an essential sound in several languages, e.g. German (*unartig*, **'un'artiç**), Arabic, and where it is not essential, as in English, it is of common occurrence. (See p. 13.)

167. The glottal stop occurs in some African languages: e.g. Efik *no* is **'i'i**: Tukulor *one* is **go'o**.

Ful.	**na'i** cattle	**ə'ə** this one	**fe'a** to cut
	owi'i he said	**yi'a** to see	**mə'ən** your
	li'i fishes		

Hausa. **a'a** no

Bari. In Bari many words end with the glottal stop, though this is not recognized in the current orthography: **lio'**, *my*; **kwe'**, *our* (cf. **kwe**, *head*).

Note that in Bari, the glottal stop may begin words with certain speakers instead of **'b**, **'d**, (see p. 96): thus **'ayin**, *nothing*, for **'bayin**, **'iloŋ** for **'diloŋ**.

168. The glottal stop is also added to the articulation of other consonants, i.e. certain consonants can be pronounced with simultaneous closure of the glottis. In Chuana glottal closure is added to unaspirated plosives and affricates for special emphasis. Consonants articulated with this accompaniment are called *ejective*. (See Ch. XVIII, p. 96.)

CHAPTER XII

NASAL CONSONANTS

169. In the formation of all kinds of nasal consonants, the air is prevented from issuing through the mouth by a stop at some point: the lowering of the soft palate from the back wall of the throat allows it to issue through the nose. (See Ch. III, p. 15 on the function of the soft palate in speech.) The difference between one nasal consonant and another is in the point at which the mouth passage is stopped.

170. The following nasal consonants are found in European and African languages.

171. m. For **m** the stoppage of the mouth passage is made by the two lips: it is the bi-labial nasal.

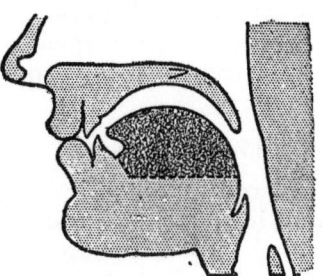

FIG. 21. **m.** Bi-labial nasal.

172. For **n,** the stoppage is made by the tip of the tongue either against the teeth, the teeth-ridge, or the hard palate (dental, alveolar, and retroflex **n**).

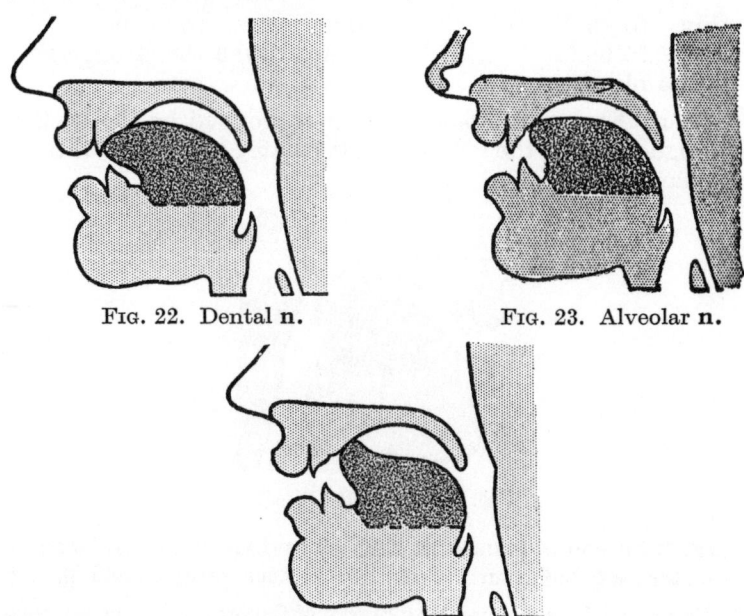

FIG. 22. Dental **n.**   FIG. 23. Alveolar **n.**

FIG. 24. Retroflex **n** (ɳ).

173. In most languages only one **n** occurs, and the alveolar variety is the commonest. Dental **n** and retroflex **n** are both uncommon in African languages.

174. Dental **n** occurs in Nuer and Dinka, together with alveolar **n,** and the difference between them distinguishes words. In the orthography decided upon for these languages, **nh** has been adopted to represent the *dental* **n** (as **th** and **dh** are used for dental **t** and **d**).

175. EXAMPLES

Dinka. **manh** son, cf. **man** mother
e manh man he is the son of his mother.
Nuer. **nhial** heaven **nhɔk** to agree, to love
ranh not close by, cf. **ran** meaning *agent* (**ranbuth** guide)

176. In Herero,[1] dental and retroflex **n** occur (and no alveolar **n**).

Dental		*Retroflex*	
nina	to swallow	**ɳua**	to drink
nuna	to be fat	**omuɳamasa**	the strong one
okona	place	**ɳenya**	with

177. ŋ. For **ŋ** the mouth passage is stopped by the back of the tongue against the velum or soft palate : it is the velar nasal consonant.

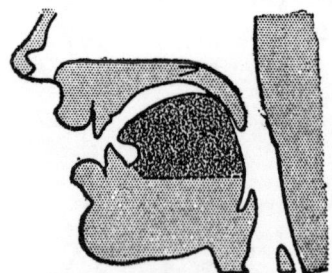

FIG. 25. **ŋ.** Velar Nasal.

178. This sound is used in English and German. In German the letters **ng** between vowels are always pronounced **ŋ,** e.g.

---

[1] We are indebted to Miss Amy Starke of Capetown for this information.

singen (**ziŋən**), *Finger* (**fɪŋər**), *länger* (**lɛŋər**).[1] In English the letters **ng** sometimes represent **ŋ**, as in *sing* (**siŋ**), *singer* (**siŋə**),[2] and sometimes **ŋg**, as in *longer* (**ləŋgə**), *finger* (**fɪŋgə**).

179. For some reason or other the sound **ŋ** has presented difficulties to writers on African languages and it has often been given meaningless names (e.g. it has been called '*the nasal n*'; this term conveys no meaning, since there is no such thing as a non-nasal **n**). An examination of the diagram above, together with the simple description given of its formation, ought to dispose of any difficulty about this sound. Some people do not find it easy to use **ŋ** initially before a vowel: this is a real difficulty to Europeans, because it is not used in this position in European languages. Those who find it difficult should say the word *singer* (**siŋə**), where **ŋ** occurs between two vowels, and try to divide the word **si–ŋə**: then say the second part **ŋə** without **si**. When this is done there should be no difficulty in saying **ŋa, ŋə, ŋɛ, ŋi, ŋu**, &c.

180. EXAMPLES

Ganda.	**eŋŋo** blossom of plantain	**eŋgo** leopard	
Kikuyu.	**ŋanə** stories market	**ŋɛɛndə** journeys	**keŋaaŋa**
Mende.	**ŋəna** bitter	**ŋəni** bird	**ŋəna** to wound
Ewe.	**ŋe** to break side	**ŋlə** to hoe	**ŋəti** nose **ŋu** outside
	ŋə to perforate		
Gã.	**ŋa** to press	**ŋa** wife	
	(**ŋ** final) **dəŋŋ** never again	**dʒogbaŋ** well (adv.).	
	nyoˑŋ night	**kaŋkaŋ** civet cat	
	nyanyoŋ tooth		
Swahili.	**ŋambo** yonder shore	**ŋombe** cow	
Efik.	**ŋko** also **saŋa** walk		

181. ny.[3] For this sound (written with two letters, but one sound) the mouth passage is stopped by the front of the tongue against the hard palate: it is the palatal nasal. It occurs in

---

[1] Final **ng** in German sometimes has a very slight **k** following on the **ŋ**, e.g. *sang* may be pronounced **zaŋk**—not so definite a **k** as in English *sank* (**sæŋk**).

[2] In the Midland dialects *ng* is pronounced **ŋg, siŋg, siŋgiŋg**.

[3] I.P.A. **ɲ**.

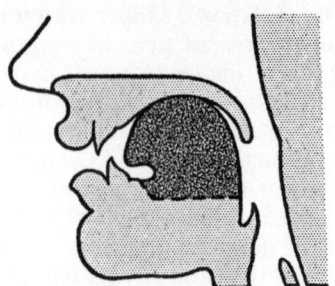

FIG. 26. **ny.** Palatal nasal.

French *agneau* (**anyo**), *ignoble* (**inyɔbl**), and in Italian *Bologna* (**bolonya**), *campagna* (**kampanya**).

182. The sound **ny** presents difficulties similar to those attaching to the palatal plosives **ty** and **dy.**

(*a*) When the tongue goes from the palatal position to that of a vowel, it goes through the position of the semi-vowel **y** (see Fig. 38, p. 90): thus **ny** sounds like a combination of **n+y.** The y-glide is naturally more noticeable when an open rather than a close vowel follows.

(*b*) When an open vowel precedes **ny,** it sounds like a diph-thong, e.g. *pany* sounds like *painy.* This is because the tongue in travelling from **a** to **ny** must go through the **i** position. But again, this is an essential glide, dependent on the palatal position, and should not be written.

183. EXAMPLES

ny is very common in African languages.

Ewe.	**nya** [˙] to know	**nya** [.] word
	nye [˙] to be	**nye** [.] my
	nyo [˙] to be good	**nyo** [.] sea cow
Swahili.	**nyama** animal	**nyota** star
	nyuki bee	**nyuŋgu** pot
Nupe.	**nya** to dance	
	nyanyanyanyayi sparkingly	
Efik.	**nyam** sell	**nyene** have
	nyime agree	**anyan** long
Gã.	**nye** yesterday	**nyo·ŋ** night
	nyeba come!	

184. ny is rare in final positions: it occurs, however, in Dinka, e.g. **piny**, *ground* (cf. **piŋ**, *to hear*), **tweny**, *to fall*, **bany**, *chiefs* (cf. **baŋ**, *to be obstinate*), **atwany**, *ill.*

185. In addition to the single sound **ny**, there can exist a combination of **n**+the semi-vowel **y**, which differs from the single sound in the same way in which **t**+**y** and **d**+**y** differ from the palatal plosives **ty** and **dy**. (*n*+*y*, and not the single sound *ny*, occurs in the English word *news*, **nyuuz**.) What has been said about these sounds (Ch. XI, p. 56) applies equally to **ny** and **n**+**y**. The difference between the two can be significant: in such a case the single sound may be written with the digraph **ny** and the combined sounds as **nyy**.

186. EXAMPLES

Karanga.	**kunyara**	to be ashamed[1]		
	kunyyara	to be tired		
Kinga.	**nyyaga**	to snatch		
	nyyala	to wither		
	enyyama	meat		
Bari.	**nye**	he, she, it	**kunyye**	others (fem.)
	kɛnya	to be torn	**kɛnyya**[2]	branch of a tree

Voiceless Nasal Consonants.

187. It was pointed out in Chapter X that the nasal consonants normally occur in their voiced form only, voiceless nasals being of comparatively rare occurrence. It is, however, possible to pronounce all nasal consonants without voice, though they are difficult to distinguish from each other, as they consist mainly of nasal breath. They are rare in African languages, but they apparently occur as significant sounds in Kuanyama. (See Tönjes, *Lehrbuch der Ovambo-Sprache*, p. 7.)

188. EXAMPLES

Kuanyama.

na with	**ṅa** quite (straight)	**ṅano** five
omunue finger	**omuṅu** man	[ṅ = voiceless **n**]
oṁepo wind	**oṁito** escape	[ṁ = voiceless **m**]

---

[1] Doke.
[2] In current orthography these are written with an **i** instead of **y**: **kɛnia**.

Homorganic Nasal and Plosive Consonants.

189. A comparison of the diagrams in this chapter with those of the plosive consonants in Chapter XI will show that the mouth articulation of the nasal consonants corresponds to that of the plosive consonants: thus, **m, p, b** are homorganic; so are **n, t, d; ŋ, k, g,** and **ny, ty, dy.** This is an important observation to note, as one of the peculiarities of African as compared with European languages lies in the frequent occurrence of words and syllables beginning with a nasal followed by a plosive consonant. The nasal and plosive are generally homorganic in these combinations, the articulation of the nasal being determined by that of the plosive (see Ch. XI, p. 49). Thus before **p** and **b** the nasal consonant is usually **m**; before **t** and **d** it is **n**; before **k, g, w,** and **h** it is **ŋ**. The nasal preceding the palatal plosives **ty** and **dy** is the palatal **ny**; the combination of palatal nasal and plosive is generally written **nty** and **ndy,** not **nyty** and **nydy**; this is mainly for the sake of simplicity, but also because the continuant part of the nasal only is heard and not the **y**-glide, and this is very **n**-like; it should be remembered, however, that the nasal is articulated where the plosive is, i.e. on the hard palate.

190. The question as to which nasal should be written before the labio-velar plosives **kp** and **gb** is difficult because of the double articulation. It is possible and even probable that a labio-velar nasal, i.e. **m** and **ŋ** together, precedes **kp** and **gb,** but it is obvious that to write both these (**mŋkp** and **mŋgb**) would be both unnecessary and clumsy. In some languages, e.g. Efik, certain words have been written with **m** and others with **ŋ,** this evidently indicating that observers have thought they heard **m** in some words and **ŋ** in others: thus **mkpa,** *death,* is generally written **m** and **ŋkpə,** *thing,* is written with **ŋ**. Goldie in his dictionary, however, under **mkpa** gives 'See **ŋkpa',** and under **ŋkpə** 'See **mkpə',** which implies that he thinks either could be used. It would make for simplification if one could be chosen.

191. Combinations of nasal and plosive consonants are not always homorganic:

Swahili. **mke**   woman   **mthu**   man[1]

---

[1] The dropping of a vowel in the first syllable has brought the **m** and **t** together: *muntu > mthu.*

Ewe.	ŋdi	morning	ŋdɔ	noon
Kru.	mriedo six			
Gã.	ŋmɔtɔ	mud	ŋmlɛ	bell
	ŋmo	field, farm	ŋmlɛtʃwa	hour
	ŋmɛnɛ	to-day	nyoŋma[1]	ten

192. Europeans find a certain difficulty in pronouncing the combinations of nasal and plosive initially. This is mainly because they do not occur in the mother tongue, but also because of a mistaken idea that it is impossible to pronounce them without a vowel (**i** or **u**) preceding them. It is quite possible and easy to say them without any vowel preceding if the sonorous and continuant nature of the nasal is realized. The easiest to begin with is **m**+a plosive: hold on **m** for some time and then add the syllable **pa** or **ba**; then try **n**+**ta** and **da**; **ŋ**+**ka** and **ga**; **n**+**tya** and **dya**; and **m** or **ŋ**+**kpa** and **gba**.

193. EXAMPLES *of Nasal+another consonant (for practice.)*

Pedi.

ŋku	sheep	ŋŋwɛ	other

Efik.

nnyin	we	ŋka	I go	ŋwan	woman
mkpa	death	nnyam	I buy	ŋkpɔ	thing
nsio	different				

Yoruba.

mbɛ	there	mbi	or		
nla	great	ŋkɔ	to be not	ŋgie	then

Nupe.

mba	a feast	mbaci	except	nda	father
ndo	another	ndondo	every	ŋgo	accept

Mende.

mba	rice	mbaka	music	mbawa	soap
nda	mouth, door	nde	brother	ndɔ	rum

Zande.

mbereke	needle	mgbaku	adze	mvuka	billhook
ŋgu	boomerang	ŋgare	crab	mbori	God

[1] From *Gã Grammar, Notes and Exercises*, by M. B. Wilkie, Oxford, 1930.

194. A nasal consonant is very sonorous and can form a syllable by itself. In English and German **m, n,** and **ŋ** are frequently syllabic, e.g. *mutton* is pronounced **mʌtn** without a vowel between the **t** and the **n**; similarly in the pronunciation of the words *open* as **oupm** and *bacon* as **beikŋ** (one possible pronunciation) the **m** and **ŋ** are syllabic. In German *reiten* is pronounced as **raitn,** *haben* is pronounced **haabm,** and *gucken* **ġukŋ**: the **m, n,** and **ŋ** respectively form the second syllable and are syllabic.

195. In African languages the nasal consonants are frequently syllabic: in the examples given above of nasal+plosive, the nasal can be syllabic or not syllabic; if it is very short and the main breath force seems to come on the plosive, it may be considered as non-syllabic, while if it is at all long, and if it bears any stress, it is syllabic.[1] The syllabic or non-syllabic character of nasal consonants must be considered with the tones of tone languages. Because of its sonorous character, a nasal consonant can and often does bear a tone: if it bears a tone it is usually considered to be syllabic. Thus if in the combinations **mp, mb, nt, nd,** &c., the nasal consonant has a different tone from that of the following vowel it is syllabic.[2] Again, when a nasal precedes or follows a vowel it may bear a tone different from that of the vowel. In this case it is generally long and syllabic, e.g. Chuana **teeŋ** [◌ ·], *there*: Kru **dza m ni** [.. ·], *bring me water*.[3]

Chapter XIII

LATERAL, ROLLED, AND FLAPPED CONSONANTS

196. The lateral, rolled, and flapped consonants are treated here in one chapter because of the peculiar nature of certain varieties of these sounds found in African languages, and their relation to each other.

Lateral Consonants.

197. Lateral consonants are formed by stopping the air passage in the middle of the mouth and allowing it to escape along one or both sides of the tongue. The stoppage is effected

---

[1] See Ch. XXI on Syllables. [2] See Ch. XXIV on Tones.
[3] See Ch. XXIV on Tones, where examples are found.

generally by placing the tip of the tongue on the teeth-ridge or teeth (alveolar or dental) : it can also be made by placing the curled-up tip of the tongue on some part of the hard palate (retroflex l), or by pressing the front of the tongue against the hard palate (palatal l). All sounds thus made are l-sounds.

198. The first kind, viz. alveolar or dental l, is the commonest, and occurs in most European and African languages.[1] The retroflex l which is found in some Indian languages is rare in African languages ; the palatal l occurs in Italian, where it is represented by the letters ǧl (as in *famiglia*).

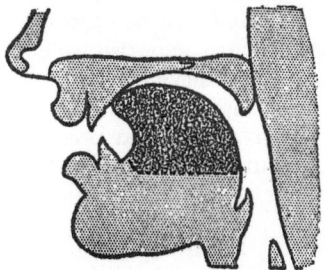
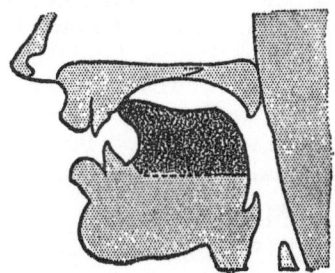

FIG. 27. Clear l.   FIG. 28. Dark l.

199. l is one of the most sonorous of the consonants.[2] As the tongue tip only is concerned in the main part of the articulation, the rest of the tongue is free to take up the position of practically any vowel sound. Thus l can be made with different vowel resonances. In English there are two main varieties of l, viz. the 'clear' l with the resonance of i, and the 'dark' l with resonance of u : in addition, a mid-variety with the resonance of ə is also heard. For clear l, the front of the tongue is raised towards the hard palate, and for dark l the back of the tongue is raised towards the soft palate.

200. In southern English these different l-sounds are members of one phoneme : the clear l is used before vowels and the

---

[1] There is no l in Efik, Twi, or Fante. (Some of the western dialects of Akan have it.)

[2] Because l is such a sonorous sound, it has developed into a vowel in many languages : thus a clear l with the resonance i has been replaced by the vowel i in Italian, *fiore* from the Latin *florem*, *piano* from *planum*; l with u resonance (dark l) has been replaced by the vowel u : Dutch *zout*, '*salt*', *hout*, '*wood*', from *holt*: French *autre* from Latin *alter*.

dark 1 finally and before consonants.[1] The student who is
untrained in speech analysis does not realize these different
1-sounds, and in learning another language he is apt to transfer
into it the phoneme usages of his own 1-sounds, whether the
two languages correspond in this point or not. A Frenchman
or a German speaking English will use clear 1 in all positions
unless he is taught how and when to use the dark 1, because
he has only one 1-sound in his mother tongue, viz. the clear
variety: thus his pronunciation of words like *all*, *old* will be
'foreign'. An untrained Englishman will use a dark 1 finally
and before consonants in speaking French and German: thus
his pronunciation of words like *belle*, *alt*, *wohl* will be 'foreign'.

201. In African languages the 1-sounds are generally clear:
French and German students, therefore, will have no difficulty
in pronouncing them correctly, but the Englishman will have
to learn to use a clear 1 in what to him is an unfamiliar position,
viz. finally and before consonants if it is found in such a position.

Syllabic 1.

202. Because of its vowel-like quality, 1 can form the most
sonorous element of a syllable and it can bear a specific tone.
Examples are given in Chapter XXII to illustrate syllabic 1 in
English and German. In Suto and Pedi, syllabic 1 occurs before
another 1: thus **lle**, past tense of **ʒa**, *to eat* (tones [˙ ˌ]); **lla**, *to
cry* (tones [˙ ˌ]); **lɛla**, *to cry for*, **mollɔ**, *fire* (tones [ˌ ˙ ˌ]). The
first two words have two syllables, the last two three syllables
each. In Chuana, there is no syllabic 1 in similar words, **lɛla**,
to cry; **molelɔ**, *fire*.

Fricative 1.

203. The normal 1 of European languages is a liquid sound:
it is the most sonorous of the consonants and is very like a
vowel.   This is partly due to the fact that the tongue is contracted in such a way as to allow a considerable space between
the sides of it and the teeth, and no friction is therefore heard.
If, however, the tongue is spread in a lateral direction, this
space is narrowed, and friction accompanies the sound. Fricative 1 is the name given to such a sound: the acoustic effect of

---

[1] See Ch. V on Phonemes. For the use of 1-sounds and their variant
pronunciations in the English-speaking world, see any good book on
English phonetics.

it is that of l and ʒ (the sound of s in *measure*) pronounced simultaneously. The special symbol suggested for this type of l is ʪ. Fricative voiced l occurs in several African languages.

204. EXAMPLES

Zulu.

uꞬweꞬwe	long staff	amalʒozi	spirits
Ꞩula	pass	iꞨelo	pasture ground

Guta (dialect of Manyika).

kuꞨya	to eat	foꞨya	tobacco

Herero. In Herero, Miss Amy Starke describes[1] a sound as 'a voiced dental fricative, the air escaping at the sides of the tongue. It sounds like an English ð with a distinct l-quality'.

oðohanya beams (noun)

Breathed or Voiceless l.

205. In the table of consonants given on p. 112, l is shown as a 'single' consonant, i.e. as a voiced sound without any voiceless counterpart. In most languages there is only a voiced l, but it is possible to pronounce l without any voice, and breathed l occurs as a speech sound in some African languages.[2] Breathed l has considerably more friction than the normal voiced l: it is the voiceless counterpart of fricative l. The special symbol suggested for this type of l is ɬ.

206. EXAMPLES

Zulu.	isiɬaɬa	bush	ɬupha	trouble
Guta.	ɬyau	whip	kuɬyora	to break law
Suto and Pedi.	ɬɛɬa	to trot	ɬapa	to wash
	ɬəla	to create	ɬola	to overpower

Rolled Consonants.

207. Rolled consonants are articulated as a succession of taps made by some elastic organ against some other organ of speech. The commonest example of such a consonant is the

---

[1] In *Le Maître Phonétique* July–Sept. 1932.
[2] Breathed l is the sound of Welsh ll: in Welsh, the air generally escapes along one side of the tongue only.

rolled lingual **r**, where the tongue tip taps against the teeth-ridge.

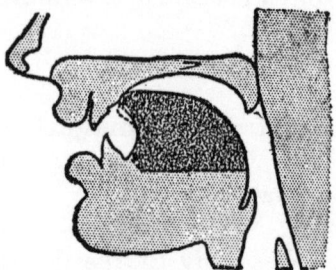

FIG. 29. Rolled lingual **r**.

208. This sound occurs in many languages, e.g. in Italian, Russian, Spanish, in some dialects of German, and in Scottish. The number of taps varies with the amount of breath force used, but in initial positions there are usually not more than two or three: and a one-tap **r** between vowels is very common. The normal **r** of southern English is a fricative, not a rolled consonant. (Some English people use a semi-rolled **r**, consisting of one tap only between vowels.)[1]

209. Another rolled consonant can be made by the uvula tapping against the back of the tongue. This is the **r** used in a large part of the north of France. The normal German uvular **r** is fricative, not rolled.

210. Most of the **r**-sounds of African languages are of the rolled lingual type and are not difficult to recognize or to imitate.[2]

Syllabic r.

211. Like **l**, **r** is a sonorous consonant and can form a syllable by itself and bear a specific tone. Syllabic **r** occurs in a number of African languages.

---

[1] See any good book on English phonetics for the varieties of **r** used in English-speaking countries.

[2] For those who cannot roll an **r**, the following exercise is suggested. Say the syllables **təda təda** with a dental **t** and an alveolar **d**, gradually increasing speed: the **d** should turn into a one-tap **r**. Now say **təra** with very vigorous breath force, holding the tip of the tongue very loosely. This should in time produce a rolled **r**, but it is not an easy sound to acquire.

212. EXAMPLES

Efik.

mbre [. . •], *game*; **ekpri** [. • .], *little*; **ntre** [. . •], *thus*
(3 syllables each); **bre** [. •], *play*; **tre** [. •], *fail* (2 syllables each)

Chuana and Pedi.

r is syllabic before another **r** in a few words:

Chuana. **rra** [. •], *father*—(2 syllables)

      rra moxolo [. • • ⌐ .], *uncle*

Pedi. **rra moɣolo**, *uncle*

213. In some African languages **l** and **r** are interchangeable. To European ears they are distinct sounds because they distinguish words, and it is difficult to realize that they can ever be thought of as anything but different. But they resemble each other in the fact that both are sonorous, liquid sounds and are articulated with the same part of the tongue in the same part of the mouth. Doke says that **l** is substituted for the usual Shona **r** in the Karanga group of languages and in some other dialects. In the Mandingo languages the word for *mountain* may be pronounced as **kulu** or **kuru**: such a difference may be dialectal, e.g. **kulu** was found more frequently with Bambara speakers and **kuru** with Malinkes, though the latter also use **kulu,** and both are often used by the same speaker. In Kru, **kuru** and **kulu** occurred for *knee*, **blable** and **brabre** for *sheep*, **sǝra** and **sǝla** for *house*.[1]

214. In Ganda **l** and **r** appear to belong to the same phoneme: the sound is **l**-like initially and after **a, o,** and **u.** It is **r**-like after **i** and **e.** The **r** is rather **d**-like, consisting of one tap only:

    okuleeta, *to bring*; **okuliira,** *to eat with* (as a relish); **efirimbi,** *whistle* (noun); **ndyiri,** *gospel.*

(See summary of Ganda, p 191.)

215. This is apparently also the case in Zande: Canon Gore writes '**r** represents "trilled" **r,** i.e. a sound between **l** and **r.** Sometimes it tends towards a pure **l**-sound, especially before **i**'. [This 'between' sound may be the flapped sound described below.]

---

[1] The sound intermediate between **l** and **r** was found in Kru (see p. 74).

Flapped Consonants.

216. The term flapped consonant is given to certain kinds of **r** and **l** sounds made by curling up the tip of the tongue and then flapping it down quickly: on the way, the underside of the tongue touches the teeth-ridge, making one tap.

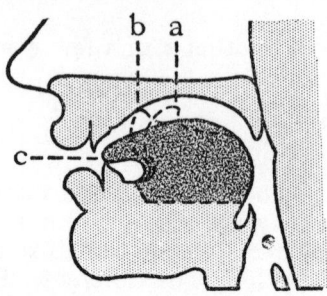

   a. Starting-point of the tongue.
   b. Underside of the tongue touching the teeth-ridge.
   c. Final position of the tongue.

FIG. 30. Flapped **r** or **l**.

217. If the sides of the tongue touch the upper teeth, the sound is a flapped **r**: it resembles a **d** made very quickly. If the sides of the tongue are free, and the air can escape laterally, it is a flapped **l**. In some languages the air escapes medially and laterally (along one side of the tongue) at the same time, and this gives to European ears an effect intermediate between that of **d** and **l** or between that of a one-tap **r** and **l**. This sound is not easy to describe accurately and it is extremely difficult to imitate: in some languages it resembles a **d** or **r**; in others it is more **l**-like. Its difficulty is also increased by the various ways it is used in different languages.

218. The following usages are found:

(1) **l, r,** and the flapped sound may occur as members of one phoneme in a language. This is apparently the case in Kru, though not enough work was done to establish this fact definitely. It was found that the flapped sound occurred with the vowel **i**, e.g. **mriedo**, *six*; **mries5**, *seven*; **bri**, *cow*; **bribrio**, *bull*. With other vowels the sound was more like the normal **r** or **l**: either satisfied the native; e.g. **blable** or **brabre**, *sheep*; **səla** or **səra**, *house*; **mlã** or **mrã**, *nose*. The **r** after a

consonant sounded very like a flapped sound. In cases of this kind, one consonant letter only is required for the orthography; **r** would appear to be the better one.

(2) The flapped sound may be the only **r**-sound of the language, the normal rolled **r** not occurring at all. In such a case the letter **r** can be used to represent it and the peculiar nature of the sound noted and learnt. This apparently occurs in Mossi. In this language the flapped sound when used between vowels resembles a flapped **r**: e.g. **kokore**, *neck*; **nyiŋere nɔre**, *upper lip*. In initial positions it is more like a mixture of l and **d** (a retroflex **d**): e.g. **rumdi**, *knee*; **ritugo**, *right*.[1] A normal l also occurs initially in **leŋdi**, *a kind of cup or dish*: in the latter case no kind of **r** or **d** was acceptable to the native informer. From these investigations, it was concluded that l and **r** belong to different phonemes, that **r** is of the flapped variety: that between vowels this sounds like a one-tap **r**, while initially it has something of an l-quality. In Herero, **r** is usually a retroflex flap, but it may be rolled: e.g. the language is **heɽeɽo**.[2]

(3) Because of its relationship to rolled **r**, the flapped sound can be a member of the **r** phoneme. In such a case it occurs only in association with particular vowels, while the normal rolled **r** takes its place in the neighbourhood of other vowels. This is the case in certain dialects of Ibo, where a rolled **r** is used between all vowels except **i** and **e**, where the flapped sound is used: thus **siri**, **sere** would be pronounced with the flapped sound, while in **sara**, **sɔrɔ** the normal rolled **r** would be used. In such cases as these also, the letter **r** can be used for both types of **r** sound and the distribution of the two varieties learnt.

(4) Because of its relationship to l, the flapped sound can occur as a member of the l phoneme. In such a case it is used only in association with certain vowels and consonants, the normal l occurring in all other positions. This is the case in Chuana: the flapped sound occurs before **i** and **u** only and the normal l before all other vowels and not before **i** and **u**. Thus **luba**, *to mix*; **lilɔ**, *things*, would be pronounced with the mixed sound, and **alebala**, *he forgot*, with the usual l. Here again

---

[1] In words like this the investigator wrote down **lumdi, litugo**—also **ditugo**.

[2] We are indebted to Miss Amy Starke of Capetown for this information. See *Le Maître Phonétique*, July–Sept. 1932.

there is no need for the introduction of a new letter, since the distribution of the two types of l sound can be learnt. In Gã, the l following **m, kp, gb** is of the flapped variety : e.g. **ŋmlɛ,** *bell*; **ŋmlo,** *laughter*; **mlɛbo,** *liver*; **mlihilɛ,** *kindness*; **mlamla,** *quickly*; **kple,** *big*; **kplɛ̃,** *agree*; **kplakpla,** *hastily*; **okplɔ̃,** *table*; **gble,** *open*; **gbla,** *draw*.

(5) In some languages the flapped sound may occur as a dialectal variant of **r** or **l**, the normal rolled **r** or the usual **l** being used in a neighbouring dialect. There is no need for the introduction of a new letter in such a case, since the nature of the sound in each dialect can be noted and learnt. Thus in Zande, in some dialects **r** is used, in others **l**, and in others the flapped sound : it is written **r** in all cases.

ri	to eat	**ira**	meat	**kuri**	rat
kpakpari	hat	**roko**	bark cloth	**koroŋgbo**	wooden bowl

(6) In some languages the flapped sound occurs as an entirely separate sound from **r** or **l** and in addition to these two ; in such cases it distinguishes words and should be written with a separate letter. Kreish (Gbaya) is an example of such a language. In this language there are the sounds **l, r,** and a flapped **r.** Dr. Tucker used temporarily the letter **ɽ** to distinguish the last named.

eɽe hen	**ere** beans
iɽi kind of tree	**iri** death

One of the present writers in investigating Kanuri came to the conclusion that the flapped sound was a separate phoneme from **r** and **l**, though it is possible that dialectal differences in its usage also occurred.[1]

This sound in Hausa appears to belong to a different phoneme from **r** and from **l** : e.g. **bara,** *begging*, and **baɽa,** *servant*, **baara,** *aiming at*, **baaɽa,** *last year*.

The words written

samlayi	youth	**amle**	marriage	**tamlalo**	star
saliki	king	**lasa**	to lack	**fali**	white
haule	tooth				

are pronounced with the intermediate sound.

219. Another flapped sound was found by Dr. Tucker in Kreish (Gbaya). 'This is rather like a **v** made by flapping the

[1] Dr. J. Lukas gives the words **kuli,** *hip*, **kuɽi,** *insect*, and **kuri,** *circle*, (the last in one dialect only).

lower lip against the upper teeth. It is written **vv** (for want of a suitable letter) and is rather rare.' [**vb** has been suggested to represent this sound.] Doke uses the symbol ɤ in his *Shona Phonetics*.

ǧevve arrow   **ǧevvumu** to shoot with a bow

220. *Note on the similarity between* **d** *and a one-tap* **r.**

The difference between **d** and a one-tap **r** is one of length only: if the stop of the **d** is momentary, it is like the striking of the tip of the tongue against the teeth-ridge for a one-tap **r.** Such a 'weakening' of **d** to **r** often takes place between vowels in unstressed positions. Say the word 'anybody' very quickly, and note how easily the **d** is replaced by a one-tap **r.** In the same way, a retroflex **d** pronounced very quickly is like a flapped **r.** See note in the summary of Bambara and Malinke.

CHAPTER XIV

FRICATIVE CONSONANTS

221. Fricative consonants are made by narrowing the air passage at some point: the air escapes through this narrowed space making a fricative sound. The voiceless fricatives are much more easily recognized as fricatives than their voiced counterparts, the fricative nature of the latter being generally somewhat obscured by their weaker articulation.

222. Fricative consonants can be made at many points. The various types of fricatives are described below, with examples from African languages.

Bi-labial and Labio-dental Fricatives.

223. In the formation of a bi-labial fricative the two lips are concerned: they are brought together (as for blowing out a candle—not necessarily with rounded lips, however), and the air passes through this narrow opening with or without the accompaniment of voice. This gives what are commonly called, bi-labial **f** (breathed) and bi-labial **v** (voiced). Labio-dental fricatives are articulated with the bottom lip against the top teeth. These are the normal **f** and **v** of most languages and present no difficulty. To the European, bi-labial **f** sounds intermediate between **f** and **h**, while bi-labial **v** sounds intermediate between **v** and **w**. As speech sounds they are not very common in European languages (bi-labial **v** is used in Germany for the sound of the letter **w** in words like *Schwester* and frequently for the sound of **b** in words like *habe, lobe*). They occur, however, in many African languages. In some, the bi-labial sounds are found and not the more ordinary (labio-dental) **f** and **v**; in others, however, the bi-labial sounds exist side by side with **f** and **v** and belong to different phonemes, and distinguish

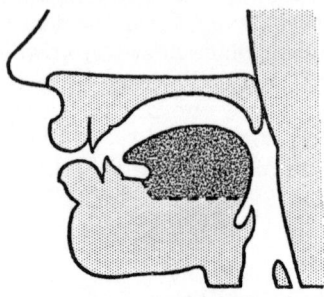
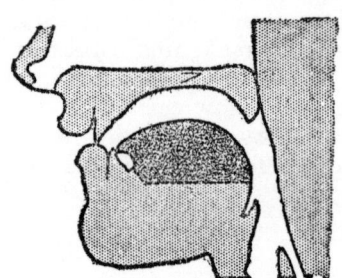

FIG. 31. Bi-labial Fricative.   FIG. 32. Labio-dental Fricative.
ƒ and ʋ   f and v

words. In such cases the two types of fricative must be carefully distinguished in pronunciation and in orthography. The letters ƒ and ʋ are suggested for the bi-labial sounds. The learner of languages where both types occur must make an effort first to *hear* and then to *make* the difference between them, since understanding depends upon it. However similar they sound to European ears, to the native they are entirely different sounds.

EXAMPLES *of ƒ and ʋ.*

224. In Chuana and Pedi, bi-labial ƒ is found, while in the related language, Suto, the labio-dental **f** is used.

Chuana and Pedi	*Suto*
ƒoƒa to fly	**foƒa**
ƒeta to pass	**feta**

225. The ordinary **f** can be used for the orthography in Chuana and Pedi, with the convention that it represents a bi-labial and not a labio-dental sound in these languages.

226. In these languages bi-labial ʋ occurs only in Pedi; it corresponds to **b** in the other two.

ʋəna to see	bəna
ʋula to open	bula

(Labio-dental **v** is a foreign sound introduced by Europeans.)[1]
In Karanga bi-labial and labio-dental **v** occur.

kuʋeŋga to hate	kuveŋga to stir up

227. In Ewe the two bi-labial and the two labio-dental fricatives occur as distinctive sounds.

ʃu bone	fu feather
ʃo beat	fo to tear off
ʋu boat	vu to tear
ʋə python	və to be finished

228. Bi-labial **ʃ** and **p** are found in some languages as alternative sounds, e.g. in Hausa, **faʃi** and **paʃi**, *to break*, are both common, though probably not used by the same speaker;[2] in Ewe **po** and **ʃo**, *to strike*, **apu** and **ʃu**, *sea*, also occur. Similarly, as has been stated above, words which in Pedi are pronounced with ʋ have **b** in Chuana and Suto. In these languages, **f** (or **ʃ**) is permuted to **ph** under certain conditions, and ʋ (or **b**) to **p**, e.g. loʃaʃa, *feather*, plural **liphaʃa** (Chuana); **ke ʋəna** (or **bəna**), *I see*, **o a mpəna**, *he sees me*.[3]

Dental or Pre-dental Fricatives.

229. A dental or pre-dental fricative is articulated with the tip of the tongue against the edge of the upper teeth. The sound of the English **th** in *thin, this*, is an example of this type of sound. The phonetic symbols commonly used to represent these are **θ** and **ð**. These sounds are not common in African languages. They occur in Swahili in loan words from Arabic and are written as **th** and **dh**. [In the following examples we retain the official spelling.]

230. EXAMPLES

Swahili.

dhahabu gold		**thuru**	to hurt
dhambi sin		**themanye**	eight
dhawadi a present		**thuluth**	one-third

[1] See Tucker, *Comparative Phonetics of Suto-Chuana.*
[2] See A. Lloyd James and G. P. Bargery, 'A Note on the Pronunciation of Hausa', *Bulletin of Oriental Studies*, vol. III, pt. iv, 1925.
[3] See Tucker, p. 36.

Note that the dental **t** and **d** in the Nilotic languages resemble the dental or pre-dental fricatives. (See Ch. XI, p. 55.) In Western Nuer **θ** occurs in a final position (see p. 205).

Kikuyu. The voiced pre-dental fricative **ð** occurs in Kikuyu in intervocalic positions where it appears to be a weakened form of **d**: iðanwa, *axe*; moðɛnya, *clay*; ɣreðaka, *bush*, *jungle*. (See Notes on Kikuyu, p. 215.) It is a member of the **d** phoneme (as ɣ is of the **g** phoneme), and should be written with **d**.

Sibilant Fricatives.

231. A number of fricative consonants can be described as sibilants—hissing or hushing sounds. The voiced counterparts are called buzzing sounds. The place where the hiss or buzz is made may vary, and consequently we have sibilants of varying acoustic properties.

232. The commonest of the sibilants is **s**, which occurs in some form or other in almost every language.[1] The most usual **s** is an *alveolar fricative*, i.e. the narrowing of the air-passage is effected by the blade of the tongue approaching the teeth-ridge. A further element in the formation of **s** is that the tongue is considerably contracted laterally and the passage through which the air passes is very narrow: it is this which gives **s** its characteristic hiss. The voiced equivalent is **z**. These two sibilants **s** and **z** can be made with the tip of the tongue up behind the upper teeth or down behind the lower teeth.

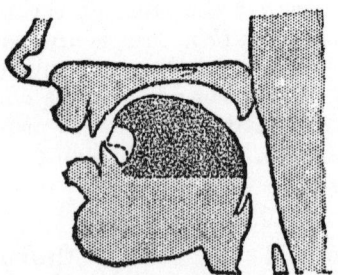

Fig. 33. Alveolar Fricative. **s, z.**

233. Another common sibilant occurring in many European and African languages is the sound represented in English by

[1] Some Nilotic languages have no **s**.

sh (*share*), in French by **ch** (*chambre*), and in German by **sch** (*Schule*). The letter suggested for the orthography of this sound is ʃ[1], its voiced counterpart is ʒ (the sound of **s** in *pleasure*, of **j** in French *jouer*). It is sometimes called the 'hushing' fricative. It is articulated farther back than **s**, i.e. near the back of the teeth-ridge, and the tongue is not contracted so much, with the result that the channel through which the air passes is wider and the sound is consequently softer. A further element in its articulation is that the front of the tongue is somewhat raised towards the hard palate: because of this palatal modification, it is called the *palato-alveolar* fricative. Like **s** and **z**, ʃ and ʒ can be articulated with the tip of the tongue up or down.

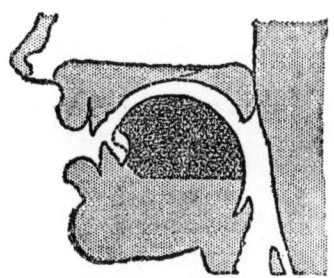

FIG. 34. Palato-alveolar Fricative. ʃ, ʒ.

234. ʃ and ʒ can be made 'clear' or 'dark', i.e. palatalized or velarized, with spread or with rounded lips. (See Ch. XX, p. 104.) For example, in Chuana two ʃ-sounds occur, the normal one, and another made with a special kind of lip-rounding (labialized ʃ). The latter is described more fully in Chapter XX on labialized sounds.

235. EXAMPLES

Gã.	ʃɛ	to reach	ʃi	but	
	ʃika	money	ʃa	to rot	
Chuana.	ʃome	ten	diʒɔ	food	
	seʃoba	bundle	ʒa	to eat	
Yoruba.	oʃe	he does	oʃo	he is obstinate	iʃu yam

---

[1] One sound in spite of its being written with two and, in German, three letters.

Fante.   ʃe   to dress   əʃe asɪ he began
Nupe.   ʃe   to fill   ʃi   to sit down   ʃita sixty
Swahili. ʃamba farm   ʃimo pit
          ʃauri counsel   ʃuʃa to let down
          ʃika   to hold

236. A further sibilant occurs in some African languages which is acoustically between s and ʃ and which bears some resemblance to the German '*ich*-laut'. This is the *alveolar palatal* fricative : its main point of articulation, i.e. where the friction takes place, is near the back of the teeth-ridge and the front of the hard palate; the front of the tongue is raised at the same time towards the hard palate, and this accounts for its resemblance to the '*ich*-laut' which is a pure palatal, and also for the slight y-glide which often follows it. It occurs in the Polish śmiać się, *to laugh.* As far as the present writers are aware, it does not exist side by side with s and ʃ and as a separate phoneme as it does in Polish, but is found as a variant of s or ʃ. For this reason no new symbol has been suggested for it.[1]

EXAMPLES *of the Occurrence of this Sound.*

237. In Mossi, what is written as s is pronounced with this softer intermediate sound, e.g. saġabo, *bread, cake*; nuġu nyɛse, *finger-nails*; mose, the name of the language. When u follows the sibilant resembles ʃ, e.g. suri, *heart*, sounds almost like ʃuri. The voiced equivalent also occurs in Mossi, e.g. zero, *soup or sauce*; zuġu, *head* (the latter sounds like ʒ).

238. With some Mandingo speakers the s resembles this alveolar-palatal sound : e.g. the word for *foot*, written sɛ, often sounds somewhat like syɛ (though there is not so much of a y-glide in it as in the word syɛ, *to scratch*).

239. In Yoruba the ʃ before a and ɛ resembles somewhat this 'middle' sibilant; and in most Ewe dialects the letter s has this sound before i, e.g. amesi, *he who*; asi, *market*, the normal s occurring before all other vowels.

240. In Zande s and z have this sound before i : in si, *to cross over*, the s is pronounced almost as ʃ; in ziazia, *pure, holy*, the z is almost like the z in *azure*.[2]

---

[1] I.P.A. ʂ, ʐ.
[2] See Gore, *Zande Grammar.*

Palatal Fricative.

241. The palatal fricative, articulated by the front of the tongue being raised till it is near the hard palate, is also a kind of sibilant. The tongue, in pass- 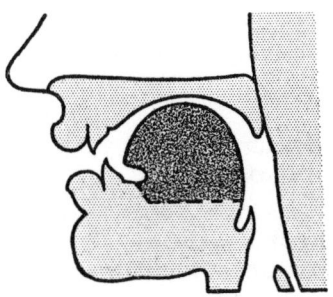 ing from this position to that of any open vowel, goes through a **y**-glide (see p. 89); this is part of all palatal consonants and cannot be avoided. The unvoiced palatal fricative is the sound of German **ch** used before front vowels (e.g. *ich, recht*).[1] The voiced sound corresponding to this is some- times called fricative **y**: i.e. it is the semi-vowel **y** held on at its starting-point and somewhat

FIG. 35. Palatal Fricative. ç.

'tightened', so that friction is heard. (See Ch. XVI on Semi- vowels.) The palatal fricative is not very common in African languages, but it occurs as a variant of **s** in some languages.

242. EXAMPLES

In Twi the words written **hyia**, *meet*; **hyira**, *bless*, are pro- nounced with the palatal fricative; in Fante these words are pronounced with ʃ.

Velar Fricatives.

243. A velar fricative is articulated by the back of the tongue near the velum or soft palate.

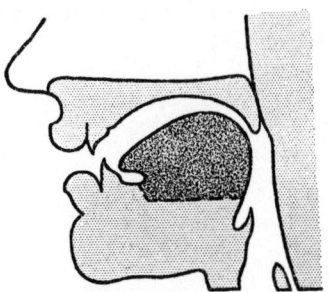

FIG. 36. Velar Fricative. **x, ɣ.**

[1] I.P.A. ç.

The voiceless velar fricative is the 'ach-laut' of German (used after back vowels, e.g. *acht*, *Woche*), and of Scottish (*loch*). Its voiced counterpart ɣ is heard in some German dialects as the pronunciation of g̈ in words like *Wage* (**vaaɣə**), and a little more forward in *liege* (**liiɣə**). The velar fricatives are very common in African languages.

244. EXAMPLES

Chuana.

maxəxə ratel   **phaxɛ** wild cat

Ewe.

g̈axə	prison	**xə**	house	**xlã**	to thrust
g̈baxle	kind of mouse	**xe**	bird	**ɣe**	sun
ɣleti	moon	**aɣe**	poverty		

Gbe.

xuli   belly   **xura** wood

Efik (it is written **h** in this language).
ədəhə pronounced **ədəxə** or **ədəɣə** he said
tuhi   early

Xosa.

.**xola**   to draw out (spelt **rola**)

Kpelle.

ɣal   to break   **ɣala** God   **ɣele** sky

Noho

'bɣam good   **mɣao** morning   **mɣaŋga** farm

Kasonke.

xele   one (in other Mandingo languages this word is **kele,
                    tele,** or **tle**)

Dagbane.

liɣa   darkness   **kuɣele** stone   **kuɣa**   chair
laɣam   to join

Kikuyu.

roɣanə story   **ɣekə** dirt   **ɣete**   stool
oruɣare heat

Uvular Fricative.

245. If the tongue is raised so as to narrow the air passage near to the uvula, i.e. farther back than the soft palate, a uvular fricative is made. The sounds articulated in this position resemble the velar fricatives. The voiceless uvular fricative is not very common, but the voiced one occurs frequently as a type of **r**-sound: this is heard in some parts of France and in Germany; it is rare in African languages.

246. Examples

In Mossi a very far back voiced fricative was heard with back vowels; since it can be considered as a back variety of velar fricative, no new symbol is required: e.g. **kwabuɣa,** 100, **paɣa,** *woman.*[1]

Pharyngal Fricative.

247. Pharyngal fricatives are made by some constriction in the pharynx. The root of the tongue is concerned in the formation of this sound, and it is possible that the walls of the pharynx are also contracted. The sounds articulated in this way occur in Arabic and in Somali. A full description of the formation of these sounds will be found in Gairdner, *The Phonetics of Arabic.* The voiced sound seems to be accompanied by what is known as 'creaky' or intermittent voice.

248. Examples

(No suggestion has yet been made for the representation of these sounds: they are shown here with the symbols of the I.P.A., viz. **ħ** for the voiceless, and **ʕ** for the voiced sound.)[2]

Somali. **saʕ·** cow **sɛɛħɔ** go to sleep
  səʕɔtɔ traveller **libæħ** lion

Glottal Fricative.

249. **h** is usually classed as a glottal fricative, i.e. friction is said to occur between the open vocal cords. A further element in its articulation is the sudden expulsion of the air from the lungs. Frequently some friction can be heard in the mouth after the sudden 'jerk'. The tongue is in readiness for the following vowel during the production of the **h**, and the friction heard is in reality a whispered vowel: thus **h** before **i** is different from that before **e, a, ɔ,** &c.

[1] I.P.A. χ, ʁ.
[2] Arabists use the letters ḥ and '.

250. A voiced **h** can be made.[1] For this sound the vocal cords vibrate along a considerable part of their length, while a triangular opening allows the air to escape with some friction.

FIG. 37. Vocal Cords in Position for Voiced **h**.

251. Many English people, especially men, use the voiced **h** between voiced sounds in words and phrases like *perhaps*, *inhabit, a house*. Voiced **h** is found in a number of African languages, but the present writers know of no case in which the difference between voiced and voiceless **h** is significant: no new symbol is suggested for voiced **h** therefore.[2]

252. EXAMPLES

Voiced **h** is found in Ewe (Gɛ̃ dialect).

ehɔ boa constrictor	**ha** pig	**hɛ̃** to draw
eha comrade	**h5** eagle	**hlɛ̃** to scatter

In this language, the voiceless sound apparently corresponding to voiced **h** is a kind of weak **x**.

Fricatives which are Ejective.

253. In certain African languages fricative consonants are pronounced with simultaneous glottal closure, i.e. they are ejective. These are described in the chapter on Ejectives, p. 96.

CHAPTER XV

AFFRICATES

254. Affricate consonants are sounds which resemble plosives in that they consist of a stop, but differ from plosives in that the stop is released slowly instead of suddenly. Thus no explosion occurs, but the fricative consonant corresponding to the stop, and made where the stop is made, is heard as the organs

---

[1] Doke says: 'Voiced **h** really indicates that the succeeding vowel is pronounced with a vibrant roughening caused by throat friction. The whole of the succeeding vowel is so affected.' [2] I.P. A.fi.

of speech separate slowly. An affricate can, therefore, be considered as a group of two sounds, stop+fricative.

255. An affricate can be made wherever a stop is made. The commonest ones which occur as speech sounds of a language are the following:

Bi-labial or labio-dental	**pf, bv,** as in South German *Pferd.*
Dental or alveolar .	**ts** as in German *Zimmer* (**tsimər**), or English *hats, rats.*
	dz as in Italian *mezzo* (**mɛddzo**).
Post-alveolar . .	**tʃ, dʒ** as in English *church* (**tʃə:tʃ**), *judge* (**dʒʌdʒ**).
Velar . . .	**kx** as in many African languages (see below).

256. The Memorandum of the African Institute recommends the writing of such sounds with two letters as above. In some cases, however, the letters **c** and **j** are preferred to represent the frequently occurring **tʃ** and **dʒ**. Where the fricative consonants **ʃ** and **ʒ** are not found and the affricates are, **c** and **j** can well be used: but where **ʃ** and **ʒ** also exist, the letters **tʃ** and **dʒ** are better for the affricates, since they show the connexion between the two types of consonant.

257. EXAMPLES

pf
Shona.

pfumo	spear	**pfuwura**	pass by

ts, dz
Fante.

Asantsı	Ashanti (people)	**midzidzi**	I eat
ətsı	he heard	**adzı**	a thing
dɛmintsir	therefore		

Ewe.

tsɔ	to take	**dzɔ**	to be straight
tsa	to walk	**dza**	to be clean

Chuana.

letsatsi	sun	**tsɛbɛ**	ear

tʃ, dʒ
Gã.

tʃɛ	father	**dʒa**	to divide
tʃi	to move	**dʒi**	to be
tʃo	to burn	**dʒu**	to wash

Chuana.

| ntʃa | dog | pitʃə | meeting |

Suto.

| tʃeka | to dance | tʃətʃə | kind of mouse |

Pedi.

| tʃe | these | tʃiɛ | locust |

Kru.

| tʃo | moon | bətʃũ | thigh |

Swahili (written **c** and **j**).

| ca | to fear | ja | to come |
| cace | little | jambo | matter |

Hausa (written **c** and **j**).

ci	to eat	ji	to hear
ce	to say	je	to go
cika	to fill	jika	bag

kx

Chuana.

mokxhalo	wacht-ein-beetje bush		
kxhosi	chief	**kxama**	hartebeest
kxhatwane	lizard		

258. In Chuana the labialized ʃ sound is also the second element in an affricate made by pronouncing **tʃ** with lip-rounding: e.g. **tʃwere**, *sparrow*. (The **w** here represents the peculiar rounding of the lips which occurs in Chuana: see Chapter XX on Labialization.) Similarly in Gã, **tʃ** and **dʒ** with rounded lips occur:

tʃwa	to strike	dʒwa	to break
tʃwãa	tough	dʒwɛi	grass
tʃwakoto	breeches	dʒweŋ	think

259. A further affricate is the group of sounds which can be made by the slow release of a **t** laterally: this is represented by **tl**.[1] (The **l** is breathed and fricative.) This affricate is found in a number of South African languages, e.g. the Suto-Chuana group of languages.

| **tlou** elephant | **tla** to come | **tləxa** to depart |

---

[1] This sound may be considered as an explosive lateral: it is classified thus in the table of consonants on p. 112.

260. In Kreish (Gbaya), an affricate is made with the curled-up tip of the tongue, somewhat like the **tr** and **dr** in English *tree* and *draw*. Tucker writes this with **c** and **j** (letters which are not used in any other way in this language).

ǵoco to pound   **uju** man

261. Affricates, like plosives, can be pronounced with or without aspiration: in many languages the presence or absence of aspiration is the only distinguishing feature between pairs of words.

Chuana.

ts : letsatsi	sun	**tsh : motshitshi**	swarm of bees
tʃ : tʃwere	sparrow	**tʃh : tʃhwere**	monkey
tl : tləla	to smear oneself	**tlh : tlhəma**	to plant
tləxa	to depart	**tlhəxa**	to spring up, begin to grow

262. Affricates can also, like plosives, be pronounced with simultaneous closure of the glottis, i.e. they can be ejective. (See Chap. XVIII, p. 96.) In many Bantu languages the unaspirated affricates are usually pronounced as ejectives.

263. In Chuana the ejective quality of **tl** is much more marked than that of the other unaspirated affricates or plosives. In Zulu the breathed affricates are all ejective : **tʃ** occurs *not* ejective also.

CHAPTER XVI

SEMI-VOWELS

264. A semi-vowel has characteristics of a vowel and a consonant. It is an independent vowel glide in which the tongue starts from the position of a close (or half-close) vowel, such as **i, u** (or **e, o**), and immediately moves to some more open position, i.e. to that of a vowel of greater sonority than itself. Thus **w** is the semi-vowel beginning from the **u** or **o** position and **y** the semi-vowel from the **i** or **e** position. The consonantal character of a semi-vowel lies in the fact that it has little sonority: it cannot have syllabic quality nor can it bear a specific tone.

265. Because of its relationship to **i**, **y** is called the palatal semi-vowel.

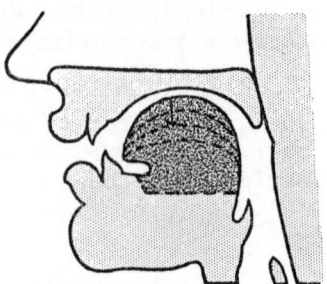

Fig. 38. The Semi-vowel **y**.

266. Examples

Efik.   **yet** wash   **yak**   allow
Ganda. **yiga** to learn   **yageenda** he went

267. In the same way, because of its relationship to **u**, **w** could be called the velar semi-vowel. But in addition to tongue position, **w** has also rounded and somewhat protruded lips: and the lips as well as the tongue move in the production of the sound: thus it has a double articulation, labial as well as velar, and is called the labio-velar semi-vowel.[1]

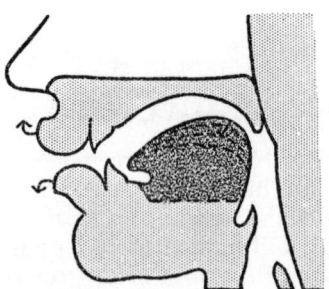

Fig. 39. The Semi-vowel **w**.

[1] It occurs in two places in the Consonant Table because of this double articulation. See Ch. XX on Sounds with more than one Articulation.

268. Examples

Efik.	**wet**	write	**wot**	kill
	awawa	green	**aŋwa**	cat
Ganda.	**ġwa**	to fall		
Fante.	**owu**	death	**kwan**	way

269. The two semi-vowels **y** and **w** occur in most languages, European and African. In some African languages, e.g. Chuana and Suto, the semi-vowel glide starts rather from the **e** and **o** positions than from **i** and **u**. Professor Jones and Dr. Tucker write them **ĕ** and **ŏ**, thus **ĕa, ŏa**, e.g. **ntŏa,** *war.* In Chuana the group **oa** also occurs as two syllables.

270. In addition to these, a semi-vowel corresponding in tongue position to the **i** vowel, *but with rounded lips* (in which it resembles **w**) can also be made.

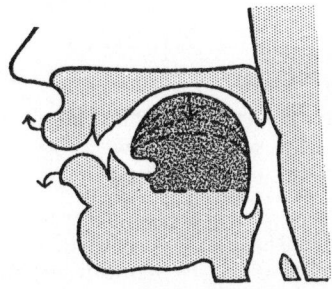

Fig. 40. The Palatal Rounded Semi-vowel.

271. This is the sound heard in the French word *huit*[1] (see p. 105). It is found in some African languages where it is usually called a palatal or palatalized **w**.[2] It is often a subsidiary member of the **w** phoneme, i.e. the normal **w** is used before back vowels and the palatalized **w** before front vowels: it is because of the proximity of the front vowel that this sound is used.[2] Thus no new letter is needed to represent it, but the student must learn its somewhat difficult pronunciation and when to use it. Say the vowel **i**, round the lips: use this new sound before the vowel **ε**. Or round the lips as for **w**: keeping the lips in this position, try to say the vowel **i**: use this sound in the same way before **i, e, ε, a,** &c. Germans should pronounce a very short **ü** and make a semi-vowel of this.

---

[1] I.P.A. **ɥ**. [2] Palatalized sounds are treated more fully in Ch. XX.

272. EXAMPLES

Gã.   **wiemɔ** speech   **awie** they speak   **wiɛ** grindstone
Twi.   **we** chew   **ewi** thief

273. The semi-vowels described above have all been voiced sounds, and in the Consonant Table they are given without any voiceless counterpart. It is possible, however, to say them all without voice. The voiceless ones resemble the breathed fricative consonants articulated at the same place: thus **y** without voice is like the German *ich*-sound (it is often used in the English word *huge*): **w** without voice occurs in one English pronunciation of **wh** as in *when* (**hwɛn**). Voiceless **y** is rare in African languages: it occurs, however, in Twi (e.g. **hyɛ,** *to put on* (clothing)). Voiceless **w** in its normal and its palatalized form is not uncommon: it is generally written **hw.**

274. EXAMPLES

Fante.   **ɔhwɛfu** governor   **hwɛ** behold

275. Very often in rapid speech, the vowels **i, e, u, o** lose their syllabic quality when followed by another vowel and become a kind of semi-vowel. Thus

    e a mpɔna, *it sees me,* is often pronounced **ĕa mpɔna,** i.e. four syllables instead of five (Suto).

    o a nthuta, *he teaches me,* is pronounced **ŏa nthuta,** i.e. four syllables instead of five (Pedi).

CHAPTER XVII

IMPLOSIVE CONSONANTS

276. Implosive consonants are sounds of a plosive nature, i.e. made by a stop and a release, in which the air is sucked inwards instead of being expelled. The sucking is produced in the following way. The organs of speech are placed in position for the stop, and at the same time the larynx is lowered considerably: this lowering, by enlarging the air-passage above, causes a rarefaction, and on the release of the stop the air momentarily rushes in to fill this rarefied space. It is immediately followed by an out-breathed vowel. In African languages only implosive **b, d, ɠ, kp,** and **ɠb** have been found.

277. Kymographic tracings of implosive **kp** and **b** (from the Arochuku dialect of Ibo) are given together with tracings of explosive **b** and **kp** (from Efik), as an illustration of their formation. The inward suction in the implosives is shown by the downward 'kick' of the needle: in the more normal explosive the 'kick' is upwards.

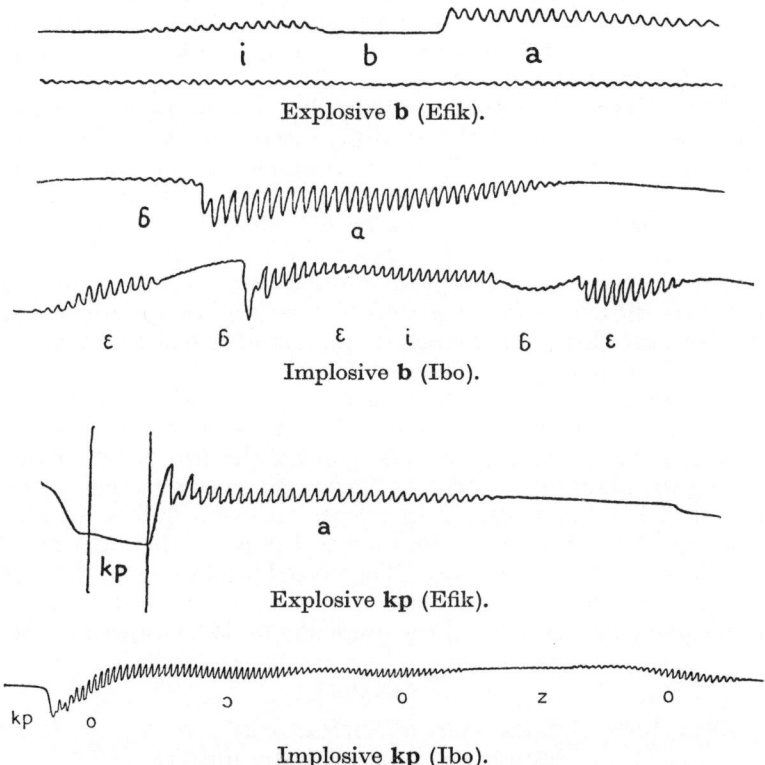

Explosive **b** (Efik).

Implosive **b** (Ibo).

Explosive **kp** (Efik).

Implosive **kp** (Ibo).

FIG. 41. Kymograph Tracings of Implosive and Explosive **b** and **kp**.

278. It should be noticed that in some languages the implosion is very slight. In one dialect of Ibo (Umanelò) the kymograph showed no explosion or implosion: the subject with whom this work was done, however, had an extremely weak articulation in all sounds: when he was induced to put some vigour into his pronunciation, the kymograph showed the difference between the implosive and explosive sounds. In Noho also, the implosion was very slight.

279. The African Institute recommends the writing of these sounds with the ordinary letters preceded by an apostrophe, if a number of them occur in a language. Thus **'p, 'b, 't, 'd, 'k, 'g** would be distinguished from the normal **p, b, t, d, k, g**. When a language contains only one implosive sound, viz. implosive **b,** the special letter **ɓ** is recommended for it : and where implosive **d** occurs, the letter **ɗ**.

280. Where an implosive and explosive consonant exist side by side in a language and differentiate words, it is very necessary to distinguish them in pronunciation and in writing. To European ears, the difference is extremely difficult to hear, but the native hears them as quite different sounds: it is a serious mistake for a foreign speaker of the language to use an explosive instead of an implosive sound. Implosives are among the most difficult African sounds to acquire, but a student who needs to use them in the language he is studying should not rest satisfied until he has mastered them. He should first have considerable practice in *hearing* the two sounds until he can recognize them with fair ease. Then he should try to make them. Begin with implosive **b,** placing the lips together and trying to enlarge the throat by lowering the larynx (he can see this in a looking-glass) : then release the stop with a sucking inwards of the breath. Implosive **d, kp,** and others if needed can be tried in the same way. The voiced implosives **b, d, g, gb** are fully voiced. A full voicing of the stop is part of the voiced implosive consonants, and the student should be aware of this.[1]

EXAMPLES

281. *Zulu.* **'ɓɛka** put (cf. **bɛka** took)
  'ɓa'ba be acrid (cf. **baba** flutter)

282. *Ful.* **'bi'də** child   **'di'di** two
  'bandu body   **'du'di** much

283. *Ibo.* In Ibo, implosive **b** and **kp** exist, together with explosive **b** (but not explosive **kp**). It is not necessary to mark

[1] An exercise is suggested on p. 14 for obtaining fully voiced consonants.

the **kp** in any way, but the two **b**'s must be distinguished. The digraph **ɠb** has been adopted for implosive **b**, since this sound corresponds to the more usual **ɠb** of other Nigerian languages.

> **ɠbu** cut (cf. **bu** carry)
> **ɛɠbɛ** hawk (cf. **ɛbɛ** gun)
> **aɠbo** gum (cf. **abo** song)

284. *Hausa.*

'bauna	buffalo	**'daki**	house
yun'bu	clay	**'da**	child
ɠwi'batʃe	dirty	**bu'da**	to open

'ba'be estrangement (cf. **babe** grasshopper)
'daka inside of house (cf. **daka** pounding)

285. *Kinga.*[1] In Kinga every **ɠ** except when following **ŋ** is implosive. **'guŋgumala** to be immovable.

'ɠa'ɠa to become large   **'gaŋgaluka** to be surprised

In such a case there is no need to mark the **ɠ** in any special way: the nature of the two **ɠ**'s and their distribution can easily be learnt.

286. *Shona Dialects.* The normal **b, d, ɠ** of the Shona dialects are implosive: explosive **b, d, ɠ** occur only in a limited number of words, most of which have been imported from English and Dutch.

Zezuru.   **'bara** bullet (cf. **bara** write)
'da'da be insolent (cf. **dada** duck)

287. *Noho.* In Noho, initial **b** was found to be implosive before every kind of vowel.

'bito	women	**'beyi**	forest
'bato	people	**'buno**	men

In intervocalic positions the contact was so weak that it was difficult to say whether the **b** was explosive or implosive: it was practically non-plosive.

ŋeba wave   **dibəlu** neck

Before the consonant **ɣ**, **b** was also implosive.

'bɣam good

[1] L. R. Wolff, *Grammatik der Kinga-Sprache,* Berlin, 1905.

When following an **m**, **b** in some words was explosive and in others it was unmistakably implosive.

Implosive.		*Explosive.*	
m'baŋo	ivory	**mboko**	yard
m'boa	prisoner	**mboa**	horse
m'bu	year	**mbɔ**	dog
m'bia	relationship	**mbia**	palm nut (same tones)

288. *Duala.* Implosive **b** and **d** also occur in Duala.

289. *Bari.* In Bari **b** and **d** are pronounced with glottal closure: they can be explosive (and because of the glottal articulation are then ejective) or implosive. But as their articulation is weak, it is often difficult to tell whether the release is explosive or implosive.

'baŋ	yard	**'dioŋ**	dog
'bayin	nothing	**'diloŋ**	meat sauce
'bö'but	water buck	**'dyakan**	however

With certain speakers, the mouth articulation of **b** and **d** is often omitted and the glottal articulation alone remains: thus **'baŋ** may be pronounced **'aŋ**, **'diloŋ** as **'iloŋ**.

CHAPTER XVIII

EJECTIVE CONSONANTS

290. In many African languages a special type of plosive is found in which the glottis is closed at the same time as the mouth closure is made. Thus **p, t, k** are formed in the mouth and the vocal cords are brought together at the same time, i.e. a simultaneous glottal stop is made. The mouth closure is generally released half a second before the glottal closure: the double closure and release give a peculiarly sharp sound to the plosive.

291. Other consonants besides plosives can be made with simultaneous glottal closure and examples of these occur in African languages: thus **s, y, ts, tʃ, pf, tl, kl** are found. For the representation of ejectives, the African Institute recommends the consonant letter (or letters) followed by an apostrophe: thus **p', t', k', s', ts', tʃ', tl'**, &c. In the case of **y**, it seems better to place the apostrophe before the letter, thus **'y**.

292. EXAMPLES

Hausa. **k'ak'a** grandfather (cf. **kaka** harvest)
   bak'i strangers (cf. **baki** mouth)
   yak'i war **ts'unts'ua** bird
   ts'oofo (and **s'oofo**) old man
   ts'ooro and **s'ooro** fear (cf. **soora** mud ceiling)
   s'aara contemporary (cf. **saara** cut down)
   'ya'ya children (cf. **yaya** older one)

293. *Suto-Chuana group of languages.* In the Suto-Chuana group of languages, the unaspirated affricates **ts, tʃ** are often —and **tl** always—ejective: the ejective nature of **tl** is much stronger and more easily recognized than in the case of the other two.

  ts'ɛbɛ ear   **ts'oma** to hunt
  tʃ'ubua to agitate **tl'isa** to bring

294. *Zulu.*

t'uɓa	soften	**iŋk'aɓi**	head of cattle
ints'aɓa	scout	**p'ət'ɛla**	eat soft fruit
ts'əɓə	smash	**nt'ant'a**	float
intl'əkə	head	**intl'ɛɓə**	secret
impf'ɛnɛ	baboon	**ikl'ume**	sapling
		tʃ'atʃ'aza	squirt

In Zulu aspiration and ejection in plosives are sometimes distinguishing features between words.

  k'ak'a encircle   **khakha** be acrid
  t'eŋga wave about **theŋga** barter

Since normal unaspirated plosives do not occur, it is unnecessary in orthography to mark both the ejection and the aspiration: thus **kaka** and **khakha** would be sufficient to distinguish the two words illustrated above, but the ejective nature of the k's in **kaka** would have to be learnt.

295. *Amharic.*

k'ëy	red	**t'ëtt'a**	drink (imper.)
t'at	finger	**as'e**	His Majesty
k'wank'wa	language	**s'ëyyaf**	erroneous, wrong
tʃ'ëdlëma	dark	**afëntʃ'a**	nose

296. *Bari.* In Bari **y** is found as an ejective: **'yur** *to burn.* **b** and **d** may be implosive or ejective (see Ch. XVII, p. 96).

Chapter XIX

CLICK CONSONANTS

297. Click consonants which occur in Zulu, Xosa, Suto, Hottentot, Bushman, and other languages, like implosives, are sounds of a plosive nature made with the breath going in instead of out. The peculiar smacking sound is due to their special formation. There are always two points of articulation, one of them being the velar stop (the k-position), and the other made by some other part of the tongue or by the lips. The air between these two points of contact is rarefied by suction: the more forward stop is released and the air rushes in from the outside to fill this rarefied space. The k-closure is released immediately after the front closure and generally quietly, so that one does not as a rule hear any k-sound. The following vowel is made on the outgoing breath and there is no perceptible pause between the click and this vowel. The tongue is tense during the production of the sound.

298. There are five main types of click heard in South African languages:

(1) The *bi-labial click*, which occurs in Bushman.

(2) The *dental click*, made by the tip of the tongue against the upper teeth and teeth-ridge. This is the sound (without the release of the k-position), used when we make an exclamation of impatience (written *tut tut*).

(3) The *palato-alveolar click*, made by the blade of the tongue against the teeth-ridge.

(4) The *retroflex click*, made by the curled-up tip of the tongue against the hard palate. This sound resembles the noise made by drawing a cork from a bottle.

(5) The *lateral click*, made by the tip and blade of the tongue against the teeth-ridge and the front of the hard palate, the edges of the tongue touching the upper teeth all round (like the alveolar click). The release of this click is made by freeing one side of the tongue, the tip remaining firmly in position, until the air has rushed in. This lateral release gives a strong l-element. This click (without the release of the k-position) is the sound used to encourage a horse to go quickly.

299. The following are diagrams of three of the commonest of these clicks. All students who are studying a language containing clicks should consult Dr. Doke's *Phonetics of the Zulu Language*, where a full description of the clicks occurring in Zulu will be found, and practical hints on acquiring these difficult sounds.

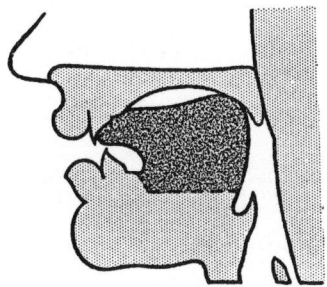

FIG. 42. Dental Click.

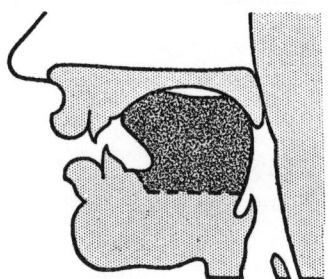

FIG. 43. Palato-alveolar Click.

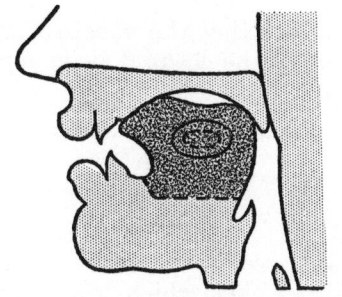

FIG. 44. Lateral Click.

Position of Lateral Release

300. The letters which are in use at present to represent these clicks are **c**, **q**, and **x**. Since these letters are used in other languages to represent quite different sounds, and since clicks are sounds of a very special nature, it has been suggested that new letters should be used for them. The Institute's Memorandum mentions

ʃ for c
ʕ ,, q
ʖ ,, x

These are the letters used by Doke :[1] Tucker also uses ʕ for the click occurring in Suto.

[1] They are the symbols used by the I.P.A.

301. Clicks can be aspirated or non-aspirated: they ·can be voiced and nasalized, and also preceded by a nasal consonant. Thus a large number of click combinations can occur. Taking the letters at present in use (**c, q, x**), the following combinations are found.

Unaspirated.	*Aspirated.*	*Nasalized.*
c	ch	ŋc
q	qh	ŋq
x	xh	ŋx

302. ŋ represents nasalization, i.e. the soft palate lowered during the whole time of the production of the click.

Voiced.	*Voiced Nasalized.*
ǵc	ŋǵc
ǵq	ŋǵq
ǵx	ŋǵx

303. ǵ here represents the fact that the vocal cords are in vibration during the formation of the click: ŋ again represents the lowering of the soft palate.

Nasal + Click.	*Nasal + Click aspirated.*
nc	nch
nq	nqh
nx	nxh

304. Here a nasal consonant *precedes* the click: this must be distinguished from the nasalized click which has nasal resonance running through the whole of the sound.

305. EXAMPLES

Zulu. Examples of Zulu clicks are given in the summary of Zulu on p. 201.

Suto (the palato-alveolar click only occurs in this language). Examples taken from Tucker.

Non-aspirated.

ç ilaç ila to stamp up and down   ç ala   to begin
ç εta   to finish   ç əkwa grass for thatching

Aspirated.

     leç heku old man   ç hala to scatter   ç huç ha to trot

306. Clicks in Nama and Bushman.
Nama, a Hottentot dialect, has four clicks for which the
following symbols have been used:

Dental /	e.g.	/ġore	to ask	/ġorasən	to separate
Alveolar ≠	e.g.	≠na	to dance	≠nou	to beat
Retroflex ./	e.g.	./am	to be green	./ami	to loosen
Lateral //'	e.g.	//ġoob	bull	//ĕib	he

Bushman has also these four clicks together with a bi-labial
click.

CHAPTER XX

SOUNDS WITH MORE THAN ONE ARTICULATION

307. Most consonant sounds have a simple articulation, i.e.
one part only of the organs of speech is concerned in making
them.[1] Thus **p** and **b** are articulated by the lips alone, **k** and **ġ**
by the back of the tongue against the soft palate: no other part
of the articulating organs is being used. There are some consonants, however, in which more than one part of the articulating organs is concerned: these are said to have a double (and
sometimes a treble) articulation. The sound of **w,** for example,
is labial and velar at the same time, in that the lips are rounded
and protruded and the back of the tongue raised to the **u**
position (see Fig. 39, p. 90). The vowels **u** and **o** have also two
articulations, labial and velar, i.e. lips rounded and the back
of the tongue raised. The 'dark l' in English is made by a velar
modification, i.e. the back of the tongue is raised to the soft
palate while the tip is touching the teeth-ridge (see Fig. 28,
p. 69). The German ʃ is velarized and labialized, i.e. the back
of the tongue raised and the lips rounded: English ʃ has less
lip-rounding (often none at all) and no velar modification. It
should be noted that in all these cases the double articulation
takes place simultaneously.

308. In some African languages there are a number of sounds
with more than one articulation, some of them involving very
complicated combinations of articulations. In previous chapters
a few examples of such African sounds have been described:
thus **kp** and **ġb** have labial and velar articulations: ejectives
have a glottal closure as a secondary added to another primary

[1] The action of the vocal cords in producing voice is neglected here.

articulation: clicks have always a double articulation, one being the **k**-stop. (See Chapters XVIII, XIX.)

309. Further combinations will be considered under the headings of Labialization, Palatalization, and Velarization. Several sounds must be considered in more than one category, since it is often found that labialization is combined with palatalization and with velarization.

Labialized Sounds.

310. Labialization is the adding of a rounding of the lips to sounds articulated in another part of the mouth. With this action, the tongue is often also concerned, i.e. the lips may be rounded and the back of the tongue raised towards the soft palate at the same time: thus labialization is accompanied by velarization. Tucker, in discussing this phenomenon as it occurs in the Suto-Chuana group of languages, calls it *back-labialization*. What he calls *front-labialization* consists of a raising of the front of the tongue in addition to the lip-rounding: this can be considered as a combination of labialization and palatalization. It must be remembered that the two articulations in each case are added to another one.

311. The following diagram and explanation may serve as an example of back labialization or labialization and velarization together.

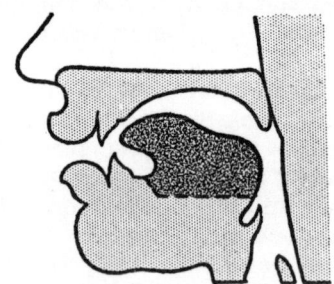

FIG. 45. Labialized and Velarized **s**.

312. Labialized and velarized **s** is found in the Suto-Chuana group of languages: the main articulation of **s** is alveolar, i.e. friction takes place between the tip of the tongue and the teeth-ridge: at the same time the lips may be rounded (labialization) and the back of the tongue raised (velarization), as is shown in the diagram above. Compare this with the diagram of normal **s** on p. 80.   When the organs of speech pass from this position to the following vowel, a kind of **w**-glide (with an **o** resonance rather than that of **u**) is heard. Many investigators have considered this fact of labialization as consisting of consonant $+$**w**, but when the native pronounces such a sound, it can be easily seen that the **w**-element goes through the whole of the consonant, i.e. the lips are put in the rounded position at the beginning of the articulation of the consonant or group of consonants: the glide is dependent upon this tongue and lip position.   If the **s** and **w** are separate sounds, the organs of speech, after articulating **s** in the normal fashion, go out of their way to make the **w**-glide, which is then an independent sound. In order to appreciate the labialization of consonants, round the lips in an exaggerated fashion as if for **u** (the tongue will be also raised towards the velum) and then try to say the word *swim* as if the **sw** were one sound.

313. Labialization (with or without velarization) such as has been described, can be added to a large number of consonants. To avoid the introduction of new letters, these sounds can be written as digraphs, with the semi-vowel letter **w** following the consonant, but it must be remembered that in many languages the digraph represents a single sound of double (or treble) articulation and not a sequence of sounds ending in **w**. Thus **sw, tw, tʃw, nw, mw, lw, fw** would represent labialized and velarized **s, tʃ, n, m, l, f**: **kw, gw, ŋw, xw** would represent labialized **k, g, ŋ, x**. (These sounds are already velar and cannot therefore be velarized.)   The student who comes across such combinations of letters should observe carefully if they represent each a velarized and labialized consonant or a group of two consonants.

314. Examples

Suto, Pedi, Chuana (taken from Tucker, p. 75).

nwa	to drink	**ŋwedi**	moonlight
nywɛka	to undress	**senywa**	to be destroyed
ʃwa	to nap	**ʒwala**	beer
lwa	to fight	**ɬwa**	to climb
xwa[1]	to die	**rwɛla**	to carry on head
ntwa	war	**kwena**	crocodile
twhala	to break	**ŋkwha**	booty

[1] Tucker writes this ʾhwa (pre-velar fricative).

ŋkwɛ	leopard	mokxwha	custom
tswa	to go out	tswhene	baboon
tʃwetso	information	tʃwhabola	to put out quickly

315. In these languages, back labialization is added to words containing consonants other than labial and to the nasals **m** and **ny** in the formation of the passive of verbs and the diminutive of some nouns.

lesa	to leave	pass.	leswa
rɛka	to buy	,,	rɛkwa
roma	to send	,,	roŋwa
rata	to love	,,	ratwa
senya	to destroy	,,	senywa or seŋwa
seʃɔ	abscess	dimin.	seʃwana
maru	clouds	,,	marwana
ŋku	sheep	,,	ŋkwana
kxhomo	ox	,,	kxhoŋwana

316. Front labialization is added for the same grammatical purposes to verbs and nouns which end in a labial consonant. For examples of these, see further, p. 107.

317. In Chuana, in addition to the normal ʃ which is pronounced without lip-rounding, there occurs a ʃ-sound with a peculiar kind of labialization. The lips are rounded and protruded and there is friction between the edge of the top teeth and the inside of the bottom lip. This can be written ʃw since no other kind of labialized ʃ occurs in the language: e.g. ʃwupa, *seven.* ʃa, *to burn,* and ʃwa, *to die* (both with high level tones), are distinguished by the difference between the two kinds of ʃ (such distinctions are extremely rare, however). The affricate tʃ with the same kind of lip-rounding also occurs: batʃwumi, *hunters.*

318. In Gã, ʃ, tʃ, dʒ occur with a similar peculiar kind of lip-rounding. These labialized sounds are also palatalized (see §§ 322–8 for explanation of palatalization). Labialization serves to distinguish words in many cases.

319. EXAMPLES

Non-labialized.		*Labialized.*	
ʃɛ	to order	ʃwɛ	to play
ʃiɛ	to preach	ʃwie	to drive away
ʃa	to sift	ʃwe	to vomit
ʃã	to burn	ʃwere	to prosper

Non-labialized.		*Labialized.*	
ʃina	door	ʃwapo	shop
ʃe gbeyei	to fear	ʃwane	afternoon
tʃina	cow	tʃwii	heart
tʃa	to dig	tʃwa	to play (same tones)
dʒa	to divide	dʒwa	to break (same tones)
dʒɛi	there	dʒwɛi	rubbish, grass

320. In Twi, palatal t and d (ty and dy) can be labialized. In the word *Twi* itself **tw** represents this sound: the main articulation is with the front of the tongue against the hard palate: to this main articulation, lip-rounding is added, i.e. it is labialized. In passing to the vowel following, the front-rounded semi-vowel glide is heard.[1] The voiced equivalent is labialized **dy**. The writing of palatal **ty** and **dy** with the addition of **w** to show labialization would be clumsy (**tyw, dyw**): **tw** and **dw** are therefore used, but it must be remembered that **t** and **d** in this case represent the palatal sounds and **w** the palatal rounded semi-vowel.[1]

321. EXAMPLES

nantwi cow   **twafo** butcher   **dwene** think
awotwe eight   **adwuma** work

Palatalized Sounds.

322. Palatalization is the raising of the front of the tongue towards the hard palate as a secondary articulation added to the main articulation of a consonant. As an example of this consonant formation, **s** pronounced with palatalization would be in the position shown in Fig. 46. The main articulation is alveolar, and the front of the tongue is raised at the same time. When the organs of speech pass from this position to that of the following vowel, a kind of y-glide is heard: this glide is dependent

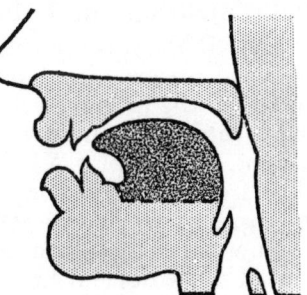

FIG. 46. Palatalized **s**.
(Compare this with the diagram of **s** on p. 80.)

upon the position described above and cannot be avoided.

[1] I.P.A. ɥ.

323. Palatalization is frequent before front (palatal) vowels. **ky** and **ģy** represent palatalized **k** and **ģ** (i.e. **k** and **ģ** with a somewhat forward articulation and simultaneous raising of the front of the tongue) in many languages.

324. EXAMPLES

In Hausa, **k** and **ģ** are palatalized, i.e. **doki,** *horse*; **dauki,** *took*, are pronounced **dokyi, daukyi.** The articulation of **k** and **ģ** in such a case is probably not so far forward as the true palatal **ty** and **dy** (see diagram, p. 53).

325. In Bambara, the word for *foot* (**sɛ̃**) sounds somewhat like **syɛ̃**, but there is not so marked a glide as in the word which is written **syɛ** meaning *scratch*. The fricative described on p. 81 as palato-alveolar is often called palatal or palatalized **s.**

326. In Kakwa (a dialect of Bari), the word **kosaŋ,** *yesterday*, is pronounced with the palatalized **s**: in Bari itself the word is **kotyaŋ.** The termination **-so** has a palatalized **s**: in Bari it is **-tyo.** The word for *child* is **ŋyɪrə** (**ŋ** is palatalized here): Bari **ŋɪrə** (with no palatalization): *revelation* is **babaŋyet**: Bari **babaŋet.**

327. In Fante, **p** is palatalized before **i, ɪ, e,** and **ɛ** in certain words (but not in all): **pɛpɛɛpɛ,** *exactly*; **apɪm,** *thousand.* [These words sound like **pyɛpyɛɛpyɛ, apyɪm.**]

Palatalization and Labialization.

328. If the lips are rounded at the same time as the tongue is raised towards the hard palate, and these two articulations added to the primary articulation of a consonant, that consonant is labialized and palatalized. Tucker calls this *front labialization.* In Chapter XVI the semi-vowel corresponding to the close front rounded vowel is described as palatal or palatalized **w** (e.g. Twi **we,** Fante **wɪ,** *chew*).

How this palatalization and labialization should be represented must depend upon whether the two types of labialization—front and back—both occur in a language in similar combinations of sounds. Thus in Twi and Fante, the semi-vowel **w** occurs before back vowels only and the palatalized semi-vowel before front vowels only. One letter, therefore, (**w**), suffices to indicate the two sounds, and the special pronunciation of **w** before front vowels can be learnt. But when both types of labialization occur irrespective of the kind of vowel which follows, the difference should be indicated.   Such a distinction is likely to be rare: there are, however, examples in Pedi of front and back labialization with the same vowels.

329. In Pedi, front labialization is added to consonants with a labial primary articulation (as back labialization is added to other consonants) to form the passive of verbs and the diminutive of some nouns.[1]

EXAMPLES

vəʃa	to tie on back	pass.	voʃwa
leʃa	to pay	,,	liʃwa
tseʋa	to know	,,	tseʋwa
phapha	to cleave	,,	phapwha
ʃɛpa	to nurse	,,	ʃepwa
kxhapha	to scoop	,,	kxhapwha
pheʃo	wind	dimin.	pheʃwana
kuʋu	hippo	,,	kuʋwana
kɛpə	spade	,,	kepwana

Velarized Sounds.

330. Velarization is the adding of a velar articulation (i.e. the back of the tongue at or near the soft palate) to some other consonant articulation.   In the first paragraph of this chapter some examples of velarization in English and German were given: on p. 101 it was also shown that velarization often accompanies labialization.   Further examples from African languages are given here.

331. EXAMPLES

The **kp** and **g̶b** of West African languages are sounds of double articulation, viz. labial and velar: it is very difficult, however, to say that one of these articulations is primary and the other secondary, since both appear to be equally important. The fact that some of these have been written **bw, g̶bw, kpw** indicates that the velar element is plainly evident.   In Kru, for

---

[1] Tucker writes this with ɥ. In broad transcription and in orthography, the letter **w** should suffice to show back labialization of all consonants other than labials and **m** and **ny** and front labialization of all labial consonants. [There are two exceptions (the only ones in the three languages), however, which Tucker found, viz. **mphɔ**, dimin. **mpwhana**, *gift*; **ɬompho**, dimin. **ɬompwhana**, *honour*. See p. 83.]

example, the word for *dog* is given by Delafosse in two dialects
as **bwe** and in a third as **ǵbwe**: one of the present writers heard
it as **ǵbe** with a very slight **w**-element: at times the **ǵ** contact
was difficult to hear. The corresponding group of nasal consonants occurred in the word for *bird*, **nuŋmwɛ**: **ŋm** were articulated at the same time with lip-rounding, which gave a **w**-glide
on passing to the vowel: also **ŋmuŋmɛ**, *bitter*. Another example
from Kru was **se mǵbati**, *daybreak*.

332. Velar labials occur in Kakwa, a dialect of Bari, e.g.
luŋmaser, *brother*; **kpen**, *birds*; **ǵbagbɛ**, *wild cat*. In this
dialect, the labialized velar consonants of Bari are replaced by
the velar-labials or by the plain consonant without either
labialization or velarization.

333. EXAMPLES

Bari.	*Kakwa.*	
kwen	kpen	birds
ǵwagwɛ	ǵbagbɛ	wild cat
iŋwan	iŋman	four
'duŋwe	'duŋe	to be cut towards
ǵirwe	ǵire	to be headed off

334. Similarly words which have labialized velar consonants
in Gbari have velar-labials in Nupe.

Gbari.	*Nupe.*	
kwe	kpe	cover
kwa	kpa	feed
ǵwa	ǵba	humble
ǵwere	ǵbere	red

335. Doke gives a number of velarized consonants in his
Unification of the Shona Dialects (pp. 55 and 56) (Zezuru).

pk:	pkere	child	**bǵ:**	ibǵe	stone
	kupka	to dry up		imbǵa	dog
mŋ:	mŋana	child	**nyŋ:**	kunyŋata	to be wet
	mŋedzi	moon		nyŋana	child
tkw:	tkwana	little children	**dɣw:**	kuti dɣwe	to drip (of rain)
	utkwu	these (class VI)			
nŋw:	kunŋwa	to drink	**ɣw:**	kurɣwa	to fight
tʃk:	kutʃka	to fear	**dʒǵ:**	fodʒǵa	tobacco
	datʃka	frog		tʃidʒǵa	thigh

CHAPTER XXI

SYLLABLES

336. It is generally easy to say how many syllables a word contains, but not so easy to define what a syllable is, nor to say exactly where one syllable ends and another begins.[1]
337. The essence of a syllable is that one sound stands out from the neighbouring sounds, i.e. it has greater prominence. More than one factor may contribute to this prominence, the most important one being the sonority of the sound compared with that of its neighbours. If of two or more consecutive sounds, one has a greater sonority, that sound is said to be syllabic. In a sequence of sounds forming a word or phrase, there may be a number of sonorous sounds surrounded by less sonorous sounds, giving the effect of waves of prominence: the crests of the waves represent the succession of sonorous sounds and the troughs the less sonorous sounds. Thus a syllable generally consists of one sonorous sound together with one or more less sonorous sounds on one or each side of it: in other words, it is a sequence of sounds containing one peak of prominence. The sound which constitutes the peak is said to be syllabic. A syllable may, of course, consist of one sound only: e.g. in **aba, mba,** the initial **a** and **m** respectively form one syllable.
338. The most sonorous sounds are the vowels. It follows, therefore, that the vowel generally forms the syllabic element. But there are a number of consonants which are also very sonorous, and these can also form syllables. It is false to think that a syllable cannot be made without a vowel. The most sonorous consonants are the voiced l-sounds and the nasal consonants. In many languages, these are frequently syllabic. The English word *little* consists of two syllables, the **i** being the prominent part of the first syllable and the final l that of the second: the two points of prominence **i** and l are separated by the consonant **t** which has no sonority. The German word *Nebel* is often pronounced **neebl,** i.e. without a vowel between the **b** and l: in such a case the l is said to be syllabic. In the English words *written* (**ritn**), *hidden* (**hidn**) there is no vowel

[1] See A. Klingenheben, 'Vai-Texte', *Zeitschrift für Eingeborenensprachen*, xvi, pp. 68 ff.

between the plosive and the **n**. There is no doubt that the words consist of two syllables and the second in each case is formed by the consonant **n** which is more sonorous than the plosive. Similarly in German, in the pronunciation of *haben* as **haabm,** the nasal forms the second syllable. Other examples of syllabic nasal consonants are **m** and **ŋ** in *open,* pronounced **oupm,** *bacon,* pronounced as **beikŋ** (one pronunciation), and in German *lecken,* pronounced as **lɛkŋ.** The consonant **r** is also sonorous and can be syllabic: in Efik, for example, the word **ekpri,** *little,* consists of three syllables, with three different tones [. ˙ .], the **r** forming one syllable.

339. Englishmen and Germans are used to the occurrence of syllabic l-sounds and syllabic nasal consonants in positions such as those illustrated above, although they are often unaware of the fact. But in African languages syllabic nasal consonants occur in positions which are unfamiliar to Europeans. One characteristic of a large number of African languages is the occurrence of words beginning with a nasal consonant followed by another consonant, e.g. **mp, mb, mf, mt, nt, nd, ns, nl, nr, ŋk, ŋg, ŋw** or **nh.** When these consonant groups are found in words like **mpa, mbə, mfu, mtu, nto, ndu, nso, nlə, ŋka, ŋgi, ŋwɛ,** &c., there are often (but not always) two peaks of prominence, the one the vowel and the other the nasal consonant, and the two are separated by the less sonorous consonant. Thus the word consists of two syllables, the nasal consonant forming one.

340. Just as a consonant may be syllabic, so a vowel may have the function of a consonant in so far as it forms the less sonorous element of a syllable: thus in the diphthongs **ai, au,** the **i** and **u** are less sonorous than **a,** and as far as syllabic function is concerned they resemble a consonant in such a combination as **an.** In a group such as **aea,** if the **e** is pronounced very short, it becomes a vowel glide, and as such has the function of a consonant.

341. It has been said that more than one factor may go to the making of a syllable. These other factors are mainly stress and pitch. The alternation of prominent and less prominent sounds may be caused by diminution and increase of breath force: for instance, the words *sofa arm* (**soufə aam**),[1] the second syllable of *sofa* is separated from the first syllable of *arm*

---

[1] Some English people would use an intrusive **r** to separate them, **soufər aam:** others a glottal stop, **soufə 'aam.**

by a decrescendo of breath force on the one and a fresh impulse on the other $><$. Similarly, nasal consonants following or preceding vowels can be made syllabic by breath force: a word like **bam** can be pronounced as one or as two syllables: in the latter case, a fresh impulse of breath is used on the **m** and this consonant is lengthened. In German the word *kommen* is often pronounced as **kɔmm̩**[1] (two syllables), and is distinguished from the imperative *komm* (**kɔm**) by the length of the **m** and the extra breath force used. *Haben* is often reduced to **haamm̩**, the second **m** having a fresh impulse of breath which makes it syllabic.

342. The syllabic quality of vowel or nasal consonant in such cases is increased if the extra breath force is accompanied by a change in pitch of the voice. Say the vowel **a** on any pitch: hold it on and drop the pitch an interval of about a third: alternate these a number of times, and the effect is of a number of syllables. Similarly, say the word **bam** with a different pitch on the **m** from that of **ba** and it will be more apparent that it consists of two syllables.

343. In tone languages or languages with a musical accent, such a use of syllabic nasal consonants is very common. A word like **ŋgom** can be pronounced as one, two, or three syllables. If it is one syllable, the first nasal consonant is very short and the major part of the stress falls on the **ɡom**. If it is two syllables, the **ŋ** is long and has a certain amount of stress: **ɡom** is pronounced with a fresh impulse of the breath. The two syllables are more clearly differentiated if the pitch of them is not the same, **ŋ-ɡom** $\left[˙. \right]$ or $\left[.˙ \right]$. If it consists of three syllables, there are three impulses of the breath, viz. on the **ŋ**, **ɡo**, and **m**; the **m** is then also lengthened. Again, if all three are on different pitches, the three syllables are more noticeable, **ŋ-ɡo-m** $\left[.˙. \right]$ or $\left[˙.. \right]$. A number of examples of such words will be found in Ch. XXIV, p. 154, in the exercises for the practice of tones.

344. The question of syllable division must be considered in connexion with these combinations of nasal+plosive consonant. Where such combinations occur in the middle of words, it should be noted whether the syllable division is before the nasal or between the nasal and plosive. For example, the

---

[1] Syllabic **m** is here shown by a vertical line underneath the letter **m**.

FIG. 47. TABLE OF CONSONANTS OCCURRING IN AFRICAN LANGUAGES

	Bi-labial.	Labio-Dental.	Dental and Alveolar.	Palato-Alveolar.	Retroflex.	Palatal.	Velar.	Labio-Velar.	Laryngeal.
Explosive	p, b		t, d		ʈ, ɖ	ty, dy ky, gy	k, g	kp, gb	ʔ
Implosive	ɓ		ɗ			ʄ	'g		
Affricative	pf, bv	pf, bv	ts, dz	tʃ, dʒ			kx		
Nasal	m		n		ɳ	ny	ŋ	ŋm	
Lateral ⎰ Explosive			tl						
Lateral ⎱ Fricative			ɬ, ɮ						
Lateral Frictionless			l			ly			
Rolled and Flapped			r, ɼ						
Fricative	f, ʋ	f, v	θ, ð s, z	ʃ, ʒ		hy	x, ɣ		h
Semi-vowel	w					y	(w)		

Notes. 1. Aspirated plosives, click consonants, and ejectives are not given in this table.
2. In some languages (e.g. Nuer, Dinka) c and j are used instead of ty, dy for the palatal plosives.
3. In some languages (e.g. Swahili, Hausa) c and j are used instead of tʃ, dʒ for the palato-alveolar affricates.
4. The capital and written forms of these letters are shown in the Memorandum on Orthography, p. 18.

word **kaŋga** can be considered as consisting of two syllables divided **kaŋ-ga** (as *finger*, **fiŋ-gə** in English): but it can also be divided **ka-ŋga**. In such a case the **ŋ** is very short. In African languages this latter method is almost always the rule, especially where the word-roots are built up on the principle of consonant+vowel.

345. Examples

Kru. **semgbati** [. ˙ .] at daybreak: here the syllable division is **se-mgbati**: the nasal consonant is the one corresponding to **gb**, i.e. **mŋ**.

Ewe.	**ekpəm**	[˙˙ .] he saw me	**ŋkə**	[˙˙]	name
	wəm	[. ˙] doing	**ŋdə**	[. ˙]	noon
Twi.	**mmom**	[˙ .˙] rather	**əmfa**	[.. ˙]	he did not take
Noho.	**mboa**	[˙˙ .] house	**mbə**	[. ˙]	dog
Efik.	**mkpa**	[. ˙] death	**mməŋ**	[˙˙]	water
Duala.	**mbəti**	[. ˙˙] clothing			
Kru.	**dza m ni**	[.. ˙] bring me water			

Chapter XXII
STRESS, LENGTH

346. Length and stress, together with pitch or intonation, are often termed sound attributes: they are elements added to the sounds composing words and syllables and are of considerable importance in every language. They may be 'significant', in that meaning is dependent upon them, and even where no semantic value is involved, a correct use of these attributes is essential if the characteristic 'accent' of the language is not to be lost. Intonation, which is specially important in a large number of African languages, is treated in Chapter XXIV.

Stress.
347. 'Stress is defined as the degree of force with which a sound or syllable is uttered. It is essentially a subjective action. A strong energy of utterance means energetic action of

all the articulating organs: it is usually accompanied by a gesture with the hand or head or other parts of the body; it involves a strong force of exhalation (except in rare cases) and consequently gives the objective impression of loudness. Weak energy of utterance involves weak force of exhalation and therefore gives the objective impression of softness.'[1]

348. In Chapter XXI it was pointed out that the formation of a syllable depended upon the relative prominence of sounds and that several elements may contribute towards this effect, inherent sonority being the chief. Additional prominence is secured by the addition of a greater force of exhalation (with a resulting more vigorous articulation). Thus certain 'peaks of prominence' stand out more than others. These are the *stressed* syllables.

349. But stress must not be confused with prominence: prominence is the general distinctness of a sound, stress is the degree of force of utterance. Nor must stress be confused with pitch. A strong stress on a syllable is sometimes accompanied by a change of pitch from that of the previous syllable, but the two elements are independent of each other, and a strong stress can occur on any pitch: thus in Twi the word **Asante** with the tones [. . ˙] has stress on the second syllable.

350. In a word or word-group consisting of a number of syllables, there are varying degrees of stress. Thus in the English word *nationality* there are five degrees of stress, shown by the numbers over each syllable, **næ ʃnæliti**. For practical purposes, we can consider this word as having a main stress on the syllable marked 1, a secondary stress on the syllable marked 2, and the rest as unstressed. In the French word *nationalité*, all the syllables have a much more even stress, the last perhaps having a somewhat heavier one than the others. In the German word *Nationalität*, the first syllable has a secondary stress, and the last a heavy one, heavier than the English main stress.

351. We mark the two degrees of stress thus: ˈ before the syllable bearing the main stress and ˌ before the syllable with secondary stress, where such marking is thought necessary.

352. Stress may be significant in some languages. In English we differentiate noun and verb in words like *object*, *subject*,

[1] From D. Jones, *Outline of English Phonetics*, new and enlarged edition, 1932, p. 227.

increase mainly by stress.[1] In German *Gebet*, 'prayer', and *gebet*, 'give', are also distinguished mainly by stress.[2]

353. In investigating the pronunciation of an African language, the stress habits must be discovered. It is often helpful to get the native speaker to tap on the syllables on which he feels he is making most effort. In some languages, the stress may fall on the last syllable of a word, as it appears to do in Bambara: in another it may fall on the penultimate syllable, as in most Bantu languages.

354. In many African languages, however, stress such as we know it in European languages, does not exist. This is especially the case in tone languages, where correct use of pitch is of far greater importance than stress. European learners of African tone languages should be very much alive to the danger of transferring their own stress habits into the new language. This is particularly easy to do, since stress is such a subjective action. Englishmen and Germans are likely to be the greatest sinners in this respect as stress plays an important part in their mother tongue: Frenchmen, on the other hand, whose language has a much more even distribution of breath force over syllables, are less likely to have this tendency.

355. In Bari, dynamic accent (accompanied by high level or high-falling tone) plays a far bigger role than syllable pitch, though the two are so interwoven as to be almost inseparable.[3] The following pairs of words are distinguished by stress rather than by tonal differences, though tone differences also exist:

Accent on the 1st syllable.   *Accent on the 2nd syllable.*

(The tone of the stressed syllables is shown by a line, of the unstressed syllables by a dot.)

ˈləkɛ	[‾ ·]	clean	pl. ləˈkɛ	[· ╲]
ˈləkwɛ	[‾ ·]	white	„ ləˈkwɛ	[· ╲]
ˈlokoŋ	[‾ ·]	clever	„ loˈkoŋ	[· ╲]
ˈlopir	[‾ ·]	fat	„ loˈpir	[· ╲]

[1] In the first two there is also some difference in vowel quality ˈɔbdʒekt and əbˈdʒekt: ˈsʌbdʒikt and səbˈdʒekt: in the last there is some difference in length: ˈinkris and inˈkriis.

[2] There is a difference in vowel quality here also, the unstressed vowel in each word being the neutral vowel ə (ˈg̊eebət, g̊əˈbeet).

[3] In Hausa, and possibly in the Mandingo language, the same tendency seems to be developing.

Note also the following verbs:

ˈNan lə ˈˈbə ˈbəg̍gu [‾ . ‾ · .] I dig

ˈNan lə ˈbə ˈˈbəg̍gu [‾ . ⌐‾ .] I dig in many places

ˈNan lə ˈkɛ kɛn dya [‾ . ‾ · .] I am talking

ˈNan lə kɛ kɛn ˈdya [‾ . · . ⌐] I am tearing

ˈNan lə kɛ ˈkɛn dya [‾ . ⌐ ‾ .] I am scolding

Length.

356. Vowels and consonants may be pronounced for a longer or shorter period of time : thus we speak of vowel or consonant *length* or *quantity*. The sounds which can have length, i.e. which can be held on, are the vowels and the continuant consonants, i.e. nasal, lateral, and fricative consonants and the stops of plosives. The plosion of plosive consonants and flapped consonants may be considered as having no appreciable length.

357. Length of vowel is often bound up with stress, the vowels of the syllables which bear the main stress being longer than those in unstressed positions. But this is not always the case, for long vowels may occur in unstressed positions and short ones in stressed positions. Here again no rules can be given, the usages of each particular language must be discovered and stated.

358. Length of vowels often occurs in African languages as a significant element of speech, one word being distinguished from another by vowel length only. Examples are given from a few languages below. In this book, long vowels are shown by writing the letters twice.

359. EXAMPLES

Ewe.

ba	mud	**baa**	wide open	(same tones)
bi	to bend	**bii**	narrow	(,, ,,)
bliba	to make dirty	**blibaa**	dirty, soiled	(,, ,,)
bala	to climb	**balaa**	moving quietly	(tones different here).

Hausa.

da	relative particle	**daa**	formerly
dafa	to cook	**daafa**	to hold
duka	all	**duuka**	to beat

Kpelle. **kali** hoe   **kaali** snake
       ti this   **tii** farm
       li to go   **lii** heart
       kpolo salt   **kpoolo** bread

Ganda.
okuzika to go out of   **okuziika** to bury (same tones)
           cultivation
okuwana to prop up   **okuwaana** to flatter (,, ,,)

Gã. **te** [.] went   **te·** [⌢] hide
      omõ [. ·] rice   **o·mõ** [. ·] you are catching
      wɔ [·] to sleep   **wɔɔ** [.] sleeping
      kpe [.] to meet   **kpee** [.] meeting

In Gã two methods of marking length of vowel have been
adopted, viz. a dot after the vowel and doubling the vowel
letter. These two methods serve to distinguish two different
grammatical functions of length : e.g.

miya· [· .] I go (habitually) **miyaa** [· ⟍] I do (or did) not go
In the latter case, the long final vowel has a falling tone :

    abi [. ·] they ask   **a·bi** [. ·] they are asking
    a·bi [⟋ ·] they will ask
    ele [. .] he knows   **elee** [. ⟍] he does not know

Dinka. The singular and plural of certain nouns are distinguished by length of vowel alone : **dhök**, *cheetah,* pl. **dhöök**;
pal, *knife,* pl. **paal**.

360. Long vowels also occur as the result of elision, either
of vowel or consonant.

361. EXAMPLES

Efik. **ke eto** *on the tree* is pronounced **keeto**
      ke ubom *in the canoe*   ,,   **kuubom**
Swahili. **kaa** *to remain* from **kala***[1]
      kukuu *old*   ,,   **kukulu***
      jaa *to be full* ,,   **jala***
Mende. **kaa** *to teach*   ,,   **kara**
      taa *scatter*   ,,   **taɣa**
Kpelle. **saa** *to cut*   ,,   **saɣa**
      waa *morning*   ,,   **wala**

[1] * Hypothetical forms.

Length of Consonants.

362. Consonants may also be pronounced with varying length. In this book, long consonants are written double, but it should be remembered that this does not mean two separate articulations but a prolongation of the one articulation. Thus **tt, dd, pp, ġġ,** &c., would mean a long holding of the stop with one release: a long affricate is written **ttʃ, ddʒ, tts, ddz,** &c., and consists of a long holding of the stop part of the sound.

363. In some African languages, length of consonant is significant.

364. EXAMPLES *of Long Consonants*

Hausa.	**babba**	big	**baabaa**	indigo
	lalle	certainly	**laale**	welcome
	cika	to fill	**cikakke**	filled
	nuna	ripen	**nunanne**	ripe
	yaye	to wean	**yayayye**	weaned
	buġa	beaten	**buġaġge**	beaten
	bata	to get lost	**batacce**	lost
	maida	to change	**maidajje**	changed
	aiki	a work	**ayyuka**	plur.
Ganda.	**okuġula**	to buy	**okuġġula**	to open (same tones)
	siġa	sow (seeds)	**siġġa**	scorpion
Twi.	**nna**	days (sing. **ɛda**)	**ŋŋo**	oil
	mma	children (sing. **ɔba**)	**oŋŋu**	he did not pour out

Note the grammatical significance of consonant length in the following examples:

ɔba	[˙ .]	he comes
ɔmma	[.. ˙]	he does not come
ɔmma	[˙˙ °]	he will come
ɔmmma	[˙ ..]	he will not come
ɔdɔ	[..]	he likes, agrees
ɔnnɔ	[.. ˙]	he does not like
ɔnnɔ	[˙˙˙]	he will like
ɔnnnɔ	[˙ ..]	he will not like

Note the four syllables and the different tones of each in the negative future.

Ful.	**holla**	to show	**lutti**	remain
	labbo	spear		
Shilḥ.	**bidd**	to stand still	**ɣwəlli**	that one
	dɛdda	uncle	**kuttu**	to prance
	ɣannu	to sing		
Nuba.	**ikke**	thus	**essi**	water
	tenna	his		
Chagga.	**mmaŋga** bell		**nnda**	banana plant

akapo wwandu he is beaten by the people
akapo ʃʃuo he is beaten with a bone (from **akapo
ŋgi ʃuo**)[1]

365. Gã has a number of words which end in **ŋŋ**: e.g. **faŋŋ**, *openly*; **ʃoŋŋ**, *afar off*; **doŋŋ** (or **dõõ**), *more*; **teŋŋ** (or **tẽẽ**), interrogative particle; **kakadaŋŋ**, *high*; **nu nɛ yɛ kroŋŋ**, *this water is clear*; **diŋŋ**, *silence*.

366. Where nasal and lateral consonants are doubled, particular attention should be paid to the tones of these words, since it is possible and even probable that these consonants may be syllabic and have a different tone.

CHAPTER XXIII
SOUNDS IN CONNECTED SPEECH

367. Changes in pronunciation often occur when words are combined into phrases and sentences. The main cause of such change is speed of utterance: the organs of speech, passing from one position to another quickly, are apt to take short cuts, such short cuts often involving an alteration in articulation. This often leads to the substitution of another sound for one of the original sounds, or to the dropping out of a sound. We shall consider these phenomena as they occur in African languages under the following heads:

1. Assimilation.
2. Similitude.
3. Vowel Harmony.
4. Vowel Elision.
5. Weakening and Elision of Consonants.

[1] I. Raum, *Versuch einer Grammatik der Dschaggasprache*, Berlin, 1909.

Assimilation.

368. In the course of the historical development of a language it is found that words change in pronunciation: these changes are due to more than one factor, but one of the main causes is known as assimilation. Assimilation may be defined as the process by which a sound came to be replaced by another sound under the influence of a third sound which is adjacent to it in word or sentence: the coalescing of a sequence of two sounds into a single new sound different from either of the two original sounds may also come under the heading of assimilation.[1]

369. There are two clearly defined kinds of assimilation, viz. *historical* and *juxtapositional*. Historical assimilation is that which has taken place in the course of the development of a language by which a word that was formerly pronounced in a certain way came to be pronounced subsequently in another way. In English, for example, the word *nation*, pronounced to-day **neiʃn,** was once pronounced **næsyon.** (There is historical evidence for this.) The assimilation which has taken place is the coalescing of **sy** into **ʃ** which is different from either **s** or **y.** The English word *chin* (**tʃin**) has developed from an earlier form *kin*, the **tʃ** having replaced **k** under the influence of the front vowel **i.**

370. *Juxtapositional* assimilation is an assimilation which occurs when words are juxtaposed in a sentence or in the formation of compounds. In this way, a word comes to have a pronunciation which is different from that which it has when said by itself.

EXAMPLES

371. The word *news*, pronounced in isolation, is **nyuuz,** but *newspaper* is often pronounced **nyuspeipə,** i.e. the voiced consonant **z** is replaced by the voiceless consonant **s** under the influence of the **p** following. The words *ten pence* are often pronounced **tempəns,** but the word *ten* alone, or in other compounds, is always pronounced **ten:** the **n** of *ten* has been replaced by **m** under the influence of the following **p** in the compound *tenpence*. In German, the word *du* is pronounced in isolation **du,** but in the phrase *hast du*, the **d** is replaced

---

[1] See Professor D. Jones, *Outline of English Phonetics*, new edition, 1932, Teubner & Co., Leipzig.

by **t** under the influence of the preceding **t** and the phrase is pronounced **hastu** or **hastə**. (The **t** of *hast* is dropped, after the preliminary stage **hast tu.**) In French, the word *prince* is pronounced **prɛ̃s** : but the phrase *Prince de Galles* is pronounced **prɛ̃z də ġal,** i.e. the voiceless **s** is replaced by the voiced **z** under the influence of the voiced consonant following.

372. All such changes as those given above follow certain definite phonetic laws: the substitution of one sound for another is usually gradual, i.e. there may be several intermediate substitutions before the present position is arrived at. The new sound generally bears some relationship either in place or in manner of articulation to one or both of the original sounds and the process of change can generally be traced phonetically.

373. Assimilation occurs as a phenomenon in all languages, but it does not work in the same way in all. The differences between one language and another allied language or between two or more dialects of one language are often due to assimilation of different kinds and at different rates. Thus certain assimilations may be made in one language or dialect and not in another: in one language assimilation may have made considerable progress, while in another the process has not reached the same stage, and in a third there may have been no change at all.

374. It is by the study of the working of the laws of assimilation in any group of languages or dialects that their origins can be traced and the relationship of one language to another can be defined. Considerable work of great importance has been done on the relationship of African languages by many scholars, chief of whom is Professor Meinhof. He has examined a large number of existing Bantu languages and reconstructed from his knowledge of phonetic development the main facts of the parent language from which presumably these many languages have descended. The name *Ur-Bantu* has been given to this ancestor. (See *Grundriss einer Lautlehre der Bantu-Sprachen,* 2nd edition.)

375. The student who wishes to learn several related languages or different dialects of one language will have to consider assimilation and the part it plays in philology. The best preparation for such study is an accurate elementary knowledge of general phonetics : this will give him an intelligent understanding of the principles upon which linguistic development has taken place. In this book, however, we are mainly concerned with describing the actual pronunciation of African languages as they are to-day and not with their historical development, and the student who has to learn to speak one language for the practical purposes of everyday intercourse will confuse himself if he tries to learn historical phonetics at the same time. A few examples of historical and juxtapositional assimilation are given here, however, to illustrate the phonetic principles upon which such linguistic development rests.

376. Historical Assimilation.

(a) When in one language the syllable **ku** appears and in another allied language the corresponding form is **ʄu**, it is safe to assume that **ʄu** has developed from **ku**; the labial character of **u** (rounded lips) has caused the **k** to be replaced by a labial articulation: the stop element is lost and a bi-labial fricative takes its place.

(b) When **ki** occurs in one language and **tyi** in another, the **ty** has probably developed from **k** under the influence of the front vowel **i**. Compare the development of **tʃin** from **kin** in English. In German, this assimilation was not made.

(c) The Fante words **nda, mba, ŋga**, in Twi are **nna, mma, ŋŋa**. Here the Fante forms may be considered as the original ones, and the Twi forms as having developed from these: in Twi a nasal consonant has replaced the original plosive, under the influence of the initial nasal consonant.

(d) In the Western dialects of the Akan language a consonant following a nasal is always voiced, whereas in the Eastern dialects the original voiceless consonant is retained.

Eastern			
ŋkatɛɛ, groundnut, is **ŋɡatɛ**		in Western Akan
ntɔrɔwa, tomato,	,, **ndrowa**	,,	,,
nsã, palm wine	,, **nzã**	,,	,,
nsu, water	,, **nzue**	,,	,,
mfẽ, side	,, **mvẽba**	,,	,,

The voiced consonant in Western Akan is probably due to the influence of the nasal. But note that this assimilation has taken place in one set of dialects only and not in another.

(e) A similar process shows itself in Ewe, where the following dialectal forms exist:

ŋkǝ and ŋgǝ, frontside
ŋko and ŋgo, front
amakpa and **aŋgba**, leaf.

(*f*) In Swahili a nasal consonant has been absorbed by a
following voiceless consonant. The latter has then become
aspirated.

khaŋga	guinea fowl	from	**ŋkaŋga***
thembe	corn	,,	**ntembe***
phaka	cat	,,	**mpaka***
mthu	man	,,	**muntu***[1]

(*g*) In Twi **tw** and **dw** before the front vowels **i, e, ɛ** have
come from an original **kw, gw,** the front vowels having influenced the place of articulation of the plosive.

377. Juxtapositional Assimilation.

(*a*) *Nuer.*

gat nath	is pronounced	**gadnath,**[2]	a Nuer boy	
mut nath	,,	,,	**mudnath,**	,, spear
wec nath	,,	,,	**wejnath,**	,, fishing village

gat child, **gadde** his child

The voiceless consonant at the end of the noun is replaced by
its voiced counterpart when **nath** follows, under the influence
of the nasal.

(*b*) *Tem.* In nouns beginning with a voiceless consonant the
latter is replaced by the corresponding voiced consonant when
a possessive pronoun ending in a vowel precedes it:

kale	to read	**ma gale**	my reading
kpao	buffalo	**nya gbao**	your (sing.) buffalo
tʃokoto	trousers	**e dӡokoto**	his trousers
to	bee	**ba do**	their bee
fɛde	hoe	**mi vɛde**	your (pl.) hoe[3]

(*c*) *Efik.* In two-syllabled verbs formed from monosyllabic
verbs ending in **p, t, k,** the **p, t, k** are replaced by a voiced

---

[1] See C. Meinh of, *Grundriss einer Lautlehre der Bantu-Sprachen*, Berlin,
1910, p. 90.

[2] Note that **th** represents dental t in Nuer (see pp. 54, 205): and **c**
and **j** the palatal plosives (see pp. 58, 205).

[3] Cf. Fr. Müller, 'Beitrag zur Kenntnis der Tem-Sprache', *MSOS*,
1905.

consonant (the plosive, **b**, **d**, **g̣** or the corresponding voiced fricative).

bɔp	tie	**bɔbɔ**	tie oneself
yet	wash	**yere**	wash oneself
siak	split	**siaɣa**	be split

The same change takes place in phrases in quick speech:

bɔp ufɔk build the house, is pronounced **bɔb ufɔk** (or **bɔʊ ufɔk**)

sɔk ikaŋ	poke the fire	,,	,,	**sɔɣ ikaŋ**
duopeba	twelve (ten, two)	,,	,,	**duobeba**
ekpat esie	his bag	,,	,,	**ekpar esie**

The forms **imaŋa, inɔŋɔ** as alternatives to **imaɣa, inɔɣɔ** (neg. of the verbs **ma, nɔ**) show an assimilation with the initial consonant of the verb: this takes place only in monosyllabic verbs whose roots consist of nasal consonant+vowel.

The infinitive prefix **ndi** is often pronounced **nni**, i.e. the **d** is replaced by **n** under the influence of the initial **n**: this occurs particularly when the root of the verb begins with **n**, e.g. **ndinam,** *to do.*

(*d*) *Ila.* **n** prefixed to a word beginning with **l** results in the substitution of **d** for **l**:

> **lwila,** fight for, **ndwila,** fight for me.[1]

(*e*) *Shambala.* A similar change takes place in Shambala: **n** prefixed to **l** results in the substitution of **d** for **l**: prefixed to **ɣ**, the resulting combination is **ŋg**:

loɣwa	to be charmed	**ndoɣwa**	killing charm
liʃa	to herd	**ndiʃa**	duty of herding
lila	to weep	**ndilo**	death wailing
ɣeleka	to give a surplus	**ŋgeleko**	a surplus
ɣoda	block of wood	**ŋgoda**	stick[2]

(*f*) *Bari.* **p, t, k** in a final position in a word are frequently replaced by **m, n, ŋ** respectively when followed by a word beginning with a nasal: **Lado ti yup nan,** *Lado doesn't believe me,* is often pronounced **Lado ti yum nan:** A kɔ mɛt nan,

[1] Smith and Dale, *The Ila-speaking Peoples,* London, 1920, vol. ii, p. 280.

[2] K. Roehl, *Versuch einer systematischen Grammatik der Schambala-sprache,* Hamburg, 1911.

he didn't see me, would be pronounced **A kɔ mɛn nan**: **A 'doro
kak ni**, *he fell down here*, **A 'doro kaŋ ni**.

378. Many examples of historical and juxtapositional assimilation such as these given here can be found in African languages. These are perhaps sufficient for the purpose of this
book and to show the phonetic principles upon which such
changes of pronunciation work.

Similitude.

379. It has been customary to consider other phenomena
of similarity in the articulation of neighbouring sounds as
examples of assimilation, but this term is better reserved for
the two types of *change* in pronunciation illustrated above.
Another type of similarity may be termed *similitude*. When
the sequence of two phonemes requires that a subsidiary
member of one of them should be used which has a greater
resemblance to the neighbouring sound than the principal
member has, there is said to be similitude between them.
Similitude describes an existing fact of language, assimilation
a process. Similitude has been illustrated fairly fully in Chapter
V (on Phonemes), where the use of the various members of
a phoneme was shown to depend mainly on the proximity of
some other sound: e.g. the use of a special kind of **t** (made on
the teeth) before the **th**-sound in *eighth*, and of another kind
·of **t** (made with the tongue-tip curled up) before the **r** of *tree*.
This cannot be said to be an assimilation, since there is no
evidence to show that any other kind of **t** was ever used in these
groups of sounds.[1]

EXAMPLES

380. In Fante (and many other African languages), the use
of **ŋ** before velar consonants is an example of similitude: the
nasal here has greater resemblance in articulation to the following consonant than the main member of the phoneme (**n**) to
which it belongs. **n** never occurs in this position.

The use in Twi of the palatalized semi-vowel (see Ch. XVI,
§§ 271–2) before front vowels, and the normal **w** before back
vowels is a further example of similitude.

---

[1] The distinction between assimilation and similitude was first made
by Professor D. Jones, to whom we are indebted for permission to use
his definition of Similitude. See *Outline of English Phonetics*, 2nd edition
(enlarged), Teubner, 1932.

381. It is possible that some similitudes have been arrived at by a process of assimilation, but this process cannot always be traced with certainty, and it is better to make the distinction between the two terms.

382. There are also sequences of sounds which have some element of their articulation in common, but which belong to different phonemes: such resemblances, however, do not come under the heading of similitude: the latter term should be used in reference to subsidiary members of phonemes only. Examples of this kind of resemblance are the ŋ and **k** in the word *ink* (**iŋk**), both velar sounds, the use of **s** as the sign of the plural of nouns and of the 3rd person singular of verbs which end in a voiceless consonant, such as *cups* (**kʌps**), *sits* (**sits**). Such sequences may be the result of historical assimilation, though it is not always possible to trace the process of development. They do not, however, come under the heading of similitude.

383. One of the chief examples in African languages of this latter type of similarity in the articulation of neighbouring sounds is the use of nasal consonants before other consonants. Thus as an example: in Efik, the 1st person singular prefix is a nasal consonant: it has not an independent existence apart from the verb. The kind of nasal consonant which is used depends upon the consonant of the root of the verb. Thus **m** is used before **b** (there is no initial **p** in Efik), e.g. **mbəp**, *I tie*: **n** is used before **t, d, s**: e.g. **nto**, *I come from*, **ndu**, *I remain*, **nsio**, *I take out*: ŋ is used before **k** and **w**, e.g. **ŋka**, *I go*, **ŋwet**, *I write*: before **kp**, **m** or ŋ is used: e.g. **mkpa**, *I die*, **ŋkpə**, *I carry on the back*. There is similarity of articulation between the nasal consonant prefix and the initial consonant of the verb.

384. The use of a nasal consonant before other consonants is very common in African languages, and for the most part the nasal and following consonant are homorganic, i.e. they are articulated in the same place. It is generally unwise to try to explain this fact, as has often been done, by making statements such as '**n** becomes **m** before **p** and **b**': there is usually no question of one sound 'becoming' another: what happens is that one variety of nasal is used in one place and another variety in another. It is, of course, possible that the original prefix had an independent existence—say **n** or **m**+a vowel: if the vowel then dropped and the **n** or **m** was brought into conjunction with the consonant following, a case of juxta-positional assimilation took place.   But in describing the pronunciation of a language, it is better to limit oneself to the actual facts of the existing pronunciation and not to confuse the issue by introducing possible historical explanations.

385. Examples

Efik.	**mkpa**	death	**ndap**	dream
	nso	what	**ŋwan**	woman
	mbak	part	**nsu**	lie
	mbre	game	**mfiori**	loud cry
Zulu.	**ŋgifuma**	I want	**ndiza**	fly
	ŋk'osi	O chief	**imp'i**	army
	int'amo	neck	**indɬala**	hunger

Vowel Harmony.

386. A further phenomenon is common in African languages, which can be considered as resulting from the grouping of syllables and words. This is vowel harmony, a principle which rules that the vowels of neighbouring syllables shall have similarity with each other. Thus in Swahili, verbs with the stems **i** and **u** have terminations **ia, ika**, while verbs with the stems **e** and **o** have the terminations **ea, eka** : these differences are due to a system of vowel harmony in this language. Similarly in Zulu, the vowels **e** and **ɛ**, **o** and **ɔ** are used accord-ing to a principle of vowel harmony, **e** and **o**, the closer of each pair being used when a close vowel follows in the next syllable, and **ɛ** and **ɔ** when an open vowel occurs in the next syllable, e.g. **leli, lolu,** *this,* **lɛlɔ, lɔlɔ,** *that.*[1]

Further Examples

387. In Efik, the prefixes of the verbs are in harmony with the root vowel in certain persons :

aka, *he goes,* **ede,** *he sleeps,* **ɔnɔ,** *he gives,* **oto,** *he comes from*

There are no **i** and **u** prefixes : the verbs with these root vowels take as prefix the next nearest vowel, viz. **e** and **o** respectively :

edi, *he comes,* **odu,** *he remains.*

[1] This is also an example of similitude, since **e** and **ɛ**, **o** and **ɔ**, respec-tively, belong to the same phoneme.

In Yoruba the object pronoun of the 3rd person singular is always a vowel and is identical with the last vowel of the verb:

mo ra a	I bought it	**mo bo o**	I peeled it
mo ʃe e	I did it	**mo bu u**	I gave it
mo ri i	I saw it	**mo bɛ ɛ**	I cut it
mo lə ə	I played it		
Twi. **mekə**	I go	**midi**	I eat
wote	you hear	**wuhũ**	you see
ɛba	it goes	**eyi**	it takes away
odi	he eats	**əba**	he comes
Ful. **yaha**	go	**yehi**	went
səta	sell	**soti**	sold

388. In Bari, which has ten vowels, five tense and five lax, there seems to be a system of vowel harmony by which the grammatical particles, prefixes and suffixes, modify their vowel in accordance with the stem vowel: thus a word with a tense vowel in the stem will have a tense vowel in the prefix or suffix, and a word with a lax vowel in the stem will have a lax vowel in prefix or suffix.

ɡirjö	to wipe a plate	but	**ɡɪrja**	to cicatrice
kurjö	to borrow	,,	**kurju**	to hoe
rembu	to stab	,,	**rɛmba**	to thatch
morju	to curse	,,	**mərja**	to collect
böndu	to shake	,,	**bandu**	to scatter
to-ɡirjö	to make wipe	,,	**tə-ɡɪrja**	to cause to cicatrize
ɡor pl. **ɡoro** spear		,,	**ɡər** pl. **ɡəra** collar-bone	
matat lo pïoŋ rain chief, chief of the water			**matat lu kak** ground chief, chief of the ground	

389. An interesting case of vowel usage occurs in Ibo which seems to be an example of a peculiar kind of harmony. In certain tenses, the prefixes are **ne** or **na**, **ɡe** or **ɡa**. The use of these alternatives depends upon the root vowel of the verb: the verbs with

close vowel root (**i** and **u**) have prefixes **ne**, **ɡe**
half-close vowel root (**e** and **ө**) have prefixes **na**, **ɡa**[1]
half-open vowel root (**ɛ** and **o**) have prefixes **ne**, **ɡe**
open vowel root (**a** and **ɔ**) have prefixes **na**, **ɡa**.

[1] **u, ө, o, ɔ** are the symbols used for the four back vowels in Ibo.

Thus the prefixes alternate ne, na, ne, na with the degree of openness of the root vowel of the verb. In addition it is extremely rare in this language to find a word of two or more syllables containing vowels which lie near to each other, i.e. close and half-close, half-close and half-open, half-open and open.[1] This curious usage is possibly due to the fact that the vowels are extremely difficult to differentiate from each other, i.e. i and e, u and ɵ, ɵ and o are respectively very near to each other acoustically and the alternating prefixes help to distinguish the root vowels. In the same way the fact that two vowels with neighbouring tongue positions do not occur in one word is probably an unconscious means of preventing vowels from falling together.

390. Christaller, writing on Twi and Fante, states that when different vowels follow each other 'the step from the first to the fourth degree of width (i.e. close to open) is too great, the steps 1–2 (close to half-close), 2–3 (half-close to half-open), 3–4 (half-open to open) are too small: the previous vowel is, therefore, brought into agreement with the succeeding vowel by assimilation, being used either of equal degree, or at least equal class'. And 'the euphonic vowel harmony existing in Twi provides against too great or too small dissimilations of vowels in successive syllables'.[2]

Vowel Elision and Contraction.

391. Vowel elision occurs in a large number of African languages. When one word ends in a vowel and the next begins with a vowel, generally either one or other of these vowels disappears, or the two are replaced by a vowel acoustically intermediate between the two. In some languages it is the first vowel which is elided, in others the second. The resulting vowel is often long, but it is not necessary generally to mark its length.

392. EXAMPLES

Efik.

ke ubom	in the canoe	is pronounced	kubom
mfɔn ye ima	mercy and goodness	„ „	mfɔn yima
owo emi	this man	„ „	owomi
ɔtɔ abia	a planter of yams	„ „	ɔtɔbia

[1] See Article in *Africa*, vol. ii, no. 1, p. 57. 'The Arochuku Dialect of Ibo', R. F. G. Adams and I. C. Ward.

[2] *Dictionary of the Asante Language, called Tshi.*

Fante.[1] **siaw** in reduplication is pronounced **sisiaw**, i.e. the **a** is elided.

The pronouns **me, ne** (in the possessive case) always drop their vowel before a noun with the prefix **a**, e.g. **m' ani, n' asõ**.

Very short vowels before an inserted **r** are frequently elided, particularly after consonants and when the following vowel is **a, ɛ,** or **ə,** or when it is long, or when the syllable ends in **m** or **ŋ,** e.g. **pra, bra, kra.** (This happens also in Efik, e.g. **efut,** *fifteen*; **iba,** *two*; **efreba,** *seventeen*.)

Ewe. The vowel **ɛ** occurs frequently as a contraction of **a** and **e** :

> **na e** to him   is pronounced **nɛ**
> **va e** come with it   ,,   ,,   **vɛ**

As in Fante, a vowel is elided in the reduplicated form :

> **bia** ask   reduplicated form **babia**
> **fia** show   ,,   ,,   **fafia**

In the following examples the final vowel is elided :

> **ele afi** is pronounced **elafi**
> **aƒe a me**   ,,   ,,   **aƒa me**
> **de asi**   ,,   ,,   **dasi**

In the following examples the initial vowel is elided :

afi mouse   **axwe** house   **axwefi** house-mouse
agble field   **ɖeti** cotton   **ɖetigble** cotton field[2]

Zulu.[3] **laɓa aɓantu** these people is pronounced **laɓaɓantu**
    ɓa eza   they come   ,,   ,,   **ɓeza**
    lolu uthi   this stick   ,,   ,,   **loluthi**
    si ala   we refusing   ,,   ,,   **sala**
    wa imithi of trees   ,,   ,,   **wemithi**
    wa umunt'u of the person ,,   ,,   **womunt'u**

393. Terminating vowels are sometimes cut off, even when there may be no vowels or words following closely after them. Thus Christaller gives as an example the post-position **mu**, which is frequently reduced to **m** : e.g. **nsam** instead of **nsamu, neŋ** instead of **ne no.** In such cases the nasal consonant is usually syllabic and bears a tone.

---

[1] From Christaller, *A Grammar of the Asante Language, called Tshi.*
[2] For the rules governing these elisions, see Westermann, *Grammatik der Ewe-Sprache.*
[3] From Doke's *Phonetics of Zulu.* Many examples of vowel elision are given in this book.

Gã. **tʃu mli**   in the house is pronounced **tʃuŋ**
      lɛ ni   it is he   ,,   ,,   **lɛŋ**
      midʒi mini it is I   ,,   ,,   **midʒi miŋ**

394. The question of writing these contracted forms has to be considered. It is generally thought better to write them in full: e.g. Efik **ke ubom, mfən ye ima**: Fante **me ani,** &c.

Weakening and Elision of Consonants.

395. In all languages in quick or slovenly speech, it is found that consonants are pronounced with less vigorous articulation and consequently tend to weaken and drop out. This is one of the main ways in which the pronunciation of words and sentences changes.

396. The normal process of weakening of articulation takes the following forms. A stop or plosive consonant is replaced by the corresponding fricative consonant; a fricative gradually loses its friction and tends to be replaced by a semi-vowel or h, and in certain positions to disappear. Voiceless consonants when they weaken are sometimes replaced by voiced consonants and then these weaken further.

397. EXAMPLES

Efik. The consonant **t** in intervocalic positions has been replaced by **r**: Ik**ət** Ekpene (name of a place) is pronounced Ik**ə**rekpene: *evening* (from **mbubit** and **eyo**) is pronounced **mbubreyo.** The steps are probably **t>d>r,** i.e. the voiceless consonant is weakened to its voiced counterpart: the **r** is a weakening of **d.** The negative suffix **ke** is often reduced to **xe** or **ɣe**: **iduxe, idiɣe, adaɣa. Sək ikaŋ,** *poke the fire,* is pronounced **səɣ ikaŋ**: **siak afia,** *chop wood,* is pronounced **siaɣ afia.**

Dinka.[1] A similar thing occurs. The sentence **Ɔk aci cək nək,** *we are killed by hunger,* would be pronounced by many Dinkas as **Ɔɣ aji cəg nək.**

Nzima (a member of the Akan group of languages):

bulɛ	stone	has pl.	**awulɛ**
doka		,,	**aloka**
duma	name	,,	**aluma**
fuke	porcupine	,,	**avuke**

[1] See Summary on p 211.

Bambara and Malinke. The verb *go* is pronounced as **taka,
taga, taɣa, ta**: this shows four steps in the weakening of a
consonant, the **g** being weaker in articulation than the
voiceless **k**, the fricative **ɣ** a further weakening: the next
step is the gradual reduction in the amount of friction of **ɣ**,
till none remains and a long vowel is the final stage.

Kasonke has **x** where the other Mandingo languages have **k**:
e.g. **xele**, *one*, **xononto**, *nine*, **xǝnǝ**, *belly*, **xolo**, *bone*.
(Compare Malinke and Bambara **kele, konondo, kǝnǝ,
koro.**) The **x** may be considered as a weakening of the **k**.

In *Kpelle* (a Mandingo language) **ɣ** has replaced Bambara and
Malinke **k**.

B. **kari**	M. **kati**	Kpelle **ɣal**	break
kalo		,, **ɣaloŋ**	moon
kiti	Vai **kiri**	,, **ɣili**	to tie

Similarly **w** (or **ʋ**) has replaced **b**:

B. **saba**   Kpelle **sawa** three

The existence of **h** in Mende, where Kpelle has **s**, seems to point
to a weakening of **s**:

Kpelle **saa**   Mende **haa** to-day
,, **siɣe**   ,, **hije** to arise

Hausa. The presence of the forms **sapka, safka,** and **sauka**
in different dialects of Hausa shows the weakening of the **p**
to the bi-labial fricative which ultimately changes into **u**.
The alternative pronunciations **t, ts, s,** also show weakening:
in this case **t** has become affricative, i.e. **ts**, then the **t**-contact
is lost and **s** remains.

Lotuko. **x** and **f** between vowels are often softened to **ɣ** and **v**.
The tribal name is pronounced **lotuɣo** usually: the word for
yes, spoken very slowly is pronounced **a-fɛ**, but in ordinary
colloquial speed is invariably pronounced **avɛ**.

398. The weakening of a nasal consonant[1] often results in
the disappearance of the consonant articulation, its place being
supplied by the nasalization of some neighbouring sound: e.g.
Efik **enye**, *he*, pronounced quickly is **ẽỹẽ**: here the glide is a
nasalized **y**, there being no contact for the **n** part of **ny**:

---

[1] A final nasal consonant in some languages tends to be **ŋ**.   See
examples, § 393, p. 130f.

aŋwa, *cat*, is often ãw̃ã, i.e. the velar contact is missing, and a nasalization of the w takes its place. (See also Summary of Yoruba.)

CHAPTER XXIV

TONE LANGUAGES AND HOW TO STUDY THEM

399. Every language has its own special intonation, i.e. the rise and fall of the voice in sentences, and in every language this characteristic element of speech is important. Until comparatively recent years, intonation has been somewhat neglected in the teaching and learning of foreign languages, for the following reasons. Its importance has been under-estimated: it has been thought that the student would pick up the intonation naturally, without being taught: it has been thought that an exact analysis of the intonation of any language was impossible. All these reasons have been discredited. If every language has its own tone sequences, it follows that a failure to use these characteristic 'tunes' will betray the foreign speaker of the language however well he knows the grammar and constructions, and even however well he may pronounce the sounds. Moreover, it can be shown that even in non-tone languages like English, meaning is very often dependent on tone and on tone alone.[1] Students, with few exceptions, do not pick up a correct intonation naturally: their normal tendency is to use the intonation of the mother tongue in learning a new language, i.e. in this particular, as in all others, they are apt to transfer into the new language the habits of their own, and they will continue to do so unless they are trained in the new intonation habits.

400. The analysis of the intonation of English, French, and German has proved not only possible, but most valuable.[2] The

---

[1] Say the sentence 'Don't tell anybody', so as to mean anybody at all: the intonation is [‾ • ＼ . . .]. (Stressed syllables marked with a line, unstressed syllables with a dot.) Then say the same sentence to mean 'Choose carefully the person you will tell': the intonation is [＼ • ＼ . . •]. The difference in meaning is indicated by the different intonation.

[2] See Klinghardt, *Übungen im englischen Tonfall, Übungen im französischen Tonfall, Übungen im deutschen Tonfall*; Palmer, *English Intonation*, Heffer & Co.; Armstrong and Ward, *Handbook of English Intonation*, Heffer & Co.; Armstrong and Coustenoble, *The Intonation of French* (in preparation).

intonation usages of these three languages have been set out
with considerable accuracy, and by a comparison of them, the
English, French, or German student can see wherein the intonation of his own language differs from that of the others,
and in this way, with training, he can learn the new tone
sequences of the other two languages.

401. What has been done for English, French, and German
can be done for African languages. Every African language
also has its own characteristic intonation, and it follows that
the student must learn this distinctive intonation if he is to
speak the language accurately and without a foreign accent.
There are additional difficulties in attacking the problem in
African languages. First, the intonation of very few African
languages has been analysed scientifically, and the student is
faced with the task of learning it purely by imitation, without
guidance. Secondly, very many African languages are *tone
languages*.

Tone Languages.

402. A tone language is one which makes a particular use
of pitch as an element of speech. This special use consists in
the employment of pitch for two purposes, viz.

(1) to indicate meaning (semantic or etymological tones);
(2) to show grammatical relationships (grammatical or
   syntactic tones).

Semantic or Etymological Tones.

403. Words alike in all other respects, but differing in tone
are different in meaning, the pitch alone indicating this difference: thus pitch is significant.[1]

404. EXAMPLES

Efik.

akpa [˙ ˙] river   akpa [. ˙] first   akpa [˙ ˙] he dies

mmɔŋ [˙ ˙] water   mmɔŋ [. .] where ?

ekere didie ? [. . ˙ . .] What is your name ?

ekere didie ? [. ˙ ˙ . .] What do you think ?

---

[1] In *Laut, Ton und Sinn in westafrikanischen Sudansprachen*, Westermann shows the connexion that exists between tone and meaning in
a large number of examples.

Ibo.

　isi [· .] smell　　isi [· ·] head　　　　isi [. ＼] six
　ibɛ [· ·] place　　ibɛ [· .] companion
　ɔnɛ ɛbu ibu [· .. · · ·] he is carrying loads
　ɔnɛ ɛbu ibu [· · · . .] he is fat

Kpelle.

　nya [.] he　　　　nya [·] I
　nyɛ [.] he said　　nyɛ [＼] I said
　ŋə [.] his part　　ŋə [＼] my part

Chuana.

　bua [＼ ·] to skin　　　bua [＼ .] to speak

Ewe.

　havi [. ·] a young pig　havi [· ·] friend

Duala.

　mbəti [· ·] garment　　mbəti [. .] unripe bananas
　ya [.]　　　to come　　ya [＼]　　to give birth
　koka [· .] to dry　　　koka [. .] to grow

Yaunde.

　nəŋ [.]　　to take　　　nəŋ [＼]　to rain
　bə [＼]　　they　　　　bə [.]　　to make
　ayaŋ [. ⌣] bulbous plant　ayaŋ [. ·] kind of snake

For further examples, see the phonetic summaries of special
languages at the end of the book.

Grammatical Tones.

405. Grammatical forms in some languages are indicated
by tone alone.

406. EXAMPLES

Efik.　eto [· ·] tree　　　etiŋe eto [. · · · .] top of the tree
　The genitive has a different tone from that of the nomi-
native.

　　　anam utom [· · · ·] he works (he does work)
　　　anam utom [. · · .] a worker (a doer of work)

The difference between the 3rd singular of the verb and the noun agent is one of tone. The word **utom,** *work,* has a genitive tone after the noun agent.

aka [˙ ⌄] he goes   **yak enye aka** [₍ₓ ˙˙ ＼] let him go
The subjunctive idea is shown by a change in the tone of the verb.

Ibo (Arochuku dialect).

onɛzu [˙ ₍ ˙] he steals   **onɛzu** [₍ₓ ˙] does he steal?
onɛzu [₍ ＼ ˙] he does not steal

The affirmative, interrogative, and negative are here distinguished by tone alone.

Dinka.[1] **pany** [˙] wall (singular)   **pany** [₍] walls (plural)
The difference between singular and plural in this word is shown by tone alone.

ɣɛn aci cɔk nɔk [₍ₓ ˙ ₍ ＼] I was hungry
ɣɛn aci cɔk nɔk [₍ₓ ˙˙ ＼] I am not hungry

The negative is shown by the different tone of **nɔk.**

Gã. **mi le** [₍ ⌐] I know
mi le [₍ ＼] I don't know
e le [₍ ⌐]   he knows   **e le** [₍ ＼] he doesn't know
The relation between the tones of the two syllables is the same in each case: but the height is different.

o le [₍ ＼]   you know   **o le** [₍ ＼] you don't know
mi nla [˙˙]   I am singing
mi nlaa [˙ ＼] I am not going to sing
mi nu [˙˙]   I drink
mi nuu [˙ ＼] I do not drink

Ewe.

tsə [˙] take   **tu** [˙] gun: **tsə tu** [＼ ˙] take a gun
kpo [˙] oven   **dzo** [₍] fire: **kpodzo** [˙ ⌄] oven-fire
lə [˙] pick up **azi** [₍ₓ] egg: **lə azi** [˙˙ ₍] pick up egg
to [˙] pound **aɡbeli** [₍ₓ₍] cassava: **to aɡbeli** [˙˙ ₍ₓ]
pound cassava

---

[1] See Summary of Dinka, pp. 212, 213.

Twi.

wafa [˙.]   he has taken   **na wafa** [. ˙] let him take

əmfa [˙ ˙ ˙]   he must take **əmfa** [. ˙]   he did not take

əmmfa [˙ ˙ . ˙] he must not take

əkə [˙.]   he goes   **əkə** [..] he is away

wakə [˙.]   he has gone **na wakə** [. ˙] let him go, he
                                                  must go

Duala.

a mabola [....] he gives   a mabola [. ˙ ..] he has given

a si boli [. ˙ ..] he has not a si boli [. ˙ . ˙] he has not
                      given   yet given

bato ba longi ndabo [.. ˙ ˙ . ˙ .] The people have built a
                                               house

bato ba longi ndabo [.. ˙ ˙ ˙ ˙ .] The people who have
                                               built a house

Yaunde.[1]

mayen [. ◝]   I see   mayen [◞ ◝] I saw

məngayen [. ˙ ◝] I saw

məngayen [. ◝ ˙] I shall (probably) see

məngayen [◞ . ◝] I am (was) seeing

bəkalara [˙ . ˙ ˙] books and **mintaŋan** [. ˙ ˙] European

bəkalara mintaŋan [. ˙ ˙ ˙ ˙ ˙ ˙] the books of Europeans

407. From the above examples, it will be seen that a wrong
use of tone may indicate three things :

(*a*) wrong meaning,

(*b*) bad tonal grammar,

(*c*) a foreign accent.

408. Tone in most African languages is an extremely complicated matter, and from the few examples given above, it
will be easily recognized that it demands as accurate an analysis
as any other linguistic phenomena, and that the rules of pitch
should be studied as carefully as those of grammar and
phonetics. It is usually found, moreover, that on scientific

---

[1] From Heepe, *Jaunde-Texte.*

analysis, these tone rules are as definite as grammatical rules and that it is possible to classify them and set them out with considerable accuracy. Moreover, an analysis of tones often throws light on grammatical usages which have hitherto been unknown: in this way unsuspected richness of construction in a language may be revealed.[1]

The few examples given above illustrate the use of tone as a bearer of meaning, and as indicating grammatical relationships. In a tone language, however, though there are usually large numbers of words which are differentiated in meaning by tone, not every sequence of sounds which forms a word is said on varying tones with a corresponding varying meaning. But every word has its inherent tone whether it distinguishes it from another or not, and this pitch is as much part of the word as the sounds which compose it. Every verbal tense and mood also has usually its own tonal pattern which is distinctive,[2] i.e. a special arrangement of the tones of the elements forming the tenses—prefix, root, suffix, or auxiliary or verb particle.

409. It is difficult for the European to realize this, for he is not accustomed to thinking of intonation as part of the word itself. The student, however, should try to develop a tone memory just as he develops a grammatical memory, a memory for vocabulary and idiom, &c. He should learn the inherent tone of every word as he adds it to his vocabulary, just as in learning French and German the student learns the articles with the nouns in order to remember the genders. When learning the grammar of the language he should note the changes made in the inherent tones for different grammatical forms.

410. It is the work of the investigator to find out all the tone variations of a language and to set them out as clearly as possible for the learner. It is the learner's business to try to use the tone patterns accurately; in doing this he will convey a right meaning, he will be using good tonal grammar and will speak the language with the correct musical accent.

411. The student needs preliminary training in the appreciation and reproduction of tones. A good musical ear is naturally

---

[1] In Efik, for example, the Aorist form has been found to have five different tonal patterns, each used regularly under certain conditions.

[2] Cf. Christaller: 'This different intonation inherent in the original formation of words, is still more diversified in the conjugation of the verb, and by syntactical combinations of words and sentences.'

a great asset in this work, but it should not be thought that with an indifferent ear for music, it is impossible to learn to speak a tone language. Any ear can be improved by training, especially if the training is systematic and graduated in difficulty. The number and variety of tones to be learnt is small in most languages. (See § 415.) Where books have been written on the tones of a special language, or where dictionaries and grammars have indicated the tones in some manner, the work is somewhat simplified. The learner can study the tone usages of his new language and practise the examples which are given in the books : thus he is trained on the special tones he needs. Where such an analysis has not been made, or where it is inadequate, his training must be more general : if he is exercised in hearing and making the various well-recognized types which occur in most tone languages, he will be able to make his own observations of how these are used in his special language. A certain number of tone ear-training exercises have been drawn up to assist such a student and are appended to this chapter.

412. A large number of African languages are tone languages, i.e. they make extensive use of tone as illustrated above. Many West African languages (e.g. Akan, Ewe, Ibo, Yoruba, Efik), Zulu, Chuana, Ganda, Dinka, are examples of tone languages. In addition to these, there seem to be a number of languages which are in the process of changing from tone to non-tone languages. Such languages may still have a number of words distinguished by tone alone, but the number is apparently diminishing and words are now distinguished either by context or by the addition of other qualifying words. One reason for this may be the use of these languages by other than native speakers as a kind of 'lingua franca' over large areas. This use is gradually 'wearing down' the tones, and other syntactic and semantic usages are being introduced to compensate for their loss. Swahili[1] and Nuba[2] are good examples of languages which were probably once tone languages and which are said to have lost their tones. The Mandingo languages, spoken over a vast area in West Africa by more than 5,000,000 people, some 2,200,000 of whom are not native

---

[1] Dr. L. S. B. Leakey finds that distinctions of tone still exist in Swahili. The results of his observations have not yet been published.

[2] Nuba has one word left: *my* and *our* are distinguished by tones.

Mandingos, seem to be in the process of losing their tones, though they still have a number of both semantic and syntactic tones. Kikuyu and Kpelle come in the same class. Most of these languages still have a recognized musical accent which gives the impression of a tone language, a correct use of which is necessary in order to speak the language well. When such languages are investigated, an analysis of this musical accent should also be made.

413. A partial or a complete tonal analysis has been made of the following languages:

I. Sudanic.

Efik. I. C. Ward, *The Phonetic and Tonal Structure of Efik.* (Heffer, 1933.)

Ewe. D. Westermann, *Grammatik der Ewe-Sprache,* Berlin, 1907.

(English version), *A Study of the Ewe Language,* London, 1930.

Gã. J. G. Christaller, *Übungen in der Akra-Sprache,* Basel.

Gola. D. Westermann, *Die Gola-Sprache in Liberia,* Hamburg, 1921.

Kpelle. D. Westermann, *Die Kpelle-Sprache in Liberia,* Berlin, 1924.

D. Westermann and H. J. Melzian, *The Kpelle Language in Liberia,* Berlin, 1930.

Mende. A. T. Sumner, *A Handbook of the Mende Language,* Freetown, 1917.

Nuer. P.Crazzolara, *Outlines of a Nuer Grammar,* Mödling, 1933.

Nupe. A. W. Banfield, *Dictionary of the Nupe Language,* Shonga, N. Nigeria, 1914.

Temne. A. T. Sumner, *A Handbook of the Temne Language,* Freetown, 1922.

Sherbro. A. T. Sumner, *A Handbook of the Sherbro Language,* Freetown, 1921.

Shilluk. D. Westermann, *The Shilluk People, their Language and Folklore,* Berlin and Philadelphia, 1913.

Tiv. R. C. Abraham, *The Grammar of Tiv.*

Twi. J. G. Christaller, *A Grammar of the Asante and Fante Language,* Basel, 1875.

Yoruba. A. Lloyd James, 'The Tones of Yoruba', *Bulletin of Oriental Studies,* vol. iii, part i, 1923.

II. Bantu.

Bena. C. Schumann, 'Der musikalische Ton in der Bena-Sprache', *Zeitschrift für Kolonialsprachen*, viii, x, p. 145.

Duala. H. J. Melzian, *Die Frage der Mitteltöne im Duala*, Dissertation, Berlin, 1931.

Jaunde. P. H. Nekes, *Lehrbuch der Jaunde-Sprache*, Berlin, 1911.

M. Heepe, *Jaunde-Texte*, Hamburg, 1919.

Kongo. K. E. Laman, *The Musical Accent of Intonation of the Kongo Language*, Stockholm.

Chuana. D. Jones, 'Words distinguished by Tone in Sechuana', *Festschrift Meinhof*, p. 88.

The Tones of Sechuana Nouns, Memorandum of the African Institute, London.

D. Jones and S. Plaatje, *A Sechuana Reader*, London, 1916.

Shambala. K. Röhl, *Grammatik des Schambala*, Hamburg, 1919.

Suto. K. Endemann, *Wörterbuch der Sotho-Sprache*, Hamburg, 1911.

A. N. Tucker, *The Comparative Phonetics of the Suto-Chuana Group of Languages*, London, 1928.

Teke. K. E. Laman, 'The Musical Accent of the Teke Language', *Festschrift Meinhof*, p. 118.

Zulu. C. M. Doke, *The Phonetics of Zulu*, Witwatersrand, 1926.

III. Hamitic.

Hausa. G. P. Bargery, *Dictionary of the Hausa Language*, Oxford, 1933.

G. P. Bargery and A. Lloyd James, 'A Note on the Pronunciation of Hausa', *Bulletin of Oriental Studies*, London, vol. iii, pt. iv, 1925.

Nama. D. M. Beach, *The Phonetics of the Hottentot Language*. (Accepted for the degree of D.Lit., London: not yet published.)

IV. General.

E. M. Hornbostel, 'Laut und Sinn', *Festschrift Meinhof*.

D. Westermann, 'Laut, Ton und Sinn in Westafrikanischen Sudansprachen', *Festschrift Meinhof*.

Types of Tones found in African Languages.

414. The tones of a language must be considered in relation to syllables. The vowel of a syllable generally bears the main

part of the tone, and it is on the pitch of the vowels that the
student must first concentrate. Where a consonant is syllabic
(see Ch. XXI, on Syllables) the tone of this consonant must be
noted too, particularly when it is different from that of the
preceding or following vowel. See further, pp. 154, 155.

415. Tones are found to be *level*, i.e. the voice continuing
on one pitch for the main part of the syllable, *rising*, i.e. the
voice gliding from a lower to a higher note in one syllable,
falling, i.e. gliding from a higher to a lower note in one syllable,
falling-rising, i.e. the voice falling from a higher to a lower
note and back again to a higher one in one syllable, *rising-
falling*, i.e. the voice rising from a lower to a higher note and
back to a lower one in one syllable. In most languages there
are two heights of level tones, viz. a *high level* and a *low level*:
in many a *mid level* tone also occurs. See below on Tonemes.
There can also be falling tones of various types, i.e. a fall from
high to low, from mid to low, from high to mid, &c.,[1] and
rising tones from low to mid and mid to high. It should be
noted that it is somewhat difficult to say a level tone, holding
the same pitch all the time: thus a high level tone sometimes
rises slightly towards the end, and a low level tone often has
a slight fall at the end of it.[2] But for all practical purposes
these small variations can usually be neglected and the tones
considered as level.

416. It must be remembered that tones are *relative*, not
absolute, i.e. the actual pitch is not important so long as the
relationship between one tone and another is kept. See further
on tones in connected speech, p. 146. The intonation of a sense
group is continuous, and if two syllables have different tones,
the pitch of each one is connected with that of the next by
a glide: thus, when a high level tone in one syllable is followed
by a low level tone in the next, there is a falling glide between
them: when a low level tone on one syllable is followed by
a mid level tone on the next, there is a rising glide between
them. The difference between these rising and falling glides
and an independent rising or falling tone on a syllable is not

---

[1] In Chuana there is a low falling tone, starting low and falling lower.
[2] This can be plainly heard in the Efik gramophone records made by
E. I. Ekpenyon, when the tones are illustrated in isolation: in the
sentences, the rise at the end of a high tone, and fall at the end of a low
tone are not made.

difficult to hear : for the latter the voice rises or falls during the whole of the syllable. The glides which, because of the continuous nature of intonation, cannot be avoided are slight and can be neglected, since it is the intonation of the main part of the syllable which is important, and the transition is made naturally.

The Investigation of Tones.

417. It is possible to investigate and record with scientific accuracy the tones of any language. This is done by making kymographic tracings of words and sentences : the number of vibrations per second can be counted and a graph made showing the exact pitch of the voice at every point in the sentence. Another method of exact analysis is by enlarging the vibrations of a gramophone or phonograph record and finding out the exact pitch from these. Methods such as these are necessarily slow, and they record more variations in pitch than are observable by the ear : for example, what strikes the ear as an essentially level tone is shown to consist of a series of small rises and falls going more or less in a level direction. Such tone analysis as this is extremely valuable for scientific purposes, but a more rough-and-ready method of recording tones is essential for the student who has to learn to use the tones of any language quickly and correctly. The best way of doing this is for some one with a trained ear and some experience to note down the tones of isolated words and sentences in some graphic fashion which is easy to interpret.

The Marking of Tones.

418. There are various ways of marking tones, and the method chosen should be suitable to the purpose for which such marking is designed. For example, a conventional marking can quite well be adopted for dictionary purposes and for indicating the tones of isolated words for reference, while a more graphic method which bears some relationship to the tones themselves would be more convenient in recording the tones of continuous sentences. Again, the marking of tone for the native reader is a different problem from that of marking the tones for the foreign learner.

Methods of Marking Tones.

419. The method of marking tones in this book is as follows. The tones of single words and short sentences are given between square brackets, after the word or sentence: the arms of the brackets represent the upper and lower limits of the voice. Between these lines the relative pitch of each syllable is indicated by a dot or a curved line. Thus [•] represents the tone of a monosyllable with a high level pitch, as in Efik **di** [•]; [.] represents the low level tone of a monosyllabic word, as **nə** [.]; [＼] represents a falling tone from high to low, as **ŋwan** [＼]; and [⌣] represents a rising tone (from low to mid), as **be** [⌣]. If it is necessary to indicate a mid tone, the dot is placed in the middle between the two arms of the bracket: thus, [•], as in Yoruba, where **bu** [•], *to be mildewed*, with a mid tone, has to be distinguished from **bu** [•], *to insult*, which has a high tone. A fall-rise is shown thus [⌍], and a rise-fall thus [⌌]. In the connected texts given in the phonetic summaries at the end of the book, the tones of longer sentences are shown between two lines above the words, thus:

. . • • • •
. .   . . .
——————————

Ami ndep bia ke urua
I buy yams in the market (Efik)

420. The advantages of such a method for the student of a tone language are evident: he can see at a glance what the 'outline' of the tune of a word or sentence is, and the marks are not difficult to interpret. It should be remembered that although we represent the tune by disconnected dots and lines, the intonation of a sense group is continuous and could be represented by a continuous line. But practical experience has proved that a continuous line is more difficult to interpret.

Other Methods of Tone Marking.

421. 1. One of the methods of marking tones in the *Memorandum on Orthography*, and which has been used by many scholars of African languages is as follows:

á is used for a high level tone.
à is used for a low level tone.
ȧ is used for a mid level tone.
ǎ is used for a rising tone.
â is used for a falling tone.

422. This method is used in many dictionaries. It may be simplified by the following rules:

1. Every syllable not provided with a tone mark has the tone of the last syllable which *has* a tone mark.
2. Every initial syllable of a word, not having a tone mark, is low, and in the same way, those following, should they have no tone mark, are also low.

Thus, in Ewe:

kɔ́kɔ = kɔ́kɔ́ high   kɔga = kɔ̀gà neck iron.
megayi = mègàyì I went again.
ameǵá = àmèǵá an elder.
wógàyi = wógàyì they went again.
atízɔti = àtízɔ̀tí walking stick.

423. These tone marks are conventional marks bearing no relationship to the tones themselves, but they can easily be learnt and are not inconvenient for dictionaries and grammars where single words are mainly referred to. The disadvantage of these marks is that the outline of the word or sentence cannot be seen as a whole, nor can the various members of a toneme be shown.

424. 2. A more comprehensive system is suggested in the Memorandum by Professor Daniel Jones as follows:

ā represents a high level tone.
a̱ represents a low level tone.
á represents a rising tone.
à represents a high-falling tone.
a̱ represents a low-falling tone.
â represents a rising-falling tone.
ǎ represents a falling-rising tone.

The marking here bears some relationship to the tones, but the outline of the tune cannot be seen. This method has been used by Professor Jones in his Sechuana Reader.

425. 3. Dr. Doke uses numbers above each syllable to indicate Zulu tones, thus

2-4 4-3   9
iziimu ogre.

Although the numbers show with great accuracy the nature and height of the tones, they are given in such detail as to render them difficult to interpret and to remember. Christaller uses this method for Twi and Gã.

426. 4. In his *Unification of the Shona Dialects*, Dr. Doke recommends the marking of high and low tones only, as follows:

à high.
ạ low.
a (unmarked) mid.

427. 5. It is also possible to mark the intonation of a language by the notes of a musical scale. Laman, in his *Musical Accent of the Kongo Language*, uses this method.

428. It should be pointed out that in any diacritic method of marking tones, the number of marks required is one less than the number of essential tones, since one can be left unmarked: the mid tone is the one usually chosen to be left unmarked. It is also often possible to simplify further, as has been shown under (1), § 422.

Tones in Connected Speech: Tonemes.

429. The previous paragraphs in this chapter have shown that in tone languages each word has its own inherent tone, and that in some cases this tone is modified to indicate certain grammatical constructions. Further modifications of tone often take place in connected speech. A comparison can be drawn with the behaviour of sounds in connected speech. In Ch. V it was explained how speech sounds can be grouped into phonemes, and that members of one phoneme are used in accordance with very definite rules, dependent largely upon the nature of neighbouring sounds. In the same way tones can be grouped into what are called *tonemes*,[1] i.e. one main tone or tone-sequence together with other tones or tone-sequences which take its place under certain circumstances: these circumstances are generally the nature of surrounding tones. Illustration is the best way of explaining this phenomenon, and how it works can be shown by reference to the tones of special languages. Efik, Gã, and Duala are used here as examples; the student of other languages should test the tone usages of the language he is studying to see if similar or other rules hold.

430. (*a*) A word which has an inherent high tone is not

[1] This term was first used by Dr. D. M. Beach with reference to Mandarin Chinese.

always pronounced on the same pitch: it is often pronounced on some kind of *mid* tone. The substitution of a mid for a high tone generally depends on a preceding low or mid tone. In fact the mid tone in many languages is often only a subsidiary member of the high or low toneme. To decide whether the mid tone is a separate toneme from the high or low toneme, the test of significance must be applied, i.e. if words alike in all other respects differ in pitch and meaning, this difference must depend upon the pitch. Yoruba is a language which has a significant mid tone. See p. 169.

EXAMPLES

431. In Efik, the tones low-high in one word are not usual: the word **ubom** *canoe*, is pronounced with low-mid tones [. •]. The mid tone here can be considered as a high tone lowered under the influence of the preceding low tone. The verb *will sink*, **eyedeŋ**, is pronounced with the tones [••• •] (two high, followed by a slightly lowered high tone: this is the normal tone pattern of the 3rd person of the future of high-tone verbs). In the sentence *The canoe will sink*, **Ubom eyedeŋ** [. •••• •], the high tone of the first part of **eyedeŋ** is lowered to the level of the last syllable of **ubom**; the last syllable of the verb must be lowered still more. Compare **Owo eyekpa**, *the man will die*, where the noun has two high tones, [••••• •].

432. (*b*) When a succession of words bearing the tones high-low [• .] follow each other, they are not all pronounced with the first syllable on the same pitch, i.e. the high pitch of the second and third words is lowered under the influence of the preceding low tones. e.g.

Efik. **ndo ndo oro** [• . • ..] at that moment

433. (*c*) An inherent low tone may be replaced by a mid tone under the influence of a following high tone: thus a word with the inherent tones [. .] followed by a high tone may be pronounced with two mid tones [••]. e.g.

434. *Efik*. **Ami ndep ekpat** [•• •• ..] I buy a bag (Such a raising of low tones takes place frequently at the beginning of sentences.)

435. (*d*) When a language contains one falling tone only, it can usually fall from high to low, from high to mid, and from mid to low, according to the tones which surround it. In many languages, these varieties of falling tones belong to one toneme.[1] e.g.

436. *Efik.* The word *good*, **eti** is pronounced [˙ ↘] with a high fall, and the word *cat* is **aŋwa** [. ↘] with a fall from mid to low. The high fall follows the high tone on the first syllable of **eti,** the lower fall in **aŋwa** follows the low tone of the first syllable.

437. In the verbs **mmokut** [˙ ↘ ·], **mmodu** [˙ ↘ .], **mmaka** [˙ ↘ ↗], the syllable **mo** (**ma**) falls only slightly in the first example because the root of the verb is high, **kut** [˙], while in the other two it falls low because the verb roots are low and rising respectively, **du** [.], **ka** [↗].

438. *Duala.* The following examples from Duala, for which we are indebted to Dr. Melzian, show the influence of one tone on another in that language.

Jɛnɛ [↗ .] to see (infin.) : **na mɛndɛ jɛnɛ** [. . ˙ .] I shall see. Here a rising tone has been replaced by a mid tone when following a high tone.

> **a bi** [. ↘] he knows : **mə** [˙] him
> **a bi mə** [. ˙ ·] he knows him

Here two changes have taken place, the fall of **bi** has been converted into a high tone, and the high tone of **mə** is replaced by a mid tone.

Compare *Gã.* **enyee** [. ↘] he cannot
> **enyee emomo** [. ˙ · · ·] he cannot catch

439. From these few examples, it will be seen that such changes make for variety in the musical intonation of a language : they can be paralleled to a certain extent in European languages. Take the following English sentence as an example :

One summer morning, | before the sun was up, | and when the dew was still white on the grass, | I got up and walked out into the garden.

---

[1] But not in all. Chuana has a low falling tone which is distinctive from a high fall.

The first three groups marked are phrases or subordinate clauses with the intonation of an unfinished group, i.e. with a rise at the end. But the intonation of these groups, although essentially the same, is not mechanically repeated on the same pitch: the pitch of the whole of the second group is lower than that of the first, and the third is lower still. Thus the intonation is ‾·._.|.‾·↘.↗|...‾·‒·‒‒..↗|

and not ‾·._.|.‾·↘.↗|.·‾·‒...↗

Similar shifting of the intonation of the whole of a sense-group also takes place in tone languages (as shown under (b) above) and thus monotonous repetition is avoided.

440. In the recording of tones for grammar and dictionary purposes, the main member of the toneme only needs to be marked, since the subsidiary members are used in accordance with definite rules which can be learnt. In the early stages of learning a language, the student will find it useful to have all the tone usages indicated in connected texts, so that he may grow accustomed to these usages and develop a tone memory.

Tones in Vowel Elision.

441. Vowel elision is extremely common in African languages and its influence on tones must be considered. Where the two original vowels have the same tone, the tone of the syllable when elision has taken place will not be affected. Thus **ke eto** [˙ ˙ ˙], *on the tree* (Efik), when the **e** of **ke** is elided becomes **keto** [˙ ˙]. When the two original vowels have different tones, however, the effect of elision must be noted. It is impossible to make a statement which can apply to all tone languages, but from those which have come under our observation, we find that generally speaking the tone of the elided vowel is not dropped entirely, but is often combined with that of the vowel which is retained, and forms a new tone. This new tone keeps some characteristic of both tones. Thus if the vowel in one of two neighbouring syllables bearing the tones high-low [˙ .] is elided, the resulting syllable has a falling tone [↘], e.g. **ke ubom** [˙ . ·], *in the canoe*, is pronounced **kubom** [↘ ·], and not [˙ .] or [. ·] or [↘ ·], i.e. the high beginning of the

fall represents the high tone of **ke,** while the low end of it
represents the low tone of the first syllable of **ubom. ke urua**
[˙ ₌₌], *in the market,* is pronounced **kurua** [➘ ₌]. In Ganda,
the tone of the elided vowel is adopted by the following vowel.
See Text, pp. 195f.

Suggested Exercises for the Practice of Tones

442. The student should enlist the services of some one who
has done successful work in investigating or learning the tones
of a tone language, or failing such a person, some one with a good
musical ear. A native speaker using real words for practice
would, of course, be very valuable, particularly in the later
stages. It is better to give a number of short practices of 10–15
minutes at a time than longer periods. In the early stages the
pronunciation of the syllables should be prolonged or drawled
so that the nature of each tone—level, rising, falling—is easily
recognizable : later the pronunciation should be in a normal
manner of speaking. It is useful also to have the syllables
written and numbered with the tones marked in front of
the student : as the syllables are pronounced, he says the
number, and this makes it easy to see if he has recognized
the tones correctly : it also makes the work quicker. For the
sake of brevity, the suggestions set out below are made to the
trainer.

443. As stated in previous pages, the actual pitch is generally
of little importance : it is the relative pitch which matters. For
these exercises, take as the high level tone the pitch you would
use on the word *'what'* in a question such as 'What are you
going to do to-day ?' [‾ ˙ ˙ ‐ ˙ ➘ ₌], i.e. the highest note of the
sentence. For the low level tone, take about the pitch of the
end of the word *to-day* in the same sentence. For the falling
tone use the intonation with which you would pronounce the
word *now* in isolation [➘]. For the rising tone use the
intonation with which you would say the word *oh,* meaning
'Is that so ?' [◡].

444. The first step is to distinguish the most obvious differences between tones ; for example, high and low tones first in
isolated syllables and then in short groups. Then proceed to
more complicated combinations.

445. I. Exercises on High and Low Tones only

(a) *One syllable.*

la [˙] la [˳]

Exercise the student on these two until he recognizes them easily: this should not be difficult.

(b) *Two syllables.*

Using approximately the same pitches as before, pronounce the following syllables.

Two high tones	lala [˙ ˙]	(1)
Two low tones	lala [˳ ˳]	(2)
High-low tones	lala [˙ ˳]	(3)
Low-high (or mid) tones	lala [˳ ˙]	(4)

For number 4 make an interval of about a fourth, a little less than the difference between high and low: the tones low-high (with the same interval between them as in the high-low group) are very rare. This group can be considered as low-mid: see later.

   i. Say the syllables in the order given several times, to accustom the student to hearing them. Let the student imitate.

  ii. Say them in any order and ask the student to say after each one which number has been said.

 iii. Say the numbers in any order and ask the student to say the corresponding tone.

(c) *Three syllables.*

Three high tones	lalala [˙ ˙ ˙]	(1)
Three low tones	lalala [˳ ˳ ˳]	(2)
Two high, one low tones	lalala [˙ ˙ ˳]	(3)
Two low, one high (or mid) tones	lalala [˳ ˳ ˙]	(4)
High-low-high (or mid) tones	lalala [˙ ˳ ˙]	(5)
Low-high- (or mid) low tones	lalala [˳ ˙ ˳]	(6)
Low, two high (or mid) tones	lalala [˳ ˙ ˙]	(7)
High, two low tones	lalala [˙ ˳ ˳]	(8)

Make an exercise with these tones as suggested under (*b*) above, beginning with the first three or four and gradually introducing the later ones.

(*d*) Practise these tones in continuous groups of syllables: e.g.

lalalalala [. ˙ ˙ . ·]
lalalalala [· . · . .]
lalalalala [. . ˙ ˙ .]
lalalalalalala [. ˙ ˙ · . · .]
lalalalalalalala [· . . · . · · .]
lalalalalalalala [. · . . · · · ·]

446. Innumerable combinations of this kind can be made. The student should be asked to write down the 'outline' of the tune as it is being said: he should also be asked to say the correct tones marked on groups of this kind. Note that the sentences of European languages do not usually end on a high level tone: the student should therefore practise hearing and making this unusual ending.

447. II. Exercises introducing Falling and Rising Tones

(*a*) *One syllable.*

la [·]   (1)
la [.¡]   (2)
la [＼]   (3)
la [⌄]   (4)

'Drawl' the rising and falling tones at first to be sure that the student hears the rise and fall in the syllable itself. This is particularly necessary in the case of the falling tone, as it is difficult to hear the fall when the voice falls rapidly from high to low.

Make exercises with these four tones as suggested under I (*b*).

(*b*) *Two syllables.*

High—high-fall	lala [· ＼] (1)
Low—high- (or mid)-fall	lala [. ⌐] (2)
Fall—low	lala [＼ .] (3)
Fall—high	lala [＼ ·] (4)

High—rise   **lala** [`˙↗`] (5)

Rise—high   **lala** [`↗˙`] (6)

Nos. 4 and 6 are perhaps not very frequent. Exercise these in the same way.

(c) Three syllables.

A few combinations of high, low, rising, and falling tones only are given here: to give all the possible combinations of these would be confusing and would be far more than could be found in any language.

lalala [`˙˙↗`] (1)

lalala [`.˙↗`] (2)

lalala [`↘..`] (3)

lalala [`..↘`] (4)

lalala [`.↘.`] (5)

(d) As under I above a large number of groupings of connected syllables could be made for the student for practice: two or three only are given here.

lalalalala [`.˙.↘↗`]

lalalalalala [`˙˙.↗.˙`]

lalalalalalalala [`↘..˙˙...`]

lalalalalalalalala [`.˙˙↗˙˙↘.˙`]

448. III. EXERCISES INTRODUCING THE MID TONE

(a) To learn the mid tone, begin with the group high-low [`˙.`]. Then say [`˙·`] high-mid, with an interval of about a minor third—in any case less than that used in the high-low group. Alternate these two many times until the student hears the difference clearly and can imitate and recognize the two groups without difficulty. Then use the mid tone in three syllables groupings such as the following:

lalala [`˙˙·`] (1)

lalala [`.˙·`] (2)

lalala [`˙··`] (3)

Introduce these into the three syllables groups given under I (c).

(*b*) Use the mid tone in continuous groupings:

lalalalalala [. ˙˙˙˙ .]
lalalalalala [˙ . . ˙˙ .]
lalalalalalalala [. ˙˙˙ . . ˙˙]

449. IV. Exercises with Tones on Nasal Consonants

(*a*) Practise with the word **mba** (two syllables—**m-ba**).

mba [˙˙] (1)
mba [. .] (2)
mba [. ˙] (3)
mba [˙ .] (4)
mba [˙ .] (5)

(*b*) Practise with the word **ntoto** (three syllables—**n-to-to**): then **ŋkaba** (**ŋ-ka-ba**).

ntoto [˙˙˙]	(1)	ŋkaba [˙˙˙]	
ntoto [˙ . .]	(2)	ŋkaba [˙ . .]	
ntoto [. ˙˙]	(3)	ŋkaba [. ˙˙]	
ntoto [. ˙ .]	(4)	ŋkaba [. ˙ .]	
ntoto [˙˙ .]	(5)	ŋkaba [˙˙ .]	
ntoto [. . ˙]	(6)	ŋkaba [. . ˙]	
ntoto [˙ . ˙]	(7)	ŋkaba [˙ . ˙]	
ntoto [. . .]	(8)	ŋkaba [. . .]	

(*c*) A more difficult exercise. A nasal consonant following a vowel may bear a different tone from that of the vowel: practise the word **bam** as two syllables (**ba-m**), the **m** having a different tone from that of **a**.

bam [. ˙] (1)
bam [˙ .] (2)
bam [˙ .] (3)

Next the word **utaŋ** as three syllables (**u-ta-ŋ**).

utaŋ [. . ˙] (1)

utaŋ $[\cdot\cdot_{\textstyle.}]$ (2)

utaŋ $[_{\textstyle.}\cdot_{\textstyle.}]$ (3)

utaŋ $[\cdot_{\textstyle.}\cdot]$ (4)

450. V. Miscellaneous Tones on Invented Words

mpopo $[_{\textstyle.}\cdot_{\textstyle.}]$	aku $[\cdot\cdot]$	ŋko $[_{\textstyle.}\cdot]$	abota $[\cdot\cdot_{\textstyle.}]$
suni $[_{\textstyle..}]$	enye $[_{\textstyle.}\cdot]$	oko $[\cdot\cdot]$	ʃugɛ $[\cdot\diagdown]$
apam $[_{\textstyle..}\cdot]$	dodo $[\cdot_{\textstyle.}]$	laba $[\diagdown_{\textstyle.}]$	fogo $[\diagup_{\textstyle.}]$
peŋuma $[_{\textstyle.}\cdot_{\textstyle.}]$	sadɛfo $[\diagdown_{\textstyle..}]$	taremu $[_{\textstyle.}\diagdown_{\textstyle.}]$	ʃɛgopi $[_{\textstyle.}\cdot\cdot]$
boʒam $[\cdot_{\textstyle.}\cdot]$	zufɛ $[\cdot\diagdown]$	setazi $[\cdot\cdot\cdot]$	kwatulo $[\cdot\cdot_{\textstyle.}]$

451. VI. Exercises on the Same Word with Different Tones

(Actual words taken from African languages. Numbers can be given instead of meanings.)

Efik.

mməŋ $[\cdot\cdot]$ water	mməŋ $[_{\textstyle..}]$ where		
akwa $[_{\textstyle.}\diagdown]$ big	akwa $[\cdot\cdot]$ kind of cloth		
kere $[\cdot\cdot]$ think	kere $[_{\textstyle..}]$ be called		
akpa $[_{\textstyle.}\cdot]$ first	akpa $[\cdot\cdot]$ river	akpa $[\cdot\cdot]$ he dies	
mi $[\cdot]$ here	mi $[\diagdown]$ me	mi $[_{\textstyle.}]$ my	
ekere didie $[_{\textstyle.}\cdot\cdot_{\textstyle..}]$ What do you think ?			
ekere didie $[_{\textstyle..}\cdot_{\textstyle..}]$ What is your name ?			

Kreish (Gbaya).

kono $[\cdot\cdot]$ dog	kono $[_{\textstyle.}\cdot]$ salt		
ondʒo $[\cdot\cdot]$ strength	ondʒo $[\cdot_{\textstyle.}]$ hoe	ondʒo $[\cdot\cdot]$ brother	
ʃeʃe $[_{\textstyle..}]$ tooth	ʃeʃe $[\cdot\cdot]$ moon		
iri $[_{\textstyle.}\cdot]$ death	iri $[\cdot_{\textstyle.}]$ tree		

Duala.

mbəti $[_{\textstyle.}\cdot\cdot]$ clothing	mbəti $[\cdot\cdot\cdot]$ unripe bananas
ya $[_{\textstyle.}]$ to come	ya $[\diagdown]$ born
koka $[\cdot_{\textstyle.}]$ dry	koka $[\cdot\cdot]$ to grow

Yaunde.

nɔŋ [.]   take   **nɔŋ** [⟍]   to rain
bɔ [⟍]   they   **bɔ** [.]   make
ayaŋ [. ⤵] onion   **ayaŋ** [. ·] kind of snake
              growth

Ibo.

isi [· .]   smell   **isi** [· ·]   head   **isi** [. ⟍] six
akwa [· ·] cry   **akwa** [· .] cloth
ɛgbɛ [· .] gun   **ɛgbɛ** [· ·] hawk
ibɛ [· ·]   where ?   **ibɛ** [· .]   companion
ibu [· ·]   load   **ibu** [· .]   large fat
ɔnɛ ɛbu ibu [· . . · · ·] he is carrying loads
ɔnɛ ɛbu ibu [· . · . .] he is fat

Gã.

ŋo [⌣] to   **ŋo** [⤙] to be nice, sweet
he [·] place   **he** [.]   self
da [.] to be big **da** [·]   always
kɛ [·] and   **kɛ** [⤙] to say, tell
ġbɛ [·] pot   **ġbɛ** [.]   road

452. VII. Students are advised to read what is written
about tones in the summaries at the end of the book and to
practise the words given there as examples with their correct
tones : also to read the continuous texts and sentences with the
tones marked.

Note on the Use of the Gramophone

453. The gramophone in the future is likely to play an
important part in the teaching of languages and its use should
form part of the technique of African, no less than of European
language study. The first essential is that the records should
be good, i.e. they should be made specially for the purpose, and
should be clear and distinct, natural and unforced. The material
of the first records particularly should be chosen by an experi-

enced teacher and should illustrate as far as possible the main features of pronunciation and tone, together with the first steps in grammar and idiom. With modern methods of recording, it is now possible to eliminate distortion of sounds and to obtain excellent results.

454. The use of the gramophone for learning tones cannot be over-estimated: examples of all the types of tone used in a language, inherent tones of individual words, the changes these tones undergo for grammatical purposes, the tonal patterns of verb forms can all be recorded with the greatest accuracy, and the student will have at his disposal a model to which he can turn as often as he likes and by means of which he can fix the musical accent of the language in his memory.

455. It is hoped in time that all the main languages of Africa will be recorded in systematic fashion for the use of learners. By this means the task of the student will be considerably lightened and the results undoubtedly better.[1]

[1] See p. 218 for a list of those already recorded.

PHONETIC SUMMARIES

Short phonetic summaries are given of a number of African languages. These do not in any way pretend to be exhaustive or final, but it is hoped that they may serve as a basis for further study.

EWE (GƐ̃ DIALECT)

I. Vowels

There are seven vowels in the Gɛ̃ dialect: they are shown on the accompanying diagram.

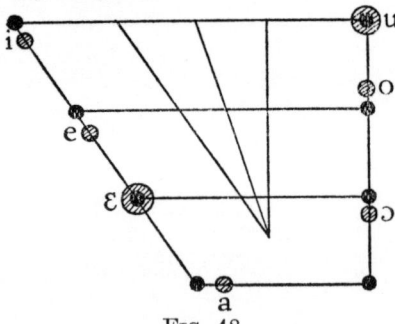

Fig. 48.

i is near to Cardinal No. 1, a close vowel.

　　ati [.ˑ] tree　　**yi** [.] go　　**efio** [.ˑˑ] monkey
　　nyi [ˑ] eight　　**ewi** [.ˑ] knife　　**eŋɔvi** [.ˑˑ] worm

e is somewhat lower than Cardinal No. 2: it is near the first element of a typical English diphthong **ei** (as in *day*), and more open than the German **e** in *beten*.

　　ede [.ˑ] palm　　**ete** [..] upright　　**ele eyi** [ˑ..] he is going

ɛ is near to Cardinal No. 3 : it occurs as a contraction of **a**
and **e** :

> **na e** to him, is pronounced **nɛ**
> **va e** come with it, is pronounced **vɛ**

Compare these two words with **ne,** *if,* and **ve,** a kind of lizard.

a is a front vowel near to Cardinal No. 4, rather like the
French **a** in *table,* further forward than the German **a** in
Vater and the English **a** in *father,* and more open than the
English **a** in *man.*

ati [. ˙] tree	**ewla ga** [˙ ˙ ˙ .] he saved money	
eza [˙ ˙] he is swaying	**axa** [. .]	side
avə [. ˙] cloth	**axwa** [. ˙]	a cry

ə is near to Cardinal No. 5, very similar to the German vowel
in *Gott.*

edə [. .] illness	**avə** [. ˙] cloth	**srɔ̃** [˙] learn
sə [˙] take	**etə** [. .] river	**ɖəɖəɖə** [. . .] gently

o is a half-close rounded vowel, closer than Cardinal No. 7,
resembling the German **o** in *rot* and the French **o** in *beau.*

efio [. ˙ ˙] monkey   **koklo** [. ˙ ↷] hen   **agbo** [. ˙] gate
wokoe [˙ . .] they laughed at him   **wodyim** [˙ .] I was born
xoxo [˙ ˙] old   **woɖii** [˙ . .] they buried him

u is a close rounded vowel, Cardinal No. 8 :

eɖu [. .] powder **munu** [. .] I drank **afu** [. .] sea
muyi [. .] I went **hɔ̃tru** [. ˙] door **nyənu** [˙ .] woman

Length of Vowel is significant.

ba [.] mud **bala** [˙ ˙] to climb **bi** [˙] to bend
baa [.] wide **balaa** [. .] moving **bii** [˙] narrow
      open   quietly
blukə [. ˙] darkness **bu** [.] to turn upside down
blukəə [. .] dark **buu** [.] with a deep hollow

Nasalization of Vowels.

All vowels are nasalized in the neighbourhood of nasal consonants. Nasalization of vowels also occurs apart from that

derived from the proximity of nasal consonants, and is significant.

Examples of all Vowels Nasalized.

edã [͙] snake **mũlɔ̃** [͙] I agree **azĭ** [ˌ ˙] peanut

ɛ̃kpɛ̃ [˙ ˌ] it is **hɔ̃tru** [ˌ ˙] door **esɔ nɛ** [˙ ˙ ↘] he gave
    heavy   to him

Examples of significance of Nasalization.

        eha [͙] song   **eɡa** [ˌ ˙] headman
        ehã [͙] pig   **eɡã** [ˌ ˙] big

efu [˙ ˙] he sieves **wolu** [ˌ ˙] you are crazy ⎱ in these examples,
efũ [͙] suffering **wolũ** [͙] you rush   ⎰ tone also differs.

II. Consonants

The following consonants occur in the Gɛ̃ dialect of Ewe:
p, b, t, d, ḍ, k, ɡ, kp, ɡb, ɣ, ty, dy, m, n, ny, ŋ, l, r, f, ʃ, s, z, x, h, y, w.

Notes on the Consonants.

i. The voiceless plosives **p, t, k,** are somewhat aspirated.

ii. **t** and **d** are alveolar: **ḍ** is retroflex, the tongue tip making contact on the front part of the hard palate. (See diagram, p. 53.)

Examples of words distinguished by **d** *and* **ḍ.**

    ede [ˌ ˙] palm   **edɔ** [͙] illness   **edu** [͙] town
    eḍe [ˌ ˙] one   **eḍɔ** [͙] fishing net   **eḍu** [͙] powder
    ade [ˌ ˙] sweat   **didi** [͙] to be long
    aḍe [ˌ ˙] tongue **ḍiḍi** [͙] ripe

iii. **t** and **d** are dental when **r** follows.

    aadrɛ̃ [˙ ˙] seven   **ewetri** [͙ ˙] moon   **hɔ̃tru** [ˌ ˙] door

iv. **p** is sometimes replaced by bi-labial **f.**

    apu [͙], *sea*: the **p** has very weak contact if contact at all: but in **apu epu** [͙ ˙ ˙], *the sea dried up*, the **p** is pronounced as **p** with some aspiration.

v. **kp** and **gb** are the usual labio-velar consonants.

       ekpe [̣ ˙] stone   **egbə** [̣ ˙]   goat

       kpə [˙]   to see   **tugbɛdyɛ** [̣ ̣ ˙] girl

vi. **ty** and **dy** are pure palatals. (See Ch. XI, p. 56.)

  mudyi [̣ ˙] I will **edyi** [˙˙] he will **wodyim** [˙ ̣] I was
                                                              born

  ŋwetyi ŋwetyi [˙˙˙˙] speckled

  enyrɔ̃ tyiḍityiḍityiḍi [˙ ̣ ˙˙˙˙˙˙] it is pitch dark

These sounds correspond to **ts** and **dz** in other dialects.

vii. **m, n, ny, ŋ,** are normal.

    ŋ occurs not only with **k, kp, g, gb,** and **w,** but before
    vowels. **ŋusu** [˙ ̣], *man, male*: also before other consonants,
    ŋde [̣ ˙], *morning.*

viii. **r** is a rolled lingual. It does not begin stems and occurs
    only when an alveolar or palatal consonant precedes. (**l**
    follows a labial or velar consonant.)

  r **srɔ̃** [˙]   learn   **enyrɔ̃** [˙ ̣] it is black

    ewetri [̣ ̣ ˙] moon   **eyrə** [˙˙] it is withered

    edyrɛ [˙ ↘] he sold it   **eyrɛ** [˙ ↘] he blessed him

l can begin stems: it does not follow alveolar and palatal
consonants.

    halo [̣ ˙] or   **mulɔ̃** [̣ ̣]   I agree

    eda hlɔ̃ [˙˙ ̣] he became guilty of murder

ix. **f** occurs in this dialect, but not in a large number of words:

  afu [̣ ̣] sea (sometimes pronounced **apu**)

  efu [̣ ˙] bone

  ema fia [˙ ̣ ̣ ̣] it (the swelling) has gone down

x. **ɣ** occurs in this dialect, but only in a few words:

  eɣe [˙˙] it is white   **ele ɣeɣe** [˙ ̣ ↘˙] it is wanting in fat

  ekə ɣe [̣ ˙˙] white clay

xi. **s** and **z** are normal.

xii. **x, h.**

    x can be described either as a weak velar fricative, i.e. with little 'scrape', or as an **h** with more than the normal friction of **h**. It is voiceless. **ɦ** is the voiced equivalent and is a pharyngal fricative with voice, i.e. a voiced **h**.

exɔ [$._{.}$]	house	**exa** [$._{.}$ ˙]	broom
ehɔ [$._{.}$]	boa constrictor	**eha** [$._{.}$ ˙]	comrade
exa [$._{.}$]	water fence	**axa** [$._{.}$]	the side
eha [$._{.}$]	song	**aha** [$._{.}$]	alcohol

x and **h** both occur before **w**.

axwa [$._{.}$ ˙] a cry		**axwe** [$._{.}$ ˙]	home
ahwa [$._{.}$] war		**yehwe** [$._{.}$]	deity

ʋ in other dialects of Ewe is represented in Gɛ̃ by **ɦ** before ɔ, o, u, and by **hw** before a, ɛ, e, i.

xiii. **w** is well rounded and often fairly long. Before **o** it practically disappears: before **u** it is very slight and before ɔ it is weak.

ewo [$._{.}$ ˙] ten is pronounced **eo**.

y before **i** almost disappears.

yi [$._{.}$] go.

III. TONES

The tones found in Ewe are high, mid, low, rising, falling.

High: **esũ** [˙˙] it tore off

Low: **esũ** [$._{.}$] clay

The *Mid* tone occurs at the end of a dependent clause: the low tones which would normally follow the last high tone are replaced by a mid tone.

le vifɛ̃ me [$._{.}$ ˙˙ $._{.}$] in childhood

eke mule vifɛ̃ me a ... [˙ $._{.}$ ˙˙˙] when I was a child ...

Falling: **koklo** [$._{.}$ ˙ ⌐] hen   **aglã** [$._{.}$ ⌐] crab

The falling tone is not very frequent in isolated words: it occurs as a syntactic tone. (See below.)

The *Rising* tone occurs as a contraction of low-high tones:

wole ewɔ [˙ $._{.}$ ˙], they are doing it, is pronounced **wolewɔ** [˙ ⌐ $._{.}$]

ele eyi [˙ $._{.}$ ˙ $._{.}$], he is going,   „   „   **eleyi** [˙ ⌐ $._{.}$]

Semantic Tones.

Tones distinguish words. A very large number of words exist distinguished by tone alone.

ehu [. ·] boat   **mi** [·] us   **ete** [. .] upright
ehu [. .] blood   **mi** [.] you (pl.)   **ete** [· ·] under it
wokoe [· · .] they skinned it   **efiɔxome** [. . · .] the King's
                                                                    homestead
wokoe [· . .] they laughed at   **efiɔxome** [. . . .] the King's
                him   family
esũ [· ·] it tore off   **egã** [. ·] big
esũ [· .] it is good, all right **egã** [· ·] he hoed
esũ [. .] clay   **egã** [· .] he has escaped from
                                                                    danger

wodɔ mi ɖoɖa [· · · · ·] they sent us forth
wodɔ mi ɖoɖa [· · . · ·] they sent you forth

Syntactic Tones.

i. As explained above, the mid tone replaces low toned syllables at the end of a subordinate clause: see examples in the text below.

ii. When a high tone verb is followed by a high tone object, the tone of the verb falls.

kpɔ [·] see **mukpɔ fiɔ ɖeka** [. ╲ · · ·] I see an axe.

iii. When a high tone verb is followed by a low tone object with the prefix **a**, the vowel of the verb disappears and the prefix **a** takes the high tone of the verb.

ekpɔ afi [· · . .], he saw a mouse, is pronounced **ekpafi** [· · .]

iv. The interrogative is shown by tone.

wokpɔ [. ·] you saw   **nuka wokpɔ** [· . . ╲]   What did
                                                                you see ?

eva [· ·]   he came   **ame ka va** [. . . ╲]   Who came ?
edyo [· ·] he went   **ame ka dyo** [. . . ╲] Who went
                 away   away ?

mudyi [｡ ˙] I wished　**ame ka wodyi** [... ˙ ⌐] Whom did they wish?

eva [˙˙] he came　**evaa** [˙˙｡] Did he come?

A Special Use of Tone.

A large number of reduplicative words exist on both high and low tones, the high being used of small things or meaning small, pleasant, agreeable, intensive, and the low being used of big things, or meaning big, bulky, disagreeable, extensive.

evivi ŋanaŋana [˙˙˙˙˙˙˙]	it is very sweet
evivi ŋanaŋana [˙˙˙ ｡｡｡｡]	it is not very sweet
ele bəlɔbɔlɔɛ [˙ ｡ ˙˙˙˙˙]	it is soft (as velvet)
ele bəlɔbɔlɔə [˙ ｡｡｡｡｡]	it is soft (but somewhat rougher or coarser)
edo ŋəvi ŋənyəŋənyəɛ [˙˙˙˙˙˙˙˙˙]	it is full of little worms
edo ŋəvi ŋənyəŋənyəə [˙˙ ｡ ˙ ｡｡｡｡]	it is full of bigger worms
ele g̣babaɛ [˙ ｡ ˙˙˙]	it is flat (and small)
ele g̣babaa [˙ ｡｡｡]	it is flat (and big)
ele zə g̃dɔ̃g̃dɔ̃ɛ̃ [˙ ↗ ｡ ˙˙˙˙˙]	she walks with little steps (as of a woman tripping)
ele zə g̃dɔ̃g̃dɔ̃ɔ̃ [˙ ↗ ｡｡｡｡｡]	he walks with big strides
ema ɟia [˙ ｡｡｡]	the swelling has gone down (said of a big swelling)
ema ɟia [˙ ｡ ˙˙]	the swelling has gone down (said of a little swelling)

TEXT

˙		˙ ˙		˙ ˙ ˙		˙			˙
	˙ ˙			˙	˙	˙ ˙		˙ ˙	˙
Eke	mule	vifɛ̃	mea	eye	enənye	be	nyinɛ		va
When I	was in	childhood	and	my	mother's		uncle		came

kpləm sə yi Amfɛ, eye midena agble, midona ebli
led me took went Amfe, and we tilled farm, we planted maize

sə ɖona ava, eye gbeɖekagbe eye təgbevinyea
put barn, and one day and my younger grandfather

eye eklɛ̃ bli le edyi lasə yi asi, eye ke ne
and he husked maize wanting to take market, and when

ŋdekenye eke ne mifɔ̃ a, eye wodo agbã, eye
morning when we rose, they packed load, and

təgbevinyea va yi sə yebe avə be yeasə ta,
my younger grandfather came took his cloth and dressed,

eye eto nɛ srɔ̃ nyã be yenyã nedo agbã, eye
and said to his wife she also should pack load, and

mamavinyea eye ye nyã do agbã, eye eto nam be sina
my grandmother also packed load, and she told me

la, akumɛ sətə ele eze me ne adə wum a ne mayi sə
pudding yesterday's was in pot if I was hungry I should take

akumɛa le zea me ne maku edesi ne maɖu nu, ne muɖu nua
pudding in pot and ladle soup I should eat, when I had

· · ·   · ·   · ·   · ·· · · ·

vǝa ne   masǝ   edesi kpɛtɛa sǝ ɖo zo dyi

finished eating, I should put the remaining soup on fire

·   · ···

ne be afiǝ.

so that it remained hot.

YORUBA
I. Vowels

The vowels occurring in Yoruba are **i, e, ɛ, a, ǝ, o, u.** They are shown on the accompanying figure.

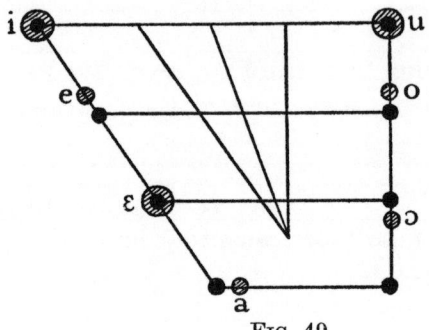

FIG. 49.

i a very close vowel.

ile [· ˙]   house   **igi** [··] tree   **iʃu** [··] yam   **bi** [˙] if

e is a little closer than Cardinal No. 2.

eeři [··] elephant   **emi** [˳ ·] I   **eji** [˳˳]   two

ile [· ˙] ˙ house   **eegũ** [··] bone   **ǝmǝde** [·· ˙] child

ɛ is near to Cardinal No. 3.

ɛjɛ [˳˳]   blood   **ilɛ** [· ˳]   earth   **rɛ** [˙] to be friendly

ɛři [˳ ·]   four   **alɛ** [· ˙]   evening

a is near to Cardinal No. 4.

aga [˳ ·]   chair   **dada** [⟍ ⟍] good   **ala** [˳˳] white cloth

awǝ [˳˳] skin   **agba** [˳˳]   adult   **alantakũ** [˳ ˙ ˳˳]

                                                     spider

ɔ is a little more open than Cardinal No. 6 : it is similar to the ɔ
in *caught* pronounced short, or to the German vowel in *Gott*.

ɔlɔr̃ũ [· ˙ ·] God ɔmɔde [·· ˙] child lɔ [·] go
ɔgɔr̃ũ [· ˙ ‿] hundred ɛɛsɔ̃ [. ‿] nine ɔr̃ĩ [. .] dysentery

o is a very close vowel, similar to the French vowel in *beau*.

oko [··] farm oto [˙ ˙] it is enough orĩ [˙ ╲] he walks
owo [· ˙] money oʃo [˙ ˙] he is obstinate ihoho [. . .] naked-
ness

u is very close, Cardinal No. 8. After t and d, it is usually
centralized.

malu [. ╲] cow okuta [. ··] stone dudu [˙˙] black
iʃu [··] yam ku [˙] die ɛru [· ˙] slave

All vowels are nasalized in the neighbourhood of nasal consonants. Nasalization of vowels is also significant, i.e. it
distinguishes words.

ru [.] carry hɔ [·] scratch
rũ [.] smell hɔ̃ [·] scream

II. CONSONANTS

The consonants occurring in Yoruba are b, t, d, kp, ɡb, m,
n, ny, ŋ, l, r, f, s, ʃ, h, j, w, y.

Notes on the Consonants.

i. kp and ɡb are the usual labio-velar consonants common to
so many West African languages.

ɡboɡbo [··] all akpo [. .] bag
iɡba [. .] when akpokpo [· ˙ ·] measure (for
cloth)

ii. ŋ. It is probable that ŋ is a subsidiary member of the n
phoneme, since it occurs only before w, k, ɡ, kp, ɡb, and
sometimes finally. If this proves to be the case, the letter
ŋ would not be needed for the orthography : n could be used
with the convention that it is pronounced ŋ in the above
circumstances.

oŋkɔ [˙ ˙] he is learning ebi ŋkpa mi [· ˙ ˙ · ˙] I am
hungry

See below under w for further examples.

ny seems to occur only as an alternative to nasalized **y**.

ỹɔmɔ̃ỹəmɔ̃ [····] soft   oỹĭ [ˑ ↘] (or **onyi**) he praises

r is generally rolled.

εri [. ↲] evidence   orε [ˑˑ] he is friendly

It occurs nasalized and then consists of one tap only, resembling somewhat a nasalized **l**.

ər̃ũ [.·] sky   εr̃ĭ [. ↲] laughter   εgbεr̃ĭ [·. ·] 800

ʃ is somewhat palatalized, i.e. accoustically it lies between **s** and **ʃ**. (This sound is described in Chapter XIV.)

oʃo [ˑˑ] he is obstinate   iʃu [··] yam

j is also somewhat palatalized and is very weak: it has little friction, and resembles **dy** particularly before **i, e, ε**: before **a, ə, o** it is like a weak English **j** as in *ridge*.

ejo [· ↘] snake   jali [· .] steal   ojε [ˑ·] he eats

w and **y** can occur nasalized and non-nasalized. The nasalized **w** and **y** seem to be alternatives to **ŋw** and **ny**: in many words it is difficult to hear whether there is actual contact of the tongue, making a nasal consonant or merely a nasalized glide. Our Yoruba assistants would generally accept either pronunciation. Thus we recorded **aw̃ɔ̃** and **aŋwə** for *they*, **εỹĭ** and **εnyi** for *palm nut*.

These must be distinguished from **ã̃ɔ̃** [·ˑ] *tongue*, and **ε̃ĭ** [. .] *back*, where there is no trace of a consonant. In the continuous tenses of certain verbs, the nasal element sounded stronger and we wrote **oŋwu** *it is swelling* and **onyi** *he is praising*. Here **ŋ** and **ny** bore a tone in careful speech. In the traditional spelling the two have been distinguished:

aɔ̃ [·ˑ] tongue	has been written	**ahon**[1]
aw̃ɔ̃ or aŋw̃ɔ̃ [. ·] they	„ „	**awon**
oũ [··] thing	„ „	**ohun**[1]
oũ [. ·] he	„ „	**oun**
oŋwu [ˑˑ] it is swelling	„ „	**owun**
ε̃ỹĭ or ε̃nyĭ [·.] palm-nut	„ „	**eyin**
ε̃ĭ [. .] back	„ „	**ehin**[1]

[1] **h** is pronounced in these words by some speakers.

Note that in orthography, it would be necessary to mark the nasalization of *one* vowel only in such combinations as õũ. In the two words for *thing* and *he*, no difference of sounds was heard: the difference was one of tone only.

When r̃, ỹ, and w̃ occur they are strongly nasalized, and in such cases the neighbouring vowels have slight nasalization only.

h is pronounced with a certain amount of friction: e.g. **iha** [. .], *side*, **hiha** [˙˙], *narrow*.

III. TONES

In the research work on which this summary is based, it was found that there are three levels of tone, viz. high, mid, low: in addition a rising and falling tone occur.

High Tone.

oto [˙˙] it is enough   **dudu** [˙˙] black

Mid Tone. The mid tone is difficult to distinguish from the high tone in isolated words. Examples are given below of high, mid, and low tone verbs with a high prefix, and of high, mid, and low tone nouns with adjectives preceding them. This shows whether the word has a high or mid tone.

Low Tone. The low tone pronounced in isolation or finally becomes low falling. It is heard best when several low tones follow each other at the end of a sense group.

Falling Tone. The falling tone can fall from high to low, high to mid, and from mid to low: **malu** [. ⟍] *cow*, **dada** [⟍ ⟍] *good*, **gũgũ** [˙ ⟍], *long, tall*.

Rising Tone. The rising tone generally rises from low to mid. **ɔga** [. ⟋] *master*. It can also rise from mid to high: e.g. **oʃee** [˙ ⟋], *he did it* (from **ʃe** [˙], *to do*).

Semantic Tones.

The following examples show that tone distinguishes meaning:

oỹi [˙˙] honey	eegũ [⟋ ˙] country devil	tu [˙] untie
oỹi [˙˙] it lays eggs	eegũ [˙˙] bone	tu [·] spit
oỹi [˙ ⟍] he praises	egũ [. .] Dahomey people	tu [.] ease

əkə [. .] spear   ɛwa [· ⌐] beauty
əkə [· .] canoe   ɛwa [⌐ ⌐] ten (cowries) in
əkə [. ⌐] dog   (counting)
əkə [· ˙] hoe   ɛwa [. ⌐] ten (in count-
əkə [· ·] husband   ing)
əba [· ·] king   ɛwa [. .] bean
əba [. .] name of tow   ɛwa [· ˙] come! (pl.)
əba [· ⌐] name of river   arũ [⌐ ⌐] five (cowries)
   arũ [. .] sickness
   arũ [. ⌐] five (in counting)

The three levels of tone in verbs can be illustrated by the 3rd person singular of the verb, i.e. the root preceded by a pronoun. The prefix, **o,** *he*, is high.

otu [˙ ˙]   he unties   obu mi [˙ ˙ ·] he insults me
otutə [˙ · ˙] he spits   obu [˙ ·]   it is mildewed
otu [˙ .]   it ceases to pain   obu [˙ .]   it is cut

The three levels of tone in nouns can be illustrated from nouns and adjectives: the adjective **gũgũ,** *tall, long*, has the tone [˙ ⌐] (high—mid-fall): **tĩtũ,** *new*, has two mid tones [· ·].

eegũ gũgũ [⌐ ˙ ˙ ⌐] tall devil   akpako tĩtũ [· ˙ ˙ · ·] new board
eegũ gũgũ [· · ˙ ⌐] long bone   awə tĩtũ [· · · ·]   new leather
egũ gũgũ [. . ˙ ⌐]   tall Dahomey people

   awə tĩtũ [. · ·]   new skin

It will be seen from the above examples that

tu [˙] to untie and **bu** [˙] to insult   have high tones
tu [·] to spit ,, **bu** [·] to be mildewed have mid tones
tu [.] to ease ,, **bu** [.] to take out have low tones.

Of the nouns:

eegũ [⌐ ˙]   devil   has two high tones
eegũ [· ·]   bone   ,,   mid ,,
egũ [. .]   Dahomey people   ,,   low ,,

akpako [· ˙˙] board   has tones mid-high, high

awɔ [··]   leather   has two mid tones

awɔ [. .]   skin   „   low   „

Professor Lloyd James, in an article on the tones of Yoruba (*Bulletin of Oriental Studies*, vol. iii, part i, 1923), recognizes a further level of tone. The work done for this short summary was not sufficient to verify this.

Syntactic Tones.

For syntactic tones which are very important in this language, the reader is referred to Mr. Lloyd James's article.

TEXT. PROVERBS

Adã dorikodo oŋwo ʃee ɛyɛ ǵbogbo.

The bat hangs head to earth : he is watching birds all. |

Ibi ki ju bi bi a ti bi ɛrũ ui abi ɔmɔ.

Birth not surpasses birth : as they bore slave, so it is they bore child.

Bi aja ba ni enia lɛyi (lɛhĩ) akpa ɔbɔ.

If a dog has a person behind, he kills monkey.

Ebi ko kpa imale oli oŋ ki jɛ aya.

Hunger not kills Mohammedan : he says he not eat monkey.

Ojukokoro baba ɔkã jua.

Covetousness is the father of unsatisfied desires.

Ori mi lɔmɔde otu mi jɛ iǵbamba daǵba ma· sã fũɔ̃.

You see me as a child, you cheat me. When I grow up, I will have my revenge.

Bi ɛya ba di ɛkũ ɛr̃ã ni ŋkpa jɛ.

If the wild cat becomes a leopard, it will devour beast.

FANTE

I. Vowels

Fante has nine significant vowels. The symbols here representing these sounds are **i, ɪ, e, ɛ, a, ə, o, ʊ, u**. Their tongue positions are shown on the accompanying diagram.

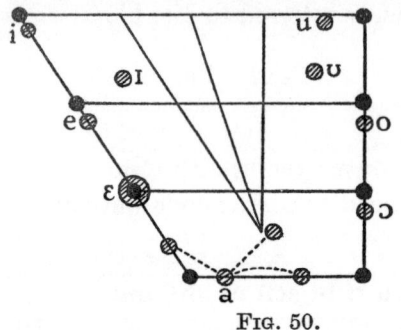

Fig. 50.

i is close.

ofi [.ˑ]   home   **dzi** [ˑ]   eat   **nyim** [ˑ] know

enyim [.ˑˑ] face   **nyimpa** [ˑˑ] person

ɪ is a vowel with a retracted tongue position, resembling the **i** in English *bit*, *sin* and German **i** in *bist*. When it is lengthened and when it is final it sounds very **e**-like, i.e. it resembles Cardinal No. 2 vowel: in these cases it is difficult to distinguish from **e** in this language. When **n** or **m** follows ɪ or ʊ, it is difficult to distinguish these two vowels.

dadzɪ [ˑˑ]   ground ətʃɪ [..] he catches əhɪn [.ˑ] king

dadzɪ [.ˑ]   iron   **adzɪ** [.ˑ] thing   ədɪʃɪ[.ˑˑ]free-

apɪm [.ˑ]   1,000   **fɪ**[ˑ]   vomit   born

əhɪmba [.ˑˑ] prince   **wɪ** [ˑ] chew

e is a little more open than Cardinal No. 2. This vowel is extremely difficult to distinguish from ɪ. That it is a separate phoneme from ɪ is shown by the existence of the following

pair of words, which are distinguished in meaning by the
final vowel only. **fɪ** [ˑ] vomit **fe** [ˑ] longing

se [ˑ] say **pe** [ˑ] waken   **tse** [ˌ] listen (cf. **tsɪ** [ˑ] hear)
Very few words have been found, however, in which **e** occurs
in the root of a word. It occurs as a prefix before words in
which **i** or **u** are the root vowels, and also preceding a palatal
consonant.

etʃir [ˌˑ] back, behind **efur** [ˌˑ] belly **enyampa** [ˌˌˑ] wilfulness
This is the result of vowel harmony, the usual prefix being **ɛ**.
(There are some words with the root vowel **i** and **u** which have
the prefix **ɛ**—i.e. the principle of vowel harmony apparently breaks down: these can be shown to be related to Twi
words which have **a** as prefix, e.g. **ɛbibifu** [ˌ ˌ ˌ ˑ], *black men*.)

ɛ is a little more open than the **e** of English *bed*—about
Cardinal No. 3.

tʃɛ [ˑ] present **ɛkur** [ˌˑ] one **ɔbɛba** [ˌ ˑˑ] he will come
mfɛfu [ˌˌˑ] comrades **ɔpɛtɛ** [ˌ ˑˑ] vulture
In final positions and before the letter **w**, the **ɛ** is often considerably retracted.

fɛw [ˑ] beauty

a. There are three (or possibly four) members of the a-phoneme:
  i. The principal member is a little farther back than Cardinal
     No. 4 and resembles the **a** in German *Vater*: this occurs
     when the vowel is stressed or long.

ɔbaa [ˌˑ] woman **mba** [ˌˑ] children **Praasu** [↘ˑ] name of a
place

  ii. When **a** occurs in an unstressed position, it is somewhat
      centralized and resembles the English vowel in *but* (ʌ): in
      a final unstressed position (short) it sounds like the neutral
      ə (as in *sofa*, **soufə**). The centralized variety of **a** also
      occurs before a nasal consonant.

edan [ˌˑ] house **ɔna** [ˌˑ] mother **ndua** [ˌˌˑ] trees

  iii. In the neighbourhood of velar consonants, the **a** is much
       farther back.

ŋwaŋwa [ˑˑ] wonder

iv. A variety resembling the English vowel in *man* (**æ**) occurs occasionally as a result of vowel harmony.

ɛtwadzɪ [. . •] measure

ə is near to Cardinal No. 6, a little more open than the German ɔ in *Gott*, similar to the English vowel in *caught*, but usually short.

əba [. •]   child   əkɔr [• .]   he has gone
waŋkə [. •] he did not go   əsəfu [. • •] minister

o is a little more open than Cardinal No. 7. Like e it is not very common in the roots of words, but there exist pairs of words distinguished by o and ʋ, which show that it is a distinct phoneme of the language. (There are apparently more words containing o as the root vowel than e.)

pʋ [•] wither   sʋ [•] on   pʋw [•] refuse
po [•] even   so [•] seize   pow [•] bark

o occurs, like e as a prefix before words which have the root vowel **i** or **u** and before palatal consonants. (Before other vowels the prefix is ə.)

odzii [. • •] he ate

okua [. • •] industry (cf. əkuaa [. ⟍] farm)   owi [. ⟍] he died

ʋ is a vowel similar to the English vowel in *pull* and to the German vowel in *Kunst*, i.e. it has a tongue position advanced from the full back position. When long or final, it is very o-like and is difficult to distinguish from o. The pairs of words given above under o show it to be a separate phoneme. It occurs more frequently in the root of the word than o.

ɛkʋr [. •]   one   ɛnʋm [. •] five   əsʋr [. ⟍] above
əsəfu [. • •] minister   mfantsɪfʋ [. . . •] Fante people
əkʋntʋmponyi [. • • • •] boastful person   abua [. • •] animal
əwʋfu [. • •] woman who bears a child (cf. owufʋ [. • •] dead person)

u is somewhat advanced from a back position, especially when preceded by an alveolar consonant: it is then similar to the

Scottish **u**. When preceded by a velar consonant it is fully
back, near to Cardinal No. 8 position.

apentu [. . ˙] kind of plantain   **sum** [˙] darkness

suma [. ˙]   hide (cf. **suma** [. ˙] send)

u and ʊ followed by a nasal consonant are extremely difficult
to distinguish: cf. the two vowels in **hʊntuma** [˙ ˙ ˙], *dust*.

Further Notes on the Vowels.

1. Note the following set of words illustrating the use of the
four back vowels:

su [˙] image **tu** [˙] pull out   **sum** [˙] darkness

sʊ [˙] on   **tʊ** [˙] meet   **pʊ** [˙] cuff,   **sʊm** [˙] serve
                                                 wither

so [˙] seize   **po** [˙] ever   **som** [. ˙] lift, hold

sə [˙] kindle   **tə** [˙] buy

2. These four back vowels are also found as the first element
of a diphthong. (The second element, written with a **w** is
really a very close **u**.)

suw [˙] rot   **fuw** [˙] rot   **puw** [˙] spit

sʊw [˙] yield   **fʊw** [˙] ascend   **pʊw** [˙] refuse

sow [˙] hatch, bear   **fow** [˙] hack   **pow** [˙] bark
           fruit

səw [˙] catch, solder **fəw** [˙] wet, moisten **pəw** [˙] be proud

u+w and ʊ+w are extremely narrow diphthongs and are often
difficult to recognize as diphthongs and to distinguish from
u and **ʊ**. Compare

             su [˙] image and **suw** [˙] rot

             sʊ [˙] on   ,,   **sʊw** [˙] yield

(When these four vowels occur as the first element of a diphthong
their quality is not exactly the same as when they are pure.)

3. All vowels occur nasalized:

esĩã [. ˙ ˙] six   **kũ** [˙] kill   **kʊ̃** [˙] fight

mĩpɛ [. . .] I want   **afĩ** [. ˙] comb (cf. **afɪ** [. ˙] year)

nsã [. ˙]   wine (cf. **nsa** [. ˙] hand)

4. Length of vowels is very important: it distinguishes meaning.

əbaa [.ᐧ] woman   əba [.ᐧ] child

əbaa [..] he came   əba [.ᐧ] he comes—Tone differs in
these two

waakaa [ᐧ╲] he has remembered⎫
waaka [ᐧ.] he has bitten,   ⎬ Here tone also differs.
he has been left out⎭

II. CONSONANTS

The consonants occurring in Fante are: **p, b, t, d, k, g̍, m, n, ny, ŋ, r, f, s, ʃ, h, ts, dz, tʃ, tw, dw, w, y.**

Notes on the Consonants.

p, t, k are generally aspirated, especially in stressed positions. When **k** occurs before nasalized **u** and **ʊ**, it is exploded in part nasally, and the aspiration of the **k** is heard as nasal breath. **p** in a number of words is palatalized before **i, ɪ, e, ɛ,** and **r,** but not in every case. Examples are given below showing words in which palatalized **p** was found and those in which no palatalization was heard.

Palatalized p		*Non-palatalized p*	
pɛpɛɛpɛ [ᐧᐧᐧ] exactly		**petu** [.ᐧ] owl	
p(ɪ)rɛkũ [...] at once		**əpɛtɛ** [.ᐧ·] vulture	
apɪm [.ᐧ] thousand		**apentu** [.ᐧᐧ] flasks	
pii [..] much			
mĭpɛ [..] I want			
pɪpɪrɪ [...] thick, rough			
pɛn [ᐧ] ever			
pĭã [.ᐧ] push			
əp(ɪ)rɛm [..ᐧ] cannon			
op(ɪ)rim [.ᐧ] it is hard, struggling			

Note that in palatalized **p+r** there is a suspicion of an **ɪ** vowel between the two. Note also that the palatalization is not so easy to distinguish before **i.**

ʃ has the quality of the English ʃ as in *ship*, i.e. it is 'clear', not
'dark' as the German ʃ.

    ʃɛ [ˑ] dress   ʃia [.ˑ] meet   ʃira [.ˑ] bless

h has considerable friction.

f was found to be palatalized in some words:

    few [ˑ] kiss   fɛw [ˑ] beauty   mfɛfu [..ˑ] comrades

ts as in German *Zimmer*, but with not quite so much friction.

dz is very weak: it is sometimes difficult to hear the d contact.

    Asantsɪ [..ˑ] Ashanti people   mɪdzi [ˑ.] I eat

    mɪtsɪ [..]   I hear   dadzɪ [.ˑ] iron

tʃ is like the English tʃ as in *church*.

    tʃɛ [ˑ] present   ɔtʃɪ [..] he catches

dʒ is like the English dʒ as in *jump*.

tw represents a palatal t with simultaneous lip-rounding. When
    it is followed by a vowel, a glide sound is heard: this is the
    semi-vowel corresponding to a close front rounded vowel,
    i.e. the palatal w (see p. 91). Compare the French *huit*.
    It is not the normal w sound. In the combination tw it is
    voiceless.

    nantwi [.ˑ] cow   awɔtwe [..ˑ] eight

    ɔtwafu [..ˑ] butcher   ɔtwafu [.ˑˑ] measurer

        etwɪr [.ˑ]   ladder

        etwadzɪ [.ˑˑ] measure thing

dw is the voiced equivalent of tw: the glide following the
    plosive articulation is voiced. When a close back rounded
    vowel follows, the glide is not heard:

idwu [.ˑ]   louse edwuma [.ˑˑ] work dwɪn [ˑ] think
ndwum [.ˑ] songs

ŋ occurs only in the neighbourhood of velar consonants.[1]

    waŋkɔ [.ˑ] he did not go   ŋkwã [.ˑ] life

w. There are two values of the letter w, viz. a real velar w
    which occurs before back vowels, and a palatal semi-vowel
    which is used before front vowels. (See p. 91.)

---

[1] In orthography the letter n could be used with the convention that
it is always pronounced ŋ when preceding velar consonants.

Velar. **waakaa** [˙ ⟍] he has remembered   **owu** [˳ ˙] death
ŋkwã [˳ ˙] life   **kwan** [˙] way

(In **owi** [˳ ⟍], *he died*, there has been vowel elision—**owu-i**,
hence the velar pronunciation of **w** before a front vowel **i**.)

Palatal **w**. **əwɪ** [˙ ˳] he chews   **əwɪɪ** [˳ ⟍] he chewed
The voiceless palatal **w** occurs very frequently: it is
written **hw**.

ɪhwɛdʊ [˳˳ ˙] government **əhwɛfʊ** [˳ ˙˙] guide **hwew** [˙] sip
Exception. The word written **əhuɛ** [˳ ˙˙] is pronounced
əhwɛ with a palatal **w** (cf. **əhwɛ** [˙ ˳], *he looked*, in which
the semi-vowel is voiceless).

III. Tones

There seem to be three levels of tone, viz. high, mid, and
low: in addition there is a rising tone and a falling tone.

edan [˳ ˙]   house (low-high)
bedzidzi [˙ ˳ ˙˙] come and eat (high-low-mid)
Praasʊ [⟍ ˙] Name of a place (fall-mid)
afãfã [˳ ⌣ ˙]   halves (low-rise-high)

Semantic Tones occur in Fante.

apentu [˳ ˙˙] flasks   **apentu** [˳˳ ˙] kind of plantain (pl.)
əba [˙ ˳]   he is coming **əba** [˳ ˙] a child

Syntactic Tones occur very frequently.

əkəm dzɪn [˳ ˙ ˳] he is hungry **əkəm dzɪn** [˳ ˙ ⟍] he was
hungry

əhwɛ [˙ ˳]   he looks   **əhwɛɛ** [˳ ⟍]   he looked

Text

Obirɛmba bi wəfrɛn   Kwɛɛku-anansĩ əyɛ odzifuu-
A certain man they called him Kwɛɛku anansĩ he is glutton-

dzıpɛfʊ a   sɛ   əkəm dzın   a   əpɛ dɛ odzi nadzı nyına
ous   who when he is hungry who likes that he eats all his food

prɛkŭ, dɛmıntsir da kʊr bi əkəm dzın mã   ədwın
at once, therefore   one day when he was hungry so he thought

dɛ ne dziban a əwə   nyına əŋkəsʊn dzi.   Dɛmıntsir
that his food which he had all would not satisfy him. Therefore

nʊdʊ   a   əwə   əsan dʊ   nyına əpra   gu
his yam which he had in the barn all   he collected put

əputum na ənũaa,   abıra əbınyıın,   ətsı naası na
in a pot and he cooked, when it was cooked, he sat down and

ətʃɛ ası dɛ   ərıdzidzi.   Wantʃɛr biara nna əmĩĩ,
he began that he was eating. Not long at all then he was

ədʊ a   ənũaa   nyına yɛ dʒan   efei
satisfied, the yam which he had cooked all was worthless now

əbə   mbədzın dɛ ntʃɛ ədzı   bɛʃɛ
he tried   that in that case, he would take put them back

əsan dʊ bio, na   wentumın   əfa   adwın fofʊr.
in barn again, and as he could not, he took idea   new.

əkɛʃeʃia   nı mfɛfʊ   na abıra
He went and invited a company of his friends, and at the time

wobeʃiaan, ose hɔn   dɛ wɛnyã   asaası fofʊr bi
that they met, he told them that he has got property new some

na ədu a   əpɛ   efʊa   ənyĩ   afınaa   dzı
and yams which he wants to plant which is last year's own

ıyi   ntsi   nna   mbeʃeʃia hũm. Obiara əwɔ dɛm
because of this so that I invited   you.   Whoever has then

ədʊn   əmãm bi   mã mʊntɔ.   mfɛfʊun pii
this yam he may give me some that I may buy. Friends many

bə anũhʊba etʃirin   wɔkɔ hwɛ   nũ san dʊ,
made a promise afterwards they went and looked on his barn,

na wohũn dɛ   ədʊ-n ədʊ-n a nna ũa na   ogu
and they saw that the cooked yam yam   which were

dʊ.   Wobisɛn   tsir   na ose   dɛ
lying on.   They asked him reason and he said that

ənam dɛ   wɔrıba   ha   ntsir nna   mʊnũaa.
owing to that you were coming here that is why I cooked.

ɔyɛ nu　mfɛfuun　ahũbuw　dɛ　wanũa
He made his friends　astonishment that he has cooked

nudu nyına.　Iyi　na　əmã　　wəmã nu
all his yams.　This　is　why　he made them they give him

ədu a ətʃɛn　　ndızın.
yams more than his own.

BAMBARA AND MALINKE

The following outline of the phonetics of Bambara and
Malinke was made after working with a number of native
speakers of these languages at the Colonial Exhibition in Paris
during part of June and July 1931. In no way does it pretend
to be exhaustive or conclusive; it is a statement of what was
found during the short time at our disposal, and may perhaps
serve as a basis for further investigations. Professor Labouret
has kindly verified our conclusions—a fact which makes the
work of far more value than it otherwise could have been.

I. Vowels

There are seven (possibly eight) vowel phonemes in Bambara
and Malinke : they can be represented by the letters i, e, ɛ, a, ə,
o, u (with ü as the eighth). Their positions are shown on the
accompanying vowel figure.

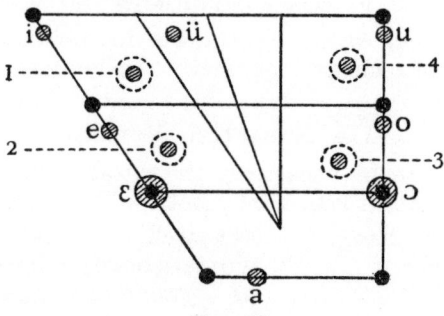

Fig. 51.

Examples.

i, kili	call	**fili** lose	**bi** fall
e, bere	stick		
ɛ, bɛrɛ	stone, pebble		
a, balo	food, feed		
ə, kərə	old, elder brother		**dəɣə** little, young, younger brother
o, dogo	hide	**ko** wash	**tolo (tlo)** ear
u, tulu	oil	**ku** yam	
ü, sünəɣə	to sleep (Dyula dialect)		

In addition to these main positions, there occur vowel sounds at the positions marked ⊙ on the figure : the first resembles the English vowel in *it, pity* : it is probable that this is a subsidiary member of the i-phoneme, e.g. **mani,** *four*; **ni,** *this one*: this kind of **i** is difficult to distinguish from close **e.** The second lies about half-way between **e** and **ɛ** and may be found to be a subsidiary member of the e-phoneme or a dialectal variant of **e** or **ɛ.** Among the back vowels there occur also two intermediate sounds, viz. a lowered **o** (3) and a lowered **u** (4), the latter resembling the English vowel in *put.* This sound is of very frequent occurrence. The vowel **ü,** resembling the French **u** in *vu* was found in Bambara and Malinke after **s,** e.g. **süfɛ,** *at night*; **sünəɣə,** *to sleep.* (Dialectal variants of this word are **sinəɣə, sunəɣə**: the latter is always used in Dyula.) The distribution of these sounds has not yet been worked out : they may be subsidiary members of other vowel phonemes or very probably dialectal differences.

II. Diphthongs

The diphthongs **ai, au, ɛi, ou, əu, iu** were found generally as the result of contractions, or of two vowels following each other.

III. Nasalized Vowels

All vowels can be nasalized : the nasalization is often very slight. Nasalization is specially noticeable in Bambara.

ǵwɛ̃ (ǵbɛ̃) chase	**kəlɔ̃** well	**nyĩ** teeth
dyakumã cat	**worõ (ǵborõ)** chimpanzee	
sɛ̃ (sɛ̃) foot	**dĩ** young of animal, fruit	
nũ nose		

Nasalization is significant in a small number of words:

woro kola nut   **worõ** chimpanzee (tones the same)

When a word ending in a nasalized vowel is followed by another word in close connexion, the nasalization of the vowel often gives rise to an intrusive nasal consonant: **m, n, ny, ŋ** according to the following consonant (homorganic nasal), or **ŋ** between vowels. The nasalization of the vowel in such cases is considerably reduced.

bakoronĩ (m)fla	two goats
worõ (m)ba	big chimpanzee
ta filɛ̃ (ŋ)ko	go and wash the calabash
fɛ̃ (n)tɛ̃ (m)fɛ	I have nothing
fɛ̃ (n)tigi do	he is a possessor of things
dõ (ŋ)o dõ	each day

In the text given here, these nasal consonants are shown in brackets. In an orthography for the native speaker of the language, it would be necessary to mark the nasalization of the vowel only. For French students, it might be helpful to insert this consonant in order to remind them to use it: English and German students would tend to do this naturally.

IV. LENGTH OF VOWELS

Not sufficient work has been done to say what the rules of vowel length are. One point may be noted: vowels with the tone rise-fall [$\frown$] and with the falling tone [$\searrow$] appear to be longer than others.

V. CONSONANTS

The following consonants are found: **p, b, t, d, ty, dy, k, g, gb, m, n, ny, ŋ, l, r, f, s, z, (x), ɣ, h, y, w.**

Notes on the Consonants.

p, t, k unaspirated as in French.

t, d alveolar. A kind of retroflex **d** similar to a flapped **r** occurs in Malinke, where Bambara has **r** (see below).

ty and **dy** are true palatals. When followed by the close vowels **i** and **u**, there is slight affrication and they sound like **tʃ** and **dʒ**, e.g. **dyi**, *water*, sounds like **dʒi**. **ky** and **gy** also occur as alternatives to **ty** and **dy**.

b intervocalic is sometimes weakened to the bi-labial fricative **ʋ**: **saba, saʋa, sawa,** *three* (the last is Dyula).

ǵb, ǵbɛ̃, *hunt* (M. ǵwɛ̃).

m, n, ny, ŋ all occur. ŋ appears most frequently before k, ǵ, ǵb, and w and only rarely between vowels and finally: e.g. dõ (ŋ)o dõ, *each day*; fiŋ, *black* (radical): it is probably not a separate phoneme from n.

The nasal consonants can be syllabic: mbɛ [˙ ＼] (two syllables).

l and r. r is a rolled lingual, occurring in intervocalic positions but apparently not initially. l occurs initially as well as in intervocalic positions. l and r are interchangeable in a great many words, dialectally and even with individuals. In the case of one or two of the subjects with whom these investigations were carried out, there were apparently some regular differences between l and r. For example, the words for *mountain*, *bowl*, and *canoe* were examined carefully with both Bambara and Malinke speakers with the following results:[1]

M. kuru [. ＼] mountain　　　B. kulu [. ＼] mountain
　　kudu [. ＼] bowl　　　　　　kuru [. ＼] bowl
　　kulũ [˙ ＼] canoe　　　　　　kurũ [˙ ＼] canoe

(The word written kudu was spoken with a kind of retroflex r, very much like ḍ: one Bambara used kuru [. ＼] for *mountain* when he was not thinking about it, but when comparing it with *bowl*, he used kulu.)

f and v. f occurs very frequently; v (pronounced more as a bi-labial (ʋ) than a labio-dental) less frequently: the latter is often heard as an alternative to w (which is Dyula), e.g. iniʋula, a greeting between 2 o'clock and evening: i fa ka kɛnɛ ʋa, *your father, is he well?*

s in the pronunciation of many is somewhat palatalized. (See Ch. XX, §§ 322, 325.) sɛ̃, *foot*.

z. sõzã, *hare*; sunzani, *hare, little one*.

ɣ occurs only in intervocalic positions: it appears to be the weakened form of k or ǵ, e.g. mɔɣɔ, *human being*: the verb *go* is pronounced taka, taǵa, taɣa, ta. [The root of the verb is taka: taɣa, taǵa are dialectal variants: ta is a Bambara contraction.]

---

[1] In Malinke of the south kutu is found for *mountain* and *canoe*. The forms kulu, kulũ, kuru, kurũ, kutu, kutũ all occur.

h occurs but rarely, e.g. **hɛra,** *happiness*; **hakili,** *spirit,*
intelligence, memory. [These words are borrowed from Arabic.]
w and **y** occur initially, and in intervocalic positions: intervocalic **w** resembles the bi-labial fricative *v*.

Consonant Combinations.

In addition to the combination of consonant + semi-vowel
(**fy, ky, kw,** &c.), the following combinations are found in
Bambara: **tl, fl, kl,** e.g. **fla,** *two*; **tle,** *sun* (elision from the
fila, tila of Malinke); it is often difficult to distinguish whether
tl or **kl** is being used: both are accepted. Similarly in Bambara
a plosive + nasal consonant occurs as the result of elision:
tuma, *moment, time,* is often pronounced **tma** or **kma;**
kũ, *head,* occurs as **kŋu**; **tny** was found in **tnyɛ tnyɛ ro,** *in the*
sand. The nasal here is somewhat devocalized under the
influence of the voiceless plosive.

VI. Tones

The Mandingo languages appear to be half-way between tone
and non-tone languages, i.e. they may be in the process of
losing their tones.[1] There are still a considerable number of
words which are distinguished by tone, though the context,
together with qualifying words, would usually prevent mis-
understanding if the correct tones were not used. Sentences
could be constructed, however, in which the sole distinction of
meaning is one of tone.

Significant Word Tones.

so [⌣]	(low rise-fall) horse		**ba** [⌣]	goat	
so [＼]	house		**ba** [＼]	river, big	
kɔ [⌣]	stream (Dyula **kwɔ**)		**su** [⌣]	corpse	
kɔ [＼]	back		**su** [＼]	night	
bã [⌣]	kind of palm		**bɔ** [⌣]	bamboo	
bã [＼]	end, refuse		**bɔ** [＼]	go out	
kɔnɔ [.＼]	bird		**woro** [.＼]	kola nut	
kɔnɔ [˙＼]	belly, stomach		**woro** [˙＼]	thigh	

[1] It is noteworthy that a large number of words pronounced in isolation or at the end of a group had falling tones in the final syllable. This
seems to confirm the opinion that tones are no longer as important as
they were formerly.

Certain verbs seem to have definitely high tones; others definitely low tones:

> **a bɛ do** [. ˙ .]   he is eating
> **a bɛ bo** [. ˙ ˙]   he is going out
> **a bɛ na** [. ˙ .]   he is coming
> **a bɛ taɣa** [. ˙ ˙ ˙] he is going

The personal pronouns seem to have their inherent tones:

> **m' bɛ taɣa** [˙ ˙ ˙ ˙] I am going
> **i bɛ taɣa** [˙ ˙ ˙ ˙]   you are going
> **a bɛ taɣa** [. ˙ ˙ ˙]   he is going
> **am bɛ taɣa** [˙ ˙ ˙ ˙] we are going

[The tones of 2nd and 3rd person plural pronouns were not fixed.]

Tones in connected speech are not the same as in isolated words:

> **woro** [. ↘] kola nut   **woro ba** [. . ↘] big kola nut
> **woro** [˙ ↘] thigh   **woro ba** [˙ ˙ ↘] big thigh

No rules of the changes in tone in connected speech were worked out and no examples of syntactic tones were found in the time given to these investigations.

The language has a definite musical accent: it *sounds* like a tone language, and the cadences are entirely different from those of a European language. An analysis of this accent would involve a considerable amount of work.

TEXT

Tyɛ Saba (*Three Men*)

Tyɛ kelẽ (m)fa y'a ǵwɛ̃   k'a, nya ka   di
Man one   father has him driven out, said to him sight is piercing

kodyuǵu.   Tyɛ kelẽ (m)fa   y'a   ǵwɛ̃   k'a,
very much.   Man one father has him driven out, said to him

tlo ka di kodyuǵu.   Tyɛ kelẽ (m)fa   y'a   ǵwɛ̃
ear is fine very much.   Man one father has him driven out,

k'a,   ye danĭ (n)də (or ndɔ̃ or nlɔ̃).   Tyɛ saba   nĭ
said to him his power of counting knows.   Men three these

(n)taɣara nyɔ̃ mbɛ̃   bada   la,   u ye nyəɣə
went together to meet river on the bank of, they have

nyiniŋka.   Də nĭ   (ŋ)ko,   k'ale   fa   y'a
together asked.   One, this one said, that to him father has

ǵwɛ̃,   k' a tlo   ka di; də nĭ   (ŋ)ko   k' ale
him driven out, says his ear is fine; one this one says, that his

fa   y'a   ǵwɛ̃   k' a   ye   danĭ
father has him driven out, says to him his power of counting

(n)də.   Ai   ko: 'an (ŋ)ka ta sɛnɛkɛ.'   Ai ye fani   si
knows.   They say 'we that go out to farm.'   They have grain

saǵi   lulu   sã.   Ai   y' a   kɛ   kurũ (ŋ)kənə: ai
baskets five buy.   They have that put canoe into: they

sera   ba   tyɛ-mã-(n)tyɛ̃ la,   fani kise kelɛ̃ (m)bira dyi
arrived river middle   in the,   grain   one   fell   water

ra.   Tolo dumã (ŋ)ko ko fani kise kelɛ̃ (m)bira: dani(ŋ)kɛ
in.   Ear   fine   said that grain   one   fell: counter

baɣa ko ka: 'i lo, m'b'   a   dã.'   A   ye   saǵi
said: that you stop I am going that to count. He has baskets

lulu da,   a ko k'o   kelɛ̃ y'a dyɛ̃.   Nya
five counted, he says that of that one is missing.   Sight

dimã (ŋ)ko a ka taɣa   tə   flɛ.   O dona
piercing says he that goes the rest to see. This one entered

dyi   ro, a y' tnu,   a ye fanĭ (ŋ)kise kelɛ̃ (n)ta kinyɛ̃ ro.
water in, he has dived, he has   grain   one taken sand in.

     Ko: nĭ   məɣə saba, ko dyɔ̃ ye ko   lɔ̃ ?
     Say: these   men three that which is things know ?

GANDA

I. Vowels

In Ganda there are five vowel phonemes. They are shown on the accompanying diagram:

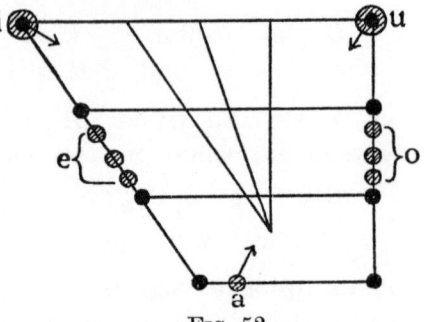

Fig. 52.

i is very close when long and when final: **evviivi** [·· ⌐], *knee*; **ekitiiyo** [····], *shovel*; **okusiima** [····], *to approve*; **eggi** [· ⌐], *egg*; **embalaasi** [····], *horse*. It is not quite so close before a nasal consonant: **okutiinda** [····], *to bridge over*. When short and non-final i sounds a little more open and retracted: **ekitabo** [····], *book*; **ekisibo** [····], *herd*; **okusima** [····], *to dig up*.

e is close (*a*) when final: **fe** [·], *we, us*; **tuzze** [·⌐], *we have come*; **ekke** [·⌐], *scent*; **ente** [··], *cow*; (*b*) when long: **feembi** [··], *we two*; **nteeka** [···], *I place*; **nteese** [···], *I have placed*; **mweenda** [·⌐], *nine*; **tuleega** [···], *we tighten*; **eeka** [·⌐], *at home*.

e is open when short and non-final: **ekke** [·⌐], *scent*; **nedda** [··], *no*; **evviivi** [··⌐], *knee*; **ekko** [·⌐], *dirt*; **ettu** [··], *small packet*; **eggi** [·⌐], *egg*. The most open variety is used when the sound is short and precedes a nasal consonant: **em** [·⌐], *one*; **ente** [··], *cow*; **enno** [··], *blossom of plantain*; **omulema** [····], *lame person*. In **ente yiye** [···⌐], *the cow is his*, three varieties of e are heard: the last is the closest, the first the most open.

a has the open position shown in the diagram (intermediate between the vowels of *have* and *halve*) when it occurs long: **na kaakano** [· · • ·], *to this day*; **aali** [· ↘], *he is*; **okusaaba** [· • • •], *to smear*. It has a central position (with a rather ə-like quality) when short: **okudda** [· • •], *to go back*; **ebbwa** [· •], *ulcer*; **bba** [↘], *husband*; **satu** [• •], *three*; **ente yamwe** [· · • •], *the cow is yours* (cf. **ente yaabwe** [· · • •], *the cow is theirs*); **nabbye** [• ↘], *I stole*.

o is close when final (a little more open than Cardinal No. 7): **ekko** [• ↘], *dirt*; **omuto** [· · ↘], *cushion*; **taano** [↘ •], *five*; **ekitabo** [• • • •], *book*; **eŋgo** [• •], *leopard*; **obuto** [· · ↘], *childhood*. It is more open when long and when initial (initial **o** often sounds rather long): **oluta** [· · ↘], *span*; **ogwaato** [· • •], *big boat*; **okwetootoola** [· • · · ·], *to go round and round*; **yooŋga** [· •], *very black negro*. It is very open when short and medial: **eŋkoko** [· • •], *fowl*; **ebboggo** [• • •], *snappishness*.

The three varieties are heard in **obwolo** [· • •], *poverty*.

u is practically Cardinal No. 8 when it is long or final: **ekkuubo** [• • •], *narrow passage*; **okutuula** [· · • •], *to sit, remain*. It sounds a little more open when short and non-final: **amakulu** [· · • •], *meaning*; **ekkubo** [· • •], *way, path*; **oluta** [· · ↘], *span*; **omuto** [· · ↘], *cushion*.

Length of Vowel is significant.
Examples.

        okuzika [· • • •]   to go out of cultivation
        okuziika [· • • •]   to bury
        okusesa [· • • •]   to cause to laugh
        okuseesa [· • • •]   to push forward, advance
        okuwana [· • • •]   to prop up
        okuwaana [· • • •] to flatter
        okusona [· • • •]   to sew
        okusoona [· • • •]   to take by surprise

  okutuma [· · **·** ·]   to send
  okutuuma [· · **·** ·] to heap up
  nasiba [╱ ╲ ╮]   Did I fasten ?
  naasiba [╱ ╲ ╮] Shall I fasten ?

In the following, the tone also is different:

  okunyiga [· **·** **·** **·**]   to press
  okunyiiga [· · **·** ·] to be offended
  okusima [· · **·** ·]   to dig a hole
  okusiima [· **·** **·** **·**] to approve of
  ekkubo [· **·** ·]   way, path
  ekkuubo [**·** **·** **·**]   narrow passage

II. Consonants

The following consonants occur in Ganda: **p, b, t, d, ty, dy,
k, ġ, m, n, ny, ŋ, l, r, f, v, s, z, y, w.**

Notes on the Consonants.

i. **p, t,** and **k** are unaspirated.

ii. **t** and **d** are alveolar, but the place of articulation is more
   retracted than that of English and German **t** and **d.** (The
   same is true of **l** and **r.**)

iii. **b** is like **ʋ** (pronounced very weak) when intervocalic and
   single. When really double it is strongly articulated. Com-
   pare the **b** of **okuba** [· · ╮], *to be*, and that of **okubba** [· · **·** ·],
   to steal. Single **b** before **w** is often extremely difficult to hear.

iv. **ty** and **dy.** For these sounds the tip of the tongue is lowered
   and the closure made by the blade and front of the tongue
   touching the back part of the teeth-ridge and the front
   part of the hard palate. Thus they are not true palatals:
   ettyuupa [· · ·], *bottle*; **okutyoppa** [· · · ·], *to be miserable*;
   okutyeketya [· · **·** · ·], *to dance*; **okutyentyena** [· · **·** · ·], *to
   break to pieces*; **okudyeedya** [· · **·** ·], *to mock*; **okuddyula**
   [· **·** · ·], *to become full of*; **eddyeŋgo** [**·** **·** **·**], *wave* (noun).[1]

---

[1] Alveolar **t** and **d**+**y** are also found: these are written here **tyy, dyy**,
e.g. **ntyya**, *I fear*; **ndyya**, *I eat*. (See Ch. XI, § 158, p. 57.)

v. l and **r** appear to belong to the same phoneme. The sound is
l-like initially and after **a**, **o**, and **u** (though it often sounds
remarkably **r**-like between vowels). It is **r**-like after **i**
and **e**. The **r** is rather **d**-like, consisting of only one tap:
okuleeta [· · · ·], *to bring*; **okuliira** [· · · ·], *to eat with* (as a
relish); **omulalu** [· · · ·], *madman*; **omulema** [· · · ·], *lame
person*; **ndyiri** [· · ·], *gospel*; **enydyaliiro** [· · · ·], *beam,
rafter*; **piripiri** [· · · ·], *pepper*; **efirimbi** [· · · ·], *whistle*
(noun); **okumiira** [· · · ·], *to swallow*.

vi. **f** and **v** are velarized, i.e. their articulation is accompanied by a simultaneous raising of the back of the tongue.
This velarization is very noticeable before front vowels:
okufeeba [· · · ·], *to diminish*; **feembi** [· ·], *we two*; **okufikka**
[· · · ·], *to be left over*; **evviivi** [· · ↘], *knee*; **okuviisa** [· · · ·],
to make a profit.

vii. **s** and **z** are made with the tip of the tongue lowered. They
are very 'clear' before **i** and **e**: **omuweesi** [· · · ·], *blacksmith*; **okusiika** [· · · ·], *to roast, fry*; **omukazi** [· · · ·],
woman.

viii. **y** and **w** are often rather long and therefore vowel-like;
but **y** is often almost imperceptible before **i**, e.g. throughout
the verb **oku(y)iga** [· · · ·], *to learn*; and **w** is very weak in
intervocalic positions before **u**: **oku(w)uga** [· · · ·], *to swim*.
It is generally absent from the pronunciation of **awo**, *then*:
aao [· ·].

Length of Consonant is significant.

naize [· · ↘]   I learned   **naiga** [· · ·]   I learned (Far Past)
naizze [· · ↘]   I hunted   **naigga** [· · ·] I hunted   „   „
okugula [· · · ·]   to buy   **siga** [· ·]   sow (seeds)
okuggula [· · · ·] to open   **sigga** [· ·]   scorpion

In the following examples, tone as well as length is different:
okuba [· · ↘]   to be   **okudyula** [· · · ·]   to be on the
                                                        point of

okubba	[· ˙ ·]	to steal	**okuddyula**	[· ˙ ˙ ˙]	to dish up
okuta	[· · ╲]	to dismiss	**okussa**	[· ˙ ˙]	to place, put down
okutta	[· ˙ ·]	to kill	**okusa**	[· · ╲]	to grind

III. Tones

The tones of Ganda are high level, mid level (these are the two most common), falling (generally from the high level to a low pitch), rising (occurring in certain interrogative forms).

High Level: **olugero** [˙ ˙ ˙ ˙], *story*; **olugeendo** [˙ ˙ ˙ ˙], *journey*; **ettuundiro** [˙ ˙ ˙ ˙], *shop*; **eggulu** [˙ ˙ ˙], *heaven*; **ekitabo** [˙ ˙ ˙ ˙], *book*; **okuddyula** [˙ ˙ ˙ ˙], *to dish up*.

Note. In each case the first tone of the above (and all similar) series may be on a lower level: **olugero** [· ˙ ˙ ˙], &c.

Mid Level: **omulasi** [· · ˙ ·], *archer*; **omuweesi** [· · ˙ ·], *blacksmith*; **okudyula** [· · ˙ ·], *to regret*.

Falling: (*a*) From the high level to a low pitch: **em** [· ╲], *one*; **mweenda** [· ╲], *nine*; **ekko** [· ╲], *dirt*; **okuta** [· · ╲], *to dismiss*; **omuti** [· · ╲], *tree*; **emiti giri** [· · ˙ · ╲], *those trees (yonder)*; **omwaana we** [· ˙ ˙ ╲], *her child*; **omwaana wuwe** [· ╲ · · ╲], *the child is hers*; **ekitabo kikye** [˙ ˙ ˙ ˙ ˙ ╲], *the book is his*.

[╲] is often replaced by the high level in non-final positions in connected speech.

(*b*) From the high level to mid level. This tone occurs in certain syllables, most of them containing the vowel **a** pronounced long preceding a syllable with the mid-level tone: **omwaana** [· ╲ ·], *child*; **taano** [╲ ·], *five*; **mukaaga** [· ╲ ·], *six*; **okusaaga** [· · ╲ ·], *to say in jest*; **okusaaka** [· · ╲ ·], *to beat bark cloth for the first time*. This fall was preferred to the high-level tone in these words, but may be found to be non-essential.

This tone is also used in certain interrogative forms, the nature of the vowel bearing it being immaterial. (See pp. 194f.)

(c) Mid falling to low. This often appears to replace the high low fall in final positions. It is used also in interrogative forms. (See below.)

Rising: **naateeka** [·‿‿], *Shall I place?* (neither [··‿] nor [··‿] was accepted); **naiga** [·‿‿], *Did I learn?*; **tunaalya** [··‿], *Shall we eat?*; **naaiga** [·‿‿], *Shall I learn?*; **naddya** [‿‿], *Did I come?* (Far Past).

Semantic Tones.

Tones distinguish words: **okuddyula** [·‿‿·], *to be full of*; **okuddyula** [·‿‿‿], *to dish up*; **okunoga** [·‿‿·], *to be rightly flavoured*; **okunoga** [·‿‿·], *to pick fruit*; **bba** [·], *steal*; **bba** [‿], *husband*.

Syntactic Tones.

In the conjugation of verbs, tone plays a large part. It should be possible to classify verbs according to the tonal patterns used in their various tenses.

1. For example, the conjugation of the verbs

	Simple Form	*Infinitive*
to come	**ddya** [·]	**okuddya** [···] or [···]
to place	**ssa** [·]	**okussa** [···] ,, [···]
to fasten	**siba** [··] or [··]	**okusiba** [····] ,, [····]
to give	**gaba** [··] ,, [··]	**okugaba** [····] ,, [····]

agrees in every detail in the matter of tone. There are doubtless many other verbs which can be placed in the same category. The verb **gwa** [·] **okugwa** [···] or [···], *to fall*, is irregular in certain tenses, but may be considered as belonging to the same class.

2. There is a different distribution of the tonal patterns from the above in the following verbs, all of which, however, have exactly the same tonal conjugation:

to learn	**yiga** [··] **okuyiga** [····]
to taste	**lega** [··] **okulega** [····]
to sow	**siga** [··] **okusiga** [····]

The following have the same tone in the infinitive as the above, but a different arrangement of the tones in the simple form:

to hunt	**yigga** [· ·]	**okuyigga** [· · · ·]
to place	**teeka** [· ·]	**okuteeka** [· · · ·]
to wander	**legga** [· ·]	**okulegga** [· · · ·]

This no doubt accounts for slight differences in one or two tenses.

3. Another class contains

to die	**ffa** [↘]	**okuffa** [· · ↘]
to eat	**lya** [↘]	**okulya** [· · ↘]
to fear	**tyya** [↘]	**okutyya** [· · ↘]
to grind	**sa** [↘]	**okusa** [· · ↘]

The verb **ba** [↘] **okuba** [· · ↘], to be, is irregular in some tenses, but obviously belongs to the same class.

4. Another class contains

to build a house	**ziimba** [· ·]	**okuziimba** [· · · ·]
to tighten	**leega** [· ·]	**okuleega** [· · · ·]
to sell	**tuunda** [· ·]	**okutuunda** [· · · ·]

It will perhaps be helpful to give as an example the 1st person singular of the Near Future of all the verbs of the different classes referred to above. The reader will then notice that the distribution of tonal patterns varies from class to class but is regular within each class:

1st Person Singular. Near Future.

	Affirmative.		Interrog.	Negative.		Interrog.
1.						
to come	naddya	[· ·]	[↗ ↘]	siddye	[· ↘]	[· ↗]
to place	nassa	[· ·]	[↗ ↘]	sisse	[· ↘]	[· ↗]
to fasten	naasiba	[· · ·]	[↗ ↘ ↘]	siisibe	[· · ↘]	[· · ↗]
to give	naagaba	[· · ·]	[↗ ↘ ↘]	siigabe	[· · ↘]	[· · ↗]
to fall	naagwa	[· ·]	[↗ ↘]	siigwe	[· ↘]	[· ↗]

	Affirmative.		*Interrog.*	*Negative.*		*Interrog.*
2.						
to learn	naaiga	[· · ·]	[· ⌐⌐]	sii(y)ige	[· · ·]	[· ⌐⌐]
to taste	naalega	[· · ·]	[· ⌐⌐]	siirege	[· · ·]	[· ⌐⌐]
to sow	naasiga	[· · ·]	[· ⌐⌐]	siisige	[· · ·]	[· ⌐⌐]
to hunt	naaigga	[· · ·]	[· ⌐⌐]	sii(y)igge	[· · ·]	[· ⌐⌐]
to place	naateeka	[· · ·]	[· ⌐⌐]	siiteeke	[· · ·]	[· ⌐⌐]
3.						
to die	naaffa	[· ⌐]	[· ⌐]	siiffe	[· ⌐]	[· ⌐]
to eat	naalya	[· ⌐]	[· ⌐]	siirye	[· ⌐]	[· ⌐]
to fear	naatyya	[· ⌐]	[· ⌐]	siityye	[· ⌐]	[· ⌐]
to grind	naasa	[· ⌐]	[· ⌐]	siise	[· ⌐]	[· ⌐]
to be	naaba	[· ⌐]	[· ⌐]	siibe	[· ⌐]	[· ⌐]
4.						
to build a house	naaziimba	[· · ·]	[⌐⌐⌐]	siiziimbe	[· · ·]	[· ⌐⌐]
to tighten	naaleega	[· · ·]	[⌐⌐⌐]	siireege	[· · ·]	[· ⌐⌐]
to sell	naatuunda	[· · ·]	[⌐⌐⌐]	siituunde	[· · ·]	[· ⌐⌐]

It will be seen from the above examples that interrogation is expressed entirely by tone.

TEXT[1]

| · (·) | · | · | · | · | · | · | · | · | · (·) | · | · | · | · | · | · · |

Aa(o)[2] oolwaatuuka Kabaka naagab(a) oomsadya erinya
Then it happened the king commanded a man name

[1] Story taken from *Engero za Baganda* by Sir Apolo Kagwa (Sheldon Press, London).
[2] Vowel (with tone) shown in brackets is not heard in reading at normal speed. The tone is always adopted by the following vowel which is generally lengthened.

•　•　•　•　•　•　•　•　•　•　(•)　•　•　•　•　•　•　•　•　•

lye Mannyowenu ookutabaal(a) Aabanyolo yageenda na
his Manyowenu   to attack   the Abanyolo, he went with

•　•　•　•　⌐＼　•　•　•　•　•　•　•　•　•　•　•　⌐

miggo myereere, naalwaana nabo   naabagoba.
sticks   only,   fought with them and drove them back.

•　•　•　•　•　•　•　•　•　•　(•)　•　•　•　(•)　•　•　•　•

Naye teyattaŋga baantu waabul(a) ookukub(a) aabakube.
But he did not kill people except to beat them   to beat.

•　•　(•)　•　•　＼　•　•　•　•　•　•　•　•　(•)

Bweyadd(a)   e Bugaanda aate Kabaka naagab(a)
When he returned to Buganda   again the King commanded

•　•　•　(•)　•　•　•　•　•　•　•　•　(•)　•　•　•　•　(•)

ooɱsady(a) oomulala ye Kimyaŋku, eer(a) ookutabaal(a)
man   another he (is) Kimyanku, also   to attack

•　•　•　•　•　•　•　(•)　•　•　•　•　•　•　(•)　•　•　•　•

Aabanyolo. Ye naatabaaz(a) aamafumu. Nay(e) Aabanyolo
the Abanyolo. He fought   with spears. Then the Abanyolo

•　•　•　•　•　•⌐　•　•　•　•　•　•　•　⌐　•　•　•　•

bwebaanulira nti Kimyaŋku ye   mugabe, buli muntu
when they heard that Kimyanku he (is) in command, each   man

(•)　•　•　•　•　•　•　•　•　•　•　⌐　•　•　•　•　•

ŋg(a) aagenda aabuulira munne nti   'Leero munywere
       went   and told his friend (that) 'This time be prepared

•　•　•　•　(•)　•　•　•　•　•　•　•　•　•　•

temuluit(a)   oolwa Mannyowenu, naye Kimyaŋku ye
don't think that it is Manyowenu,   but   Kimyanku he

mugabe.'   Aao nebamulwaanyisa   nebamugoba;
commands.'   Then they fought against   and defeated him;

aao ŋga lufuukira dala lugero na kaakano.
then   it became   true   story   to   this day.

ZULU

Zulu sounds are divided into (1) vowels, (2) plain consonants, (3) click consonants.

I. VOWELS

There are five vowel phonemes represented by **i, e, a, o, u.**

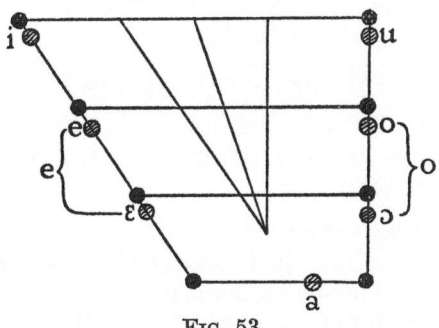

FIG. 53.

i a little below Cardinal No. 1.

      nina you   **isihambi** visitor

e has two values, viz. **e** and **ɛ**, respectively a little below Cardinal Nos. 2 and 3. The two sounds can be written with one letter (**e**), since they are members of one phoneme and used according to definite rules of vowel harmony.

    leli (e)   this   **wena (ɛ)** thou
    phezulu (e) above   **elakhe (ɛ)** his

a is nearer to Cardinal No. 5 than to No. 4: it resembles the sound in English *father*.

    thanda love   **thathu** three

o has two values, viz. **o** and **ɔ**, respectively a little lower than Cardinal Nos. 7 and 6. Like **e** and **ɛ** they can be written with one letter (o), since they are members of one phoneme and used according to definite rules of vowel harmony.

lolu (o) this **lolo (ə)** that
olubisini (o) in the milk **iŋkomo (ə)** head of cattle

u is a little lower than Cardinal No. 8.

thuma send **ulukhuni** piece of firewood

Rules for the Use of **e** *and* **ɛ**, **o** *and* **ə**.

1. The closer vowel in each case is used if the vowel in the following syllable is **i** or **u**, or if the next syllable consists of syllabic **m**.
2. The opener vowel in each case is used if any other vowel than **i** or **u** occurs in the next syllable.
3. If the phoneme occurs in a position where there is no main stress and is long, the closer vowel is always used, whatever the vowel of the next syllable.

II. Plain Consonants

The following plain consonants occur in Zulu : **p', ph, b, t', th, d, k, k', kh, ǵ, 'b, m, n, ny, ŋ, l, ɬ, ɬ, f, v, s, z, ʃ, ʒ, x, h, y, w,** and **r** (in foreign words).

Notes on the Plain Consonants.

Plosives and Implosives. **p, t, k** occur strongly aspirated and non-aspirated. The unaspirated **p** and **t** are ejective (written here **p', t'**), i.e. pronounced with simultaneous closure of the glottis (see Ch. XVIII). There are two non-aspirated **k**-sounds, however, one ejective (**k'**), and one the unaspirated **k**. The latter is very common, occurring in all infinitive prefixes (**uku-**), locatives in **ku-**, adverbs in **ka-**, and derivative verbal suffixes in **-eka** and **-akala**.

Examples.

(a) *Ejective* **p, t,** *and* **k** (**p, t, k**).

    p'euka fall over **namp'a**[1] here they are
    it'it'ihoye pewit **int'aβa** hill
    k'ak'a surround **iŋk'aβi** ox

(b) *Aspirated* **p, t, k.**

    phuma go out **thanda** love **khanya** shine

---

[1] Syllabic nasal consonants are here underlined, **m̲**.

(c) *Unaspirated* **k.**

    uthukela River Tugela   **kakhulu** exceedingly

(d) *Aspiration and Ejection distinguishing words.*

k'ak'a	encircle	**khakha**	be acrid
t'eŋga	wave about	**theŋga**	barter
k'ela	wear down	**khela**	place slantwise

b, d, and **g** have no voicing in the stop.

    beka look   **amadoda** men   **gula** be ill

6. Zulu has one implosive consonant (see Ch. XVII), the bi-labial, which is used distinctively from the explosive.

    beka look   **ɓeka** put

    boŋga roar   **ɓoŋga** praise (same tones)

Implosive **ɓ** is the common **b** of Zulu, occurring in all the **ba-** and **bu-** class prefix forms and concords. Under nasal influ-ence **ɓ** is replaced by **mb.**

Nasal Consonants.

m, n, ny are normal. Syllabic **m** occurs before all consonants and finally, but not before vowels. It is generally a contrac-tion from **mu** and sometimes from **mi**: u<u>m</u>fazi o<u>m</u>khulu, *a big woman*; isiba<u>m</u>, *gun*; u<u>m</u>ŋgane, *friend*. **ŋ** and **ŋg** are alternative dialectal forms: in **ŋk,** the **k** is ejective. The morphological influence of homorganic nasals upon succeed-ing consonants is extremely important in Zulu as in all Bantu languages.

Main Rules governing these changes.

(a) Aspirated plosives are replaced by ejectives.

uphaphe	feather	pl.	**izimp'aphe**
uthi	stick	,,	**izint'i**
ukhezo	spoon	,,	**iziŋk'ezo**

(b) Radical fricatives are replaced by ejective affricates, voiced fricatives by voiced affricates.

ufudu	tortoise	pl.	**izimpf'udu**
uvu	grey hair	,,	**izimbvu**
usuku	day	,,	**izints'uku**
uʃik'iʃi	quarrelsome person	,,	**izintʃ'ik'iʃi**
uɬo'ɓo	species	,,	**iziuɬ'oɓo**

(c) ɓ is replaced by **b**.

    uɓambo rib   pl. **izimbambo**

(d) Aspirated clicks are replaced by nasal clicks.

(e) Radical clicks   ,,   ,, voiced ,,

Laterals.

Zulu has three lateral sounds, l as the clear l in English, and two fricative l-sounds, one voiceless (ɬ) and one voiced (ɮ).

    lala to sleep   **isiɬaɬa** bush   **uɮweɮwe** long staff

Fricatives.

f, v, s, z, ʃ, ʒ are all normal, **tʃ** occurs as a dialectal variant of **ʃ** in Natal and **dʒ** of **ʒ**.

h represents a sound which varies dialectally from the glottal fricative **h** to the velar fricative (**x**) with little 'scrape'.

    hola or **xola** draw or lead

hh is used in current orthography to represent a voiced **h** which occurs seldom.

    ihhaʃi horse

Semi-vowels.

w and **y** occur normally and are used as intervocalic semi-vowels to keep syllables apart.

Affricates.

Zulu has a large number of affricates: **tʃ** as in English *church* is the only affricate that is not ejective in Zulu. All other unvoiced affricates are ejective: **ts', tʃ', kx',[1] kɬ'**: in combination with nasal consonants **mpf', nts', ntʃ', ˋntɬ'** (written respectively **mf, ns, nʃ, nl**) and their vocal equivalents **mbv, ndz, ndʒ, ndɮ**.

III. CLICK CONSONANTS.

Zulu has *three* click positions, viz. dental, palato-alveolar, and lateral: they are represented here (and in current orthography) by **c, q**, and **x** respectively. They can occur aspirated, nasalized, and voiced. (For these see Doke, *The Phonetics of Zulu*.)

---

[1] **kl** is the conventional representation of a sound which has several forms, the commonest of which is **kx'**: it is a difficult sound for Europeans to acquire.

Notes on the Click Consonants.

(*a*) Words are distinguished by the aspiration or non-aspiration of clicks.

caca	scrape a wound	**chacha**	shell beans
qatha	break up new ground	**qhatha**	cause a fight
xoxa	relate	**xhoxha**	prod

(Tones in each pair the same.)

(*b*) The radical click preceded by a nasal consonant is rare in Zulu but common in Xosa.

choŋco of being on top   **ukuǥquŋqa** to fade
ukuxaŋxatha to pound

(*c*) The digraphs **ǥc, ǥq, ǥx** represent the voiced forms of the clicks; they may be preceded by the velar (homorganic) nasal.

ǥcina	wax up a hive	**iziŋŋǥcu**	rows of beads
isiǥqoko	hat	**iziŋŋǥqoko**	wooden trays
uǥxa	digging stick	**iziŋŋǥxa**	digging sticks

(*d*) The nasal clicks are represented by **nc, nq, nx**: they are nasalized throughout the click formation, not preceded by a separate nasal as in (*b*) above. At present no means of distinguishing these two formations have been used.

uncencence a tinkling thing   **inqola** wagon   **nxa** when

IV. STRESS

This is important in Zulu. Generally the main stress falls on the penultimate syllable of each word. Stress is never used to indicate emphasis, nor is it used to differentiate words, as is done in English. Its work, as in other Bantu languages, is solely that of word-building, and each Zulu word has one and only one main stress. This holds even with certain monosyllables, but unstressed syllables can never stand alone. When a word is increased in length by the addition of suffixes, the stress almost invariably moves forward to remain on the penultimate syllable in each case.

V. LENGTH

Length of vowel is not a regular feature of Zulu to distinguish words. The stressed syllable (penultimate) is always long. Long vowels also occur as the result of some contraction of syllables.

VI. TONE

Tone in Zulu is extremely complicated. Nine levels of tone
have been recorded.[1] Tone is to a considerable extent significant
and may be (1) semantic, (2) grammatical, and (3) emotional.

(1) *Semantic.*

i6ele [⌣ ⌐ ·]	corn	i6ele [⌐ · ͵]	breast
inyaŋga [· ⌐ ͵]	doctor	inyaŋga [· ⌐ ⌣]	moon
6ona [· ⌐]	they	6ona[· ͵]	see
łanza [· ⌣]	wash	łanza [· ͵]	vomit

(2) *Grammatical.*

umunt'u [· · ͵]	person	umunt'u [͵ · ͵]	it is a person
inǥu [· ͵]	house	inǥu [⌣ ͵]	houses
wahamba [· · ͵]	he went	wahamba [͵ · ͵]	thou didst go
6asi6ona [⌐ · ⌐ ͵]	they saw us	6asi6ona [⌐ · ⌐ ·]	did they see us ?

(3) *Emotional.*

(Emphasis) m̲khulu [· · ͵] he is big   m̲khulu [· · ⌐] he is
tremendous

(Sarcastic) aŋgiyithandi [· · · ͵] I don't like it

aŋgiyithandi [· · · ⌐] I don't half like it

NUER EASTERN DIALECT

The difficulties of Nuer are:

(1) A somewhat complicated vowel system, including central
vowels.

(2) Complicated vowel changes in the stems of words for

---

[1] See Chapters on Tone in *The Phonetics of Zulu*, where Dr. Doke
shows these levels by the numbers 1–9. In this summary the numbers,
by permission of Dr. Doke, have been translated roughly into the
system of tone-marking used in this book.

different grammatical forms, changes in quality and quantity.

(3) In Western Nuer, changes in the final consonant of the stems of words.

I. Vowels

Nuer has a vowel system similar to that of Dinka. The number of significant vowels has not yet been determined: there are seven or eight front and back vowels, together with centralized forms of all these except **u**. Up to the present, it is suggested that only two of these centralized vowels need to be marked in current orthography, viz. **ä** and **ö**. Most of the central vowels are pronounced with 'breathy' voice and with wide pharynx: **ö**, however, can have both types of voice production; there are two close o-sounds, a very close variety with contracted pharynx, and an opener one with 'breathy' voice (but not centralized).

e and **ɛ**, **o** and **ɔ** respectively cover large phoneme areas and they approximate to each other: but they can be distinguished by the vowels of the genitive and other forms; words containing **ɛ** and **ɔ** have the forms **ɛa, ɔa** in declension, while those with **e** and **o** never have these. The vowel written **e** in suffixes added to words, and in pronouns, e.g. **je**, *him, it*; **de**, *his*; **ke**, *there*, is similar to the neutral vowel **ə**.

The approximate tongue positions are shown below on the Cardinal figure.

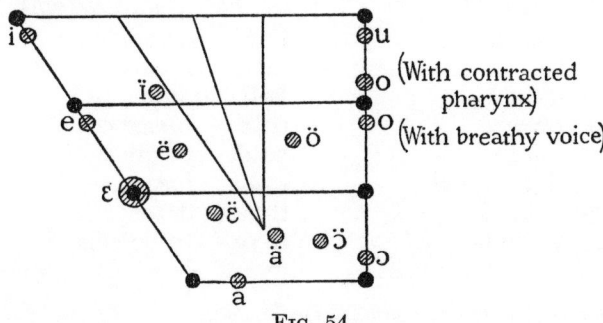

Fig. 54.

Examples.

i	**rip**	needle	**e**	**lek**	to shut	**ɛ**	**lɛp**	tongue
	lil	furrow		**dhyec**	five		**dɛl**	sheep
	jiith	scorpion						

a **raan** man   ə **jakək** crow   o **kom** to thrash
  mac fire   **kəm** chair
u **dul** clod

Centralized Vowels.

ï **elïk** noisily, suddenly   ë **ciëŋ** village
                         ǧëka neighbouring
                         bël blacksmith

ä **käp** to snatch   (cf. **kap** to put on the head)
  käm to give   (,, **kam** between)
  wäär cow-dung   (,, **waar** sheep-dung)
  päl to leave alone (,, **pal** to pray)

ɔ̈ **mɔ̈k** buffalo (pl. **mök**)   ö **löth** bell
  lɔ̈t to stake   **ǧör** kind of snake
                              cök foot (pl.)

There are two kinds of voice in Nuer: the normal voice is produced with considerable contraction in the pharynx while many words are pronounced with wide pharynx and 'breathy' voice. The difference is apparently significant, especially in declension. In many of these pairs of words, the 'breathy' voice is accompanied by centralization, but not all centralized vowels are breathy, and there is one non-central vowel which also has this peculiar voice production, viz. a mid-variety of **o**.

Examples.

	Contracted Throat		*Open Throat and Breathy Voice*
ken	to sing	**ken**	egrets
tet	to lead in singing	**tet**	hands
kek	dykes	**kek**	dyke
thiin	breast	**thin**	breasts
cook	miser	**cook**	to give
kəm	chair, stool	**kəm**	insect
thəaar	floated	**thəaar**	dates
thiak	to be heavy	**thyak**	to be close by
nyaau	cat, pl. **nyauni**	**nyau**	bead, pl. **nyauni**

Examples of Centralization in Declension.

         kwar chief, pl. **kuäär**
         rol country, pl. **röl**
         jiok dog, gen. **jiöök**, pl. **jiook**
         ciook foot, pl. and gen. **cök**

II. Diphthongs.

Nuer has all the diphthongs which occur in Dinka, and in addition əa and ɛa, both long and short.

dɛl sheep, gen. dɛaal
kəm chair ,, kəaam

The falling diphthongs have not yet been fully determined.

Rising Diphthongs.

The starting-points are i and u pronounced fully or pronounced so short as to warrant their being written y and w.

diək	three	rwom	fly
biɛl	colour	guər	elephant, pl. ġwər
ciem	kiss	duel	house, pl. dwel, gen. dweel, loc. dueel

III. Consonants

The following consonants occur in Nuer: p, b, th, dh, t, d, c, j, k, ġ, m, nh, n, ny, ŋ, l, r.

Notes on the Consonants.

th, dh, nh are dentals:

nath Nuer nhial heaven ranh close by (cf. ran agent, doer, as in ranlat worker).

c and j are true palatals, not like the English tʃ and dʒ. They occur frequently in final positions:

wic head jec to stand juəl tail

(See Notes on Dinka for the i-glide before final c and ny.)

Fricatives.

In Western Nuer, the voiceless plosives in some final positions weaken into fricatives: this is generally governed by strict grammatical rules. Thus th is replaced by θ, t by a kind of voiceless r (such as is heard in English *tree*), p by f or ʃ, c by ç (as in German *ich*), and k by h. In Eastern Nuer there is no such replacing of plosive by fricative.

duəp pl. dwəf path [Eastern Nuer duəəp pl. dwəp]
kɛaθ ,, kɛth bile [,, ,, kɛath ,, kɛth]
dit ,, diṛ big [,, ,, diit ,, dit]
cä je ŋäç I knew it cä je ŋäc I don't know it
[In Eastern Nuer, intonation alone shows the difference.]
yah, pl. yaak hyena [Eastern Nuer yak, pl. yaak].

IV. SEMI-VOWELS

The two semi-vowels **y** and **w** occur in Nuer. The correct use of these and of the vowels **i** and **u** in diphthongal combinations is important in pronunciation and spelling, since they differentiate meaning.

i. The letters **i** and **u** are *written* to represent the semi-vowels when they precede long vowels.

liɛɛth	butter	**diaar**	milking gourd
cieeŋ	villages	**kuäär**	chief
duɔɔp	path	**dueel**	at home

ii. Before *short* vowels **i** and **u** are used if the accent is on **i** or **u** (i.e. if they are falling diphthongs).

liɛl	streams	**cieŋ**	village	**ciek**	wife
ġuar	father	**duel**	house		

iii. Before *short* vowels **y** and **w** are used if the accent is on the following vowel (i.e. if it is a rising diphthong).

lyɛl	anus	**jyɛth**	scorpions	**cyɛk**	bracelet
ġwar	girl	**dwop**	paths	**dwel**	houses

V. LENGTH

Length of vowel can be significant in Nuer. It is not so important or obvious in Western as in Eastern Nuer.

ce je ŋäc	I knew it
ce je ŋääc	I milked it
ce je ŋäc	I don't know it
ce je ŋääc	I am not milking it

ŋäcä je	I milk it	Eastern Nuer
ŋääcä je	I know it	

ŋäcä je	I milk it	Western Nuer
ŋääyä je	I know it	

kɛakä je	I slash it	Eastern Nuer
kɛaakä je	I draw it	

VI. INTONATION

Tone in Nuer plays two roles: it distinguishes words, as in **bel** [.], *to sing*; **bel** [˙], *blacksmith*.

It is also used to show grammatical relationships:

cä mut pat [˙ ˙ .] I have sharpened the spear (verb, **pat**)

cä mut pat [˙ • .] I am not sharpening the spear

cä je ŋäc [˙ ˙ .]   I knew it (verb, **ŋäc**)

cä je ŋäc [˙ • .]   I don't know it

TEXT (*Eastern Dialect*)

Meedan wut kɛl a thɪn, e ɡat kwar.   Cɔal   cödë
Once   man one was there, was son (of) chief. Name is called

Lual.   Laa   bounike a camke e   yak.   Lual ce ɣɔm
Lual.   Always his-fruit was eaten by hyena: Lual has a pit

tɛt ke ɣöö   bee   yak käp.   Cu   yak pɛn   thɪn.
dug so that (he) should hyena catch. And hyena fell therein.

Mee   ci Lual ben,   cue   yak   jek.   Cue   Lual
When has Lual come, then (he) hyena found.   He (to) Lual

jyök: 'Päl   ä,   cu ɣä näk.'   Cu Lual e   päl,   ka
said: 'Spare me, do not me kill.' So Lual him spared, but

cue löth ɡwɔk   ŋwääde.   Cu   yak   jïɛn   ka caa
he a bell tied (to) his neck. So the hyena escaped, but was

löth ɡwɔk   ŋwääde.   Mee e jen i la a wee kak   ke
bell tied (to) his neck. If he always went hunting with

lei,   bɪ   lei löth liŋ, bɪke   ro   bar. Mee
animals, would animals bell hear, would themselves flee. Thus

wee teene cu yak   liu   kee bwɔth.
it went till was hyena dead from hunger.

DINKA (REK DIALECT)

I. VOWELS

The vowel system of Dinka is very complicated, since in addition to the normal vowels, there are a number of central or centralized vowels. These have not been represented in the current orthography, except in three words (**dhöl**, *path*; **köt**, *cow urine*; **dhök**, *cheetah*). The vowels are shown on the accompanying cardinal figure.

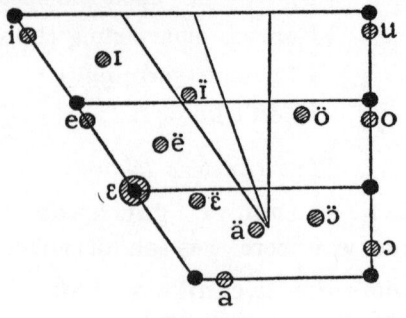

Fig. 55.

i has varieties of pronunciation between the **i** of *feet* and the vowel in *fit*. (The latter is indicated by the special symbol **ɪ** on the figure above and in the examples below.)

dın dit big bird (*lit.* bird big).

e is a little lower than Cardinal No. 2.

ɛ is near to Cardinal No. 3.

Examples to show the distinction between **e** *and* **ɛ**.

ŋwet	to scratch	**ŋwɛt**	to get thin
tweny	to fall (of rain)	**twɛny**	to break
lek	to throw spear	**lɛk**	to tell
del	skins	**dɛl**	skin
rec	fishes	**rɛc**	fish

(Note that the singular and plural of some nouns are distinguished by the difference between **e** and **ɛ**.)

a has varieties of pronunciation: one is near to Cardinal No. 4, the other near to the English vowel in *but* (shown by **a** on the figure above).

rac bad   **raan** man   **mada** our mother

ə is about half-way between Cardinal vowels Nos. 5 and 6, between the English vowels in *caught* (but not necessarily long), and in *not* (not necessarily short).

məc give as a present   **dəm** to take   **təŋ** spear

o is a little below Cardinal No. 7.

moc to sting   **dom** field   **doŋ** mortar for grinding

Examples to show the distinction between **o** *and* **ɔ**.

lor	to receive guests	**lɔr**	go!
thok	mouth	**thɔk**	goat
dom	field	**dɔm**	pilfer
lol	water channels	**lɔl**	water channel in swamp

(Note again that the singular and plural of certain nouns are distinguished by these two vowels.)

u is near to Cardinal No. 8, similar to the English **u** in *cool*.

wut	cattle kraal	**kur**	stone
wuut	ostrich		

Centralized Vowels.

ï	**kwïn**	porridge	cf.	**kwɪɪn**	(plural)
				dit	big
				dɪt	bird
ë	**ebën**	all	cf.	**ben**	again
	kwëm	break			
	wër	river			
ɛ̈	**yɛ̈k**	give			
	lɛ̈k	tell			
	kɛ̈ɛ̈t	bridge			
ä	**bär**	long	cf.	**bar**	orphan
	wäl	grass			
ɔ̈	**tɔ̈ɔ̈ŋ**	spears	cf.	**tɔŋ**	spear
	akɔ̈l	sun			
ö	**dhöl**	path			
	dhök	cheetah			
	dhöök	cheetahs			

II. DIPHTHONGS

Dinka has a large number of diphthongs: they can be represented by the following letters: **ai, ui, ei, ɛi, oi, ɔi, au, iu, ou, ɔu, ia, ie, iɛ, io, iɔ, ua, uo, uɔ, ue, uɛ.**

Note that in the falling diphthongs (the first ten), the **i** and **u** elements are nearer to **e** and **o** respectively than to **i** and **u**. In the rising diphthongs (the second ten), the **i** and **u** elements may be pronounced fully or they may be pronounced so short that they often resemble **y** and **w** respectively.

Examples.

lai	wild game	liəi	soft
lui	work (*noun*)	dau	string
wei	to breathe	kiu	to roar
wɛi	to fall	reu	two, thirst
loi	to work	rəu	hippopotamus
riak	broken	luaŋ	fly
dier	pig	muoth	greet
diɛr	shin bone	muəth	dark
tiok	deep mud	lueth	to tell a lie
thiək	near	luɛth	spittle

Note on Voice.

Two different kinds of voice are heard in Dinka : some words are pronounced with considerable contraction in the pharynx, while many are pronounced with wide pharynx and 'breathy' or 'hollow' voice. Hollow voice often goes with centralization : the difference between the two may be significant.

Contracted Throat	*Open Throat*
thoc stool	**thoc** stools
war shoe	**war** shoes
apik he pushes it towards (the speaker)	**apik** he pushes it away (from the speaker)

III. Consonants

The consonants in Dinka are : **p, b, th, dh, t, d, k, g, c, j, m, ṁh, n, ny, ŋ, l, r, ɣ, w, y.**

Notes on the Consonants.

i. **th, dh, nh** are dental sounds : **th, dh** are slightly affricated (see p. 55). They are separate phonemes from alveolar **t, d,** and **n.**

tok	one	thok	mouth
ket	song	keth	gall
duk	neg. imper.	dhuk	return
man	mother	manh	son
nial	knee	nhial	sky

ii. **c** and **j** represent true palatal sounds:[1] they are not like
tʃ and **dʒ**.

cam	to eat	**cum**	fruit
jam	to talk	**rac**	bad[1]
joŋ	dog	**toc**	swamp[1]

ny, the palatal nasal, is frequently final.[1]

beny	chief	**kony**	to help
tweny	to fall		

iii. The voiced plosive phonemes do not normally occur in a
final position but **p, th, t, c, k** at the end of a word are often
weakened to **b, dh, d, j** (or **y**), **ǵ** (or **ɣ**) when that word occurs
in the middle of a sentence. Thus

Ok aci cɔk nɔk, *we are killed by hunger*, is pronounced by
some Dinkas as

Oɣ aji cɔǵ nɔk.

iv. In some dialects (e.g. Bor), **p, th, t, c, k** are weakened in
some positions to the corresponding voiceless fricatives, i.e. **p**
is replaced by the bi-labial fricative **ʄ** (or **f**), **th** is replaced by **θ**
(the sound of **th** in English *thin*), **t** by a voiceless fricative **r**
(somewhat like the **r** in English *tree*), **c** by **y** and **k** by **h**. In
the last case, **h** tends to disappear (cf. Western Nuer).

IV. SOUND CHANGES

Complicated sound changes take place in declension, and the
vowel frequently changes (in quality, length, or pitch) for the
plural or locative of nouns and in certain parts of the verb
forms. For these no rules can be given.

Consonant Changes.

These changes apply only to the singular of nouns, not to the
plural. When a singular noun ending in a vowel or one of the
voiceless plosives (**p, th, t, c, k**) is followed by an adjective, by
a possessive or demonstrative pronoun, or by a noun in the
genitive case, the following changes take place:

The vowel is replaced (or followed) by **n**

p	,,	,,	,,	**m**
th	,,	,,	,,	**nh**

---

[1] Before final **c** and **ny**, a small **i**-glide is heard. It is not necessary to
denote this in the orthography: e.g. **rac**   sounds like **raic**

                                             kony   ,,   ,, **koiny**, &c.

(See Ch. XI, pp. 56, 64.)

t is replaced (or followed) by **n**

c   ,,   ,,   ,,   **ny**

k   ,,   ,,   ,,   **ŋ**

i.e. the homorganic nasal replaces the plosive consonant.

Examples.

buəi	net	**buən riak**	a broken net
məu	merissa	**mən diŋ**	sweet-tasting beer
nya	daughter	**nyan path**	a good daughter
liep	tongue	**liem bar**	a long tongue
alath	cloth	**alanh thith**	a red cloth
wut	cattle kraal	**wun dit**	a big kraal
məc	man	**məny dit**	an old man
jək	spirit	**jəŋ rac**	a bad spirit

buən dia my net   **liem du** your tongue   **alanh dhe** his cloth

mən tiik woman's beer   **liem kor** tongue of a lion

Examples of Vowel Changes for the Plural.

mac	fire,	pl.	**mec**
yar	leaf,	,,	**yər**
ləl	channel,	,,	**lol**
alɛl	stone,	,,	**alel**
meth	child,	,,	**mith**
miir	giraffe,	,,	**miɛr**

V. Length

There seem to be three degrees of length in vowels and diphthongs, but it is rarely necessary to mark length in orthography. It is, however, significant in a few cases.

wut	cattle kraal	**wuut**	ostrich
pal	knife	**paal**	knives
dhök	cheetah	**dhöök**	cheetahs

VI. Stress and Intonation

Stress and intonation are bound up together: few definite rules have as yet been discovered.

Tone is used for certain grammatical distinctions. The negative present differs from the positive past in tone alone. (Sometimes the vowel in the verb stem changes and the difference can be detected by this.)

Aci dhieth aci rol [˙ ˙ ˙ ˙ ˙ ＼] She does not give birth, she is
barren

Aci dhieth aci rol [˳ ˙ ˙ ˳ ˙ ˳] She gave birth, she is not barren

Xɛn aci cɔk nɔk [˙ ˙ ˙ ＼] I was hungry

Xɛn aci cɔk nɔk [˙ ˙ ˙ ˙ ˳] I am not hungry

Xan aci jal [˙ ˙ ˙ ＼] Good-bye (*lit.* I have gone)

Xan aci jal [˳ ˳ ˙ ˳] I am not going

The singular and plural of nouns are distinguished by tone in
some cases:

pany [˙] wall   **pany** [˳] plur.

TEXT

Tiik atɔ bai keɡe dhɔk.   Koor aci ben a luel:
Woman was at home with boy.   Lion   has   come   said:

'Man   Diŋ,   bar bei.'   Guk aci   luel: 'Man
'Mother of Ding, come out.' The dove has said: 'Mother

Diŋ,   biɛt!'   La piny   aci   bak,   koor
of Ding, be silent.' When the earth has grown light,   lion

aci lɔ pande. Man Diŋ   aci   dec ɡuk:
has gone home.   Mother of Ding has strangled dove (saying)

'Yin e rɔɔr   pen tene ɣɛn?'
'You would the woods forbid to me?'

SOME NOTES ON KIKUYU

I. VOWELS

Vowels: **i, e, ɛ, a, ɔ, o, u.** They occur both long and short.

Examples.

i iiriɔ [˙ ˙ ˙] food, **riikia** [˙ ˙ ˙] deepen, **motyie** [˙ ˙ ˙] village,
iriɣo [˙ ˙ ˙] banana

e kahee [˙ ˙] boy, **moðeeni** [˙ ˙ ˙] poor person, **ɣete** [˙ ˙]
stool, **mote** [˙ ˙] tree

ɛ mwɛɛri [··] moon, month, ŋɛɛndə [··] journeys, keɛha [···] sorrow, moðɛnya [···] day

a kenaaŋa [···] market, iðaanə [···] five, nyama [··] meat, ndyata [··] star

ə ndyəəhi [··] Kikuyu beer, həəta [·· .] to overcome, ɣetyikə [···] spoon, moriɣə [···] load

o moɣoonda [···] garden, field, morooði [···] lion, moɣatɛ [···] bread, roɣɛɛndə [···] journey

u tuura [·· .] to ache, muutə [··] pillow, iruɣa [···] feast, kaɣui [···] puppy

II. Consonants

The Consonants in Kikuyu are: (b), t, (d), ty, dy, k, (g), m, n, ny, ŋ, r, ʋ (or v), ð, ɣ, h, y, w.
There appears to be no **p**.

b. Mr. Mockiri, with whom this work was done, used this initially. Some speakers may use **mb**. (I heard no **m**, though Mr. Mockiri was quite willing to use **m** when his attention was called to its absence. He agreed that there was no **m** in his pronunciation.)

bori [··]   goat (Others probably say **mbori**)
bakori [·· .] bowl („   „   **mbakori**)
baraði [·· .] horse („   „   **mbaraði**)
baara [··]   battle („   „   **mbaara**)

b is used after **m** in medial positions:
roembə [···] song, ŋəmbɛ [··] cattle, kehɛɛmbɛ [···] drum

d used only after **n**. Initially **n** is *very* weak: nduka [··], *shop.*

Examples of **nd** *medially:*

keanda [···] river valley   keendo [··]   thing
ində [··]   things   ondo [··]   thing (abstract)
kahiinda [···] a moment   moondo [··]   man
roɣɛɛndə [···] journey   moɣɛɛndi [···] traveller
kɛɛnda [··]   nine

ty: ɣatyera [···] small road   **motyie** [···] village
  motyiiŋga [···] gun   **ɣetyikə** [···] spoon
  tyiara [··] fingers   **tyiuɣo** [···] cattle kraals
  tyiira [··] law case

dy. Used only after a nasal consonant which is not really **n** but
  a fronted variety of **ny**:
  ndyera [··] big road   **ndyɛɣa** [··] good
  ndyiro [··] black   **ndyata** [··] star
  ndyəəhi [··] Kikuyu beer

ny. In this there seems often to be no contact. The sound is
  then really ĩ or ỹ:
  moðɛnya [···] day   **nyɛki** [··]   grass
  inya [··]   four   **inyaanya** [···] eight

ŋ occurs as a separate phoneme:
  ŋɛɛndə [··]   journeys   **ŋanə** [··]   stories
  keŋaaŋa [···] market   **iŋaaŋa** [···] markets
  moreŋgeti [···] blanket

r is often very l-like.

ʋ (or **v**)[1] is never preceded by a nasal:
  kavori [···] small goat   **kevare** [···] sleeping-mat
  vaava [··] father   **viivi** [·.]   lady
  Very often in initial position **ʋ** (or **v**) is voiceless. In very slow
  speech it is sometimes voiceless when medial.

ð is never preceded by a nasal:
  moðeeni [···] poor person   **morooði** [···] lion
  moðɛnya [···] day   **ɣeðaka** [···] bush, jungle
  rooða [··]   holiday   **iðanwa** [···] axe
  iðato [···] three   **iðaanə** [···] five
  ð is often voiceless in slow speech.

----

[1] Mr. Mockiri seemed to prefer **v**.

ɣ is never preceded by a nasal:

roɣanə [···]	story	roɣɛɛndə [···]	journey
ɣiaðe [···]	feast, market	kaɣui [···]	puppy
ɣatyera [···]	small road	kareeɣo [···]	girl
moriɣə [···]	load	moɣatɛ [···]	bread
moɣoonda [···]	garden, field	ɣete [··]	stool
ɣeðaka [···]	bush, jungle	ɣetyikə [···]	spoon
ɣekə [··]	dirt	kiuɣo [···]	cattle kraal
iriɣo [···]	banana	riiɣe [··]	door of hut
oruɣare [···.]	heat	ɣako [··]	twig of firewood
ɣate [··]	small stick		

ɣ is often voiceless initially, and in very slow speech it is sometimes voiceless medially.

BIBLIOGRAPHY

For the guidance of the reader a few of the more important publications dealing with phonetics are given here.

PHONETICS

I. General.

Noel Armfield, G. *General Phonetics.* Cambridge.

Sievers, E. *Grundzüge der Phonetik.* Leipzig.

Panconcelli-Calzia, G. *Die experimentelle Phonetik in ihrer Anwendung auf die Sprachwissenschaft.* Berlin. 1924.

II. European Languages.

1. English.

Jones, D. *Outline of English Phonetics*, 3rd edition, 1932. Teubner, Leipzig, Heffer, Cambridge.

Ward, I. C. *The Phonetics of English*, 2nd edition, 1931. Heffer, Cambridge.

Ripman, W. *The Sounds of Spoken English*, 1932. Dent & Co., London.

2. French.

Armstrong, L. E. *The Phonetics of French*, 1932. Bell & Co., London.

Passy, P. *Les Sons du français.* Paris.

3. German.

Bremer, O. *Deutsche Phonetik.* Leipzig.

Viëtor, W. *Kleine Phonetik.* Leipzig.

—— *German Pronunciation.* Leipzig.

III. African Languages. (General)[1]

Dahl, E. 'Die Töne und Akzente im Kińamwezi', *MSOS*, vii. 3, pp. 106–26, 1904.

Homburger, L. *Phonétique Historique du bantou.* Paris.

Johnston, Sir. H. *A Comparative Study of the Bantu and Semi-Bantu languages.* London.

Klingenheben, A. 'Ablaut in afrikanischen Sprachen', *Zeitschrift für Eingeborenensprachen*, xxi. 81 ff.

—— 'Die Tempora Westafrikas und die semitischen Tempora', *Zeitschrift für Eingeborenensprachen*, xix. 241 ff.

[1] The writers on special languages and the titles of their books are quoted in this book where the languages are mentioned.

Meinhof, C. *Grundzüge einer vergleichenden Grammatik der Bantusprachen*. Berlin.

—— 'Linguistik', in G. von Neumayer, *Anleitung zu wissenschaftlichen Beobachtungen auf Reisen*. Hannover.

—— *Lautlehre der Bantusprachen*. 2. Auflage. Berlin. Pages 1–17 deal with phonetic phenomena. An English edition of this book has appeared under the title : *Introduction to the Phonology of the Bantu Languages*. Berlin. 1932.

Nekes, P. H. 'Die Bedeutung des musikalischen Tones in den Bantusprachen', *Anthropos*, vi, pp. 546–74, 1911.

—— 'Die musikalischen Töne in der Dualasprache', *Anthropos*, vi, pp. 911–19, 1911.

Schwellnus, Th. and P. 'Die Verba des Tšivenda', *MSOS*, vii, 3, pp. 12–31, 1904.

Westermann, D. *Die Sudansprachen, eine sprach-vergleichende Studie*. Hamburg. 1911.

—— *Die westlichen Sudansprachen*. Berlin. 1927.

Practical Orthography of African Languages. Revised edition, Memorandum I, International Institute of African Languages and Cultures, London. 1930.

Gramophone Records of African Languages

The following records (with texts) have been prepared for linguistic purposes.

Linguaphone Institute, 24–27, High Holborn, London, W.C. 1.
Efik　　Two double-sided records.
Hausa　　,,　　,,　　,,　　,,
Ewe, Yoruba, Ibo (to be issued shortly).
Prepared by the Department of Phonetics, School of Oriental Studies, London.

Lautbibliothek, phonetische Platten und Umschriften, herausgegeben von der Lautabteilung der Preussischen Staatsbibliothek, Berlin.

Ewe (Gɛ̃-Mundart)	L.A. 1183–5	Prepared by D. Westermann.		
Yoruba	L.A. 1188	,,	,,	,,
Fante	L.A. 1296–7	,,	,,	,,
Mandara	P.K. 275	,,	,,	A. Klingenheben.

SUBJECT INDEX

elision, pp. 129–31, §§ 391–4;
English, French, German, p. 26,
Fig. 8; harmony, pp. 127–9, §§
386–90; nasalized, p. 42, § 101;

rounded front, p. 40, §§ 97, 98;
rounded back, p. 41, § 99.

Whisper: p. 13, § 30.

INDEX OF LANGUAGES

[Numbers indicate paragraphs.]

AKAN (Gold Coast):
  assimilation of consonants, 376;
  weakening of consonants, 397;
  tone language, 412.
AMHARIC (Abyssinia):
  ë, ë, central vowels, 95;
  pharyngal fricative, 247;
  ejectives, 295.

BAMBARA (French West Africa):
  interchange of i and u, 90;
  rounded front vowel ü, 98;
  d like r, 220;
  s palatalized, 325;
  stress, 353;
  weakening of consonants, 397;
  phonetic summary, pp. 181–7.
BANDA (French EquatorialAfrica):
  kp, gb, 164.
BARI (Anglo-Egyptian Sudan):
  'lax' i and u, 86;
  interchange of i, u; ı, ʊ, 90;
  ö, central vowel, 95;
  gb and 'b, 164;
  glottal stop, 167;
  ny and nyy, 186;
  b and d with glottal stop, 289;
  y ejective, 296;
  ty, 326;
  velarized sounds, 332, 333;
  stress, 355;
  assimilation of consonants,
    377 (f);
  vowel harmony, 388.
BUSHMAN (S. W. Africa):
  clicks, 297, 298, 306;
  bi-labial click, 298.

CHAGGA (Tanganyika Territory):
  long consonants, 364.

CHUANA (S. Africa):
  k, 72;
  dy, 157;
  glottal stop, 168;
  syllabic nasal, 195;
  syllabic r, 212;
  flapped l, 218;
  bi-labial f, 224, 225, 228;
  ʃ, 234, 235;
  x, 244;
  ts, 257;
  kx, 257;
  ʃ labialized: tʃw, dʒw, 258, 317;
  aspirated affricates, 261;
  tl, ejective, 263;
  labialized sounds, 314, 315, 317;
  semantic tones, 404;
  tone language, 412.

DAGBANE (Togoland):
  γ, 244.
DINKA (Anglo-Egyptian Sudan):
  ï, ë, ä, central vowels, 95;
  diphthongs, 113, 114;
  incomplete plosive, 147;
  dental t, d, 153;
  ty, dy (c, j) final, 156, 157;
  dental and alveolar n, 174,
    175;
  ny final, 184;
  length of vowels, 359;
  weakening of consonants, 397;
  grammatical tones, 406;
  tone language, 412;
  phonetic summary, pp. 207–13.
DUALA (Cameroons):
  implosive b and d, 288;
  syllabic division, 345;
  semantic tones, 404, 451;
  grammatical tones, 406;

GA (*contd.*)
elision of final vowel, 393;
grammatical tones, 406;
tone marking, 425;
tonemes, 429, 438;
semantic tones, 451;
tone examples, 451.
GANDA (East Africa):
ŋ, 180.
l and r members of one phoneme, 214;
y, 266;
w, 268;
length of vowels, 359;
long consonants, 364;
tone language, 412;
tone in vowel elision, 441;
phonetic summary, pp. 188–97.
GBARI (Nupe, Nigeria):
velarized sounds, 334.
GBAYA: *see* KREISH.
GBE (Kru, Ivory Coast):
x, 244.
GUTA (Manyika, East Africa):
fricative l, 204;
voiceless l, 206.

HAUSA (N. Nigeria):
glottal stop, 167;
flapped l, 218 (6);
bi-labial ʃ alternating with p, (dialectal), 228;
c, j, 257;
implosives, 284;
ejectives, 292;
k, g palatalized, 324;
stress, 355, n. 3;
length of vowels, 359;
long consonants, 364;
weakening of consonants, p>
f>u; t> ts> s, 397.
HERERO (S. W. Africa):
retroflex t, d, 152;
dental and retroflex n, 176;
fricative l, 204;
flapped r, 218 (2).
HOTTENTOT (S. and S. W. Africa):
clicks, 297, 306.

IBO (S. Nigeria):
word consisting of consonants only, 43;

r, l, 72;
eight vowels, 88;
interchange of e and o, 90;
kp, gb implosive, 161;
flapped and rolled r, 218;
implosives: (Arochuku) 277, 283, (Umanelo) 278;
vowel harmony, 389;
semantic tones, 404, 451;
grammatical tones, 406;
tone language, 412;
tone examples, 451.
ILA (NW. Rhodesia):
assimilation of consonants, 377 (*d*).

KAIDIKANEM (Lake Chad region):
ə, central vowel, 95.
KAKWA (Bari):
kp, gb, 164;
palatalized s, ŋ, 326;
velarized sounds, 332, 333.
KANURI (N. Nigeria):
ə, central vowel, 95;
flapped r, 218 (6).
KARANGA (S. Rhodesia):
ny and nyy, 186;
l and r interchangeable, 213;
bi-labial ʋ, 226.
KASONKE (French West Africa):
x, 244;
k > x (weakening of consonant), 397.
KIKUYU (Kenya):
ŋ, 180;
dental fricative, 230;
ɣ, 244;
tones wearing down, 412;
notes, pp. 213–16.
KINGA (Tanganyika Territory):
ny and nyy, 186;
implosive g, 285.
KPELLE (Liberia):
ɣ, 244;
length of vowels, 359, 361;
effect of elision, 361;
ɣ < k, 397;
w < b, 397;
semantic tones, 404;
tones wearing down, 412.

APPENDIX

PRACTICAL ORTHOGRAPHY OF
AFRICAN LANGUAGES

INTERNATIONAL AFRICAN INSTITUTE
MEMORANDUM I

PRACTICAL ORTHOGRAPHY
OF
AFRICAN LANGUAGES

PRACTICAL ORTHOGRAPHY OF AFRICAN LANGUAGES

INTRODUCTION

THE first edition of the *Practical Orthography of African Languages*, consisting of 3,500 copies (3,000 in English and 500 in German) has been sold out within two years. This fact proves that the problem of finding a practical and uniform method of writing African languages has aroused widespread interest, and that the efforts of the Institute towards the solution of the problem have met with considerable response.

The second edition is being printed in English, French, and German.

Up to the present, the principles of orthography recommended by the Institute have been accepted for the following languages: Fante, Twi, Ga, Ewe on the Gold Coast; Efik, Ibo, Yoruba, and partially for Hausa in Nigeria; for Mende, Temne, Soso, Konno, Limba in Sierra Leone; Shilluk, Nuer, Dinka, Bari, Latuko, Madi, and Zande in the Sudan; in Mashonaland it is proposed for a written language to be called Shona, based on the closely related dialects of Karanga, Zezuru, Ndau, Korekore, and Manyika. In the Union of South Africa and in other parts of the continent the introduction of the new orthography is under discussion at present. A number of books for school and mission use have appeared in the new orthography in several of the above-named languages, and others are in preparation. Further information about these can be obtained on request from the Institute.

The aim of the recommendations of the Institute has been, and is, the unification and simplification of the orthography of African languages. Over large areas which have political, geographical, or linguistic unity an unsatisfactory state of affairs is found to exist at the present time owing to lack of agreement as to the general principles of writing down the languages, and as to the letters to be used and the meanings attached to them. In Africa to-day conditions of life are such that many thousands of natives leave their home districts and, either with or without their families, settle temporarily or permanently in districts where their mother tongue is not understood. Thus, for everyday intercourse, for church and school life, or in order to read a newspaper, they are obliged to learn another language. It would obviously be a great advantage if in the orthography of the new language, the value of the letters were the same, or as nearly as possible the same, as those they have already learnt for their mother tongue. Moreover, in many parts of Africa, children in the early stages of school life receive instruction through the medium of the mother tongue, and later in a language which is used over a wider area. The change from mother tongue to another language may not be very difficult for the Negro, because of his linguistic ability and because the two languages are generally closely related, and their construction, grammar, idiom, and vocabulary are often very similar. But if the two languages are written with two different systems of orthography, confusion is likely to arise, and unnecessary difficulty is placed in the path of the learner. In such cases the promotion of uniformity is clearly an important need of the moment.

Another urgent need is expressed in the second purpose of the Memorandum, viz. the simplification of orthography. The number of ways in which speech-sounds are represented to-day in Africa is overwhelming. In every case the basis is the Latin alphabet.[1] As many African languages contain sounds for which the Latin letters are inadequate and which nevertheless must be distinguished in writing, many methods of representing these sounds have been devised. The only systematic orthography which has been used to any considerable extent is that of R. Lepsius, described in his *Standard Alphabet* (2nd edition, London and Berlin, 1863). It is not necessary here to insist upon the scientific value of this alphabet, and especially of the enlarged and improved forms which Meinhof has devised for the particular needs of African languages, and the alphabets which have sprung from it (e.g. the *Anthropos* alphabet of P. W. Schmidt). It is possible by means of this system to represent speech-sounds with great accuracy.

For the practical use of the native, however, the Lepsius and *Anthropos* alphabets have notable disadvantages, in that they make extensive use of diacritic marks above and below the letters. For practical purposes in every-day life diacritic marks constitute a difficulty and a danger. In the first place it is found that in current writing these marks are liable to be altered so as to be unrecognizable and even omitted altogether, as every one who has had to read written texts in African languages will readily acknowledge. Such alterations and omissions of diacritic marks are also frequently found in print. For example, in Yoruba and in other Nigerian languages the horizontal line which Lepsius used in writing 'open' e and o has been replaced sometimes by a vertical line and sometimes by a dot. In the Lepsius alphabet, however, the dot has the opposite meaning to the horizontal line, and is used to indicate a 'close' vowel. A. T. Sumner has published handbooks in the Mende, Temne, and Sherbro languages (Freetown, 1917, 1921, and 1922). In the first of these, close vowels are represented by a dot under the letter and the open vowels are unmarked; in the Temne and Sherbro books the

---

[1] The few cases where Africans have invented their own alphabet or where a negro language has been written in Arabic characters need not be considered, as there is little likelihood of these scripts spreading further.

usage is reversed, the open vowels being represented by a dot under the letter and the close vowels remaining unmarked. In Sotho school-books open e and o have been printed in four different ways.[1]

In the Introduction to the *Standard Alphabet* (p. xii) the following statement is found: 'For the uncritical Native . . . many of the diacritical marks may be dispensed with, or will gradually drop off of themselves.' This expected dropping off has certainly taken place, but proper distinction has not been made in what may and what may not be dispensed with.

The following are some further drawbacks to the use of diacritics. Letters with diacritic marks give a blurred outline to words and thus impair their legibility. Again, a letter consisting of two, three, or four separate elements is much more difficult to grasp and much more likely to strain the eyes than a simple letter. This objection is particularly true of diacritic marks under the letters, as these are most easily overlooked in reading and forgotten in writing.[2] Some existing alphabets are so overloaded with diacritic marks that a glance at them is sufficient to show that they are unsatisfactory from a practical point of view. When native pupils are no longer under the supervision of a teacher in school they simply drop most of the diacritics in writing.[3]

Economic considerations also support the case for uniformity and for the use of letters without diacritic marks. If the types in use differ from language to language and have to be stocked to meet every special case, European printers are less likely to undertake the production of African books than if similar type can be used over large speech-areas.[4] In printing-types diacritic

---

[1] A. N. Tucker, *Suggestions for the Spelling of Transvaal Sesuto* (p. 5).

[2] 'With the spread of religion over the world, the missionaries, usually educated men, have left, as has been said, examples of their erudition: but unfortunately they have shown little knowledge of typography, as is evidenced by the selection made by them of the miscellaneously accented characters with which they have unhappily endowed the scripts of many countries.'—*Typographical Printing Surfaces*, by Legros and Grant, 1916, p. 535.

'Our use to-day of a large number of diacritical marks attests the persistent deficiencies of our alphabet.'—*The Psychology and Pedagogy of Reading*, by E. B. Huey, 1913, p. 222.

'However, all the systems of phonetic writing and marking, often most carefully worked out from the philological and logical points of view, have been conspicuously lacking in revision from the psychological and pedagogical sides.'— Huey, p. 358.

'Too often, as in the working out of systems of phonetic spelling by philologists, a system excellent from the philological or logical standpoint has lacked fitness to the psychic or hygienic conditions involved in reading.'—Huey, p. 430.

[3] At the Language Conference at Rejaf (Sudan), 1928, it was authoritatively stated that experience in the schools of the Northern Sudan showed that about 50 per cent. of the diacritic marks were omitted in the writing of Arabic script.

[4] It may be mentioned here that there are now on the market typewriters of

marks are apt to break off, and they wear out more quickly than the letter itself, so that more frequent renewals are necessary.

All these facts, together with practical experience, have led us to recommend the introduction of a few new letters, which in view of their legibility and the suitability of their cursive forms are clearly to be preferred to ordinary Roman letters with diacritic marks attached. The adoption of these letters will put an end to the multiplicity of signs in use at present; each new letter is, moreover, a simple uniform symbol and not a conglomeration of two or more elements. Diacritic marks are manifestly a makeshift, and a practical alphabet for current use should not be constructed of makeshifts. The representation of each sound (or rather each phoneme, see p. 14) by one separately designed letter should be considered as an essential principle of orthography. Such difficulty as there may be in new letters lies in the fact that for Europeans (but not for the African child who is beginning to learn to read) these letters are unfamiliar and strike us as strange. It is difficult to find any other objections to them.

Although the above objection has not much intrinsic weight, it must nevertheless be taken into consideration to some extent in constructing a system that is to be of general practical use. For this reason, in the alphabet proposed the number of new letters is reduced to a minimum, and the principle of representing each essential sound by a separate symbol is not always rigidly adhered to. Thus in some cases—as for instance in the representation of palatal consonants—it has been thought advisable to resort to 'digraphs' or groups of two letters to indicate single sounds. Diacritic marks too have not been altogether banished: they are used to show 'central' vowels, nasalized vowels, and tones. Such departures from the general principles are made for two reasons: firstly because due regard must be given to forms of spelling which have long been established in many parts of Africa, and secondly because an alphabet which involves too radical a change from existing alphabets would have little prospect of general acceptance. In many parts of Africa traditions of spelling have existed for some time, and these one should endeavour to preserve in so far as they are not inconsistent with the production of a simple, practical, and unified alphabet. For example, the writing of palatal consonants with digraphs avoids the introduction of a diacritic mark or new letters; moreover, digraphs are already commonly used for this purpose, particularly for **ny**, which occurs in so many languages.

Diacritic marks are recommended for certain purposes, and notably to indicate nasalization and tones, because in these particular cases the advantages

---

various makes containing the new letters recommended by the Institute. The difference in price between these and the ordinary typewriter is negligible. The Institute will gladly furnish further information about these machines.

resulting from their use greatly outweigh their inherent drawbacks; it would be a manifest impossibility to introduce new letters for all nasalized vowels and all vowels with special tones. The marks which we recommend for nasalization and for tones are already widely used. For many languages, however, marks to show nasalization and tone are not required; and where they are essential, it is generally possible to reduce them to a manageable number.

It will thus be seen that the intention of this Memorandum is to show how existing orthographies may be modified and improved. It is hoped that the proposals here set forth, grounded as they are on scientific phonetic principles, may serve as a working basis and bring the ideals of unity and simplicity of writing nearer realization.

This Memorandum is not a document providing ready-made alphabets for every African language. For many languages the materials requisite for drawing up satisfactory alphabets are not yet available. Even when the sound-system of a language is known, an alphabet can only be constructed by an expert in the language, who must take into consideration its phonetic and grammatical structure, and sometimes also historical and geographical facts. How far this can be done and how far existing conditions have to be taken into account is discussed in the article by D. Westermann in vol. ii of *Africa* noted below.

In this second edition recommendations are made for the writing of various sounds and sound-groups which were not included in the first edition, but which have recently been under consideration by the Institute. It is hardly necessary to add that there still remain many African sounds for which we are not yet in a position to make recommendations.

The question of the orthography of African languages is discussed in the following articles, reports, and books:

(1) A. Lloyd James: 'The Practical Orthography of African Languages', in *Africa*, i, pp. 125–9.

(2) I. Carl Meinhof, II. Daniel Jones, 'Principles of Practical Orthography for African Languages', in *Africa*, i, pp. 228–39.

(3) A. Lloyd James, 'Phonetics and African Languages', in *Africa*, i, pp. 358–71.

(4) R. F. G. Adams and Ida C. Ward, 'The Arochuku Dialect of Ibo', in *Africa*, ii, pp. 57–70.

[(5) D. Westermann, 'The Linguistic Situation and Vernacular Education in British West Africa', in *Africa*, ii, pp. 337–51.

(6) *A Common Script for Twi, Fante, Ga and Ewe*. Report by Prof. D. Westermann. Ordered by H. E. the Governor to be printed. Gold Coast Government Printer, Accra, 1927.

(7) *Report of the Rejaf Language Conference*. Published by the Sudanese Government. London, 1928.

(8) *Alphabets for the Efik, Ibo and Yoruba Languages.* Recommended by the Education Board, Lagos. London, 1929.

(9) *Alphabets for the Mende, Temne, Soso, Kono and Limba Languages.* International Institute of African Languages and Cultures. London, 1929.

(10) A. N. Tucker, *Suggestions for the Spelling of Transvaal Sesuto.* Memorandum VII of the International Institute of African Languages and Cultures.

(11) A. N. Tucker, *The Comparative Phonetics of the Suto-Chwana Group of Bantu Languages.* Longmans, Green & Co., 1929.

(12) R. A. C. Oliver, 'Psychological and Pedagogical Considerations in the making of Textbooks', in *Africa*, iii, pp. 293–304.

(13) *The New Script and its Relation to the Languages of the Gold Coast.* Published by the Crown Agents for the Colonies, London, 1930.

REPRESENTATION OF SOUNDS

1. The Institute recommends that African languages should be written on a Romanic basis according to the following scheme.

Consonants.

2. (i). **b, d, f, h, k, l, m, n, p, s, t, v, w, z** shall have their English values, subject to the General Principles mentioned in §§ 20–31, and to the following special conditions:

(a) When it is necessary to distinguish between aspirated and un-aspirated **p, t, k**, the simple letters shall be employed to represent the unaspirated sounds, and the aspirated sounds shall be represented by **ph, th, kh**. **ph** is thus to be pronounced as in *loop-hole* (and not as **f**), **th** as in *at home* (not as in *thin or then*), **kh** as in *back-hand*.

(b) When it is necessary to distinguish between dental or alveolar **t** and **d** and retroflex (cerebral) **t, d**, the ordinary letters shall be used for the dental or alveolar sounds and the special letters **ṭ, ḍ** for the retroflex sounds. (Alveolar consonants are those formed by pressing the tongue-tip against the teeth-ridge, while the retroflex consonants are those which have the tongue-tip placed somewhat further back, so that it touches the roof of the mouth just behind the teeth-ridge or even further back still.) In Ewe the words **du** (town) and **ḍu** (powder), **da** (snake) and **ḍa** (hair) must be distinguished.

(ii) **g** shall have its hard value as in *get, go.*

r shall stand for the rolled lingual (tongue-tip) **r** of Scottish pronunciation or for the fricative **r** of Southern English.

x shall be used to represent the Scotch sound of *ch* in *loch* (the German *ach*-sound). When in any language the German *ich*-sound occurs in addition to the *ach*-sound, and the use of the two is determined by the character of the neighbouring vowel, both can be written with **x**.

y shall have its consonantal value as in *you, yet.*

ty, dy, ny, ly, sy, zy may be used to represent palatal **t, d, n, l, s, z**.

ky, gy may be used to represent palatal or 'fronted' **k, g**.

When a palatal consonant is preceded by a vowel, a kind of i-sound can often be heard between the two. This arises from the palatal character of the consonant and is an unavoidable 'glide'; thus the sound-group **anya** is often heard as **ainya** and has therefore been written **ainya** by some authors. But as this **i** is only the 'on-glide' to the palatal consonant and not an independent sound, it is not necessary or advisable to write it; the group should be written **anya** not **ainya**.

kp, gb shall be used for the labio-velar consonants of many Sudanic languages.

(iii) It is recommended that the following special consonant letters be used to supplement the ordinary Roman letters (subject to General Principles, § 31):

ŋ for the 'velar *n*', i.e. for the sound of *ng* in English *sing*, German *singen*.

ƒ for 'bilabial *f*', as in Ewe ƒu (bone), ƒo (to beat), which have to be distinguished from **fu** (feather), **fo** (to tear off). The symbol **f** has also been suggested instead of ƒ.

ʋ for 'bilabial *v*', i.e. the German sound of *w* in *schweben, schwimmen*. In Ewe the words ʋu (boat), ʋə (python) have to be distinguished from **vu** (to tear), **və** (to be finished).

ʃ for the English sound of *sh*, French *ch*, German *sch*.

ʒ for the English sound of *s* in *pleasure*, French *j*. The symbol ɟ has also been recommended for this sound.

ɣ for the 'voiced velar fricative' sound as in the colloquial pronunciation of *g* in German *Lage*.

' for the 'glottal stop', as in Hausa a'a (no).

(iv) It is recommended that the Affricate Consonants be represented by groups of two letters thus: **pf** as in German *hüpfen*, **bv** the corresponding voiced sound, **ts** as the German *z*, **dz** the corresponding voiced sound, **tʃ** the sound of English *ch*, **dʒ** the sound of English *j*. In some cases it is advisable to dispense with **tʃ** and **dʒ** and use the single letters **c** and **j** in their place.

(v) It is recommended that consonants pronounced with simultaneous 'glottal stop' be represented thus: **p', t', k', s', ts'**, &c.; e.g. Hausa **k'ofa** (door). It seems preferable to write the ' before the **y** in the combination of ' and **y** occurring in Hausa, as in **'ya'ya** (children).

(vi) *Implosive Sounds.* Implosive sounds are consonants of plosive nature formed by a sucking in of the air.[1] In many languages glottal closure accompanies an implosive consonant, but the exact nature of the sound is not yet definitely known in every case. To represent the peculiar character of these sounds, the ordinary letters preceded by an apostrophe are recommended: thus **'b, 'd, 'g**.

It frequently happens that a language contains only one implosive sound, namely implosive *b*; for such a case the special letter ɓ is recom-

---

[1] The sucking in is often very weak.

mended. The letter **ɗ** is recommended for use in those languages where implosive *d* also occurs.

In many dialects of Ibo an implosive *b* is found, while in other dialects the corresponding sound is **gb**. For Union Ibo the spelling **gb** has been adopted, because this notation is used in neighbouring languages and in some of the existing Ibo literature.

(vii) *Dental Sounds.* In the new orthographies for Bari, Nuer, Dinka, Shilluk, and other Sudanic languages where the distinction between dental **t, d, n** and alveolar **t, d, n** is found, the notation **th, dh, nh** has been adopted for the dental sounds. Such a device is only possible in languages which do not contain aspirated **t**.

(viii) *Lateral Sounds.* A decision is likely to be reached in South Africa itself in the near future as to the writing of the lateral sounds and clicks which occur in South African languages. We therefore give here only the present spelling and the letters suggested by Dr. C. M. Doke.

Present Spelling.	*Doke.*	
tl	tl	for laterally exploded **t**.
tlh	tlh	for aspirated **tl**.
hl	⁜	for lateral **s** (voiceless fricative **l**).
dhl	ⅼ	for lateral **z** (voiced fricative **l**).

The current use of **hl** and **dhl** to represent single sounds is far from satisfactory. In comparison with this Dr. Doke's suggestions, even though they introduce two new letters, are an improvement.

(ix) *Clicks.* The letters at present in use in South Africa to represent clicks are:

    c for the dental click
    q for the retroflex click
    x for the lateral click.

There exist also the following click-combinations:

c	ch	nc	nch	gc	ŋc	ŋgc
q	qh	nq	nqh	gq	ŋq	ŋgq
x	xh	nx	nxh	gx	ŋx	ŋgx

(Here **nc, nq, nx** indicate n followed by a click, while **ŋc, ŋq, ŋx** denote clicks completely nasalized throughout.)

As the letters **c** and **x** are used in other languages to represent quite different sounds, and as the clicks are sounds of a very special nature, it has been suggested that special signs should be used for them. The following letters have been recommended:

    ʇ for **c**
    ɕ for **q**
    ƅ for **x**

It should be noted, however, that the only important languages containing clicks are found in South Africa. Moreover, even if the new symbols for the clicks were adopted, it would still be necessary to use the letters g and ŋ in special conventional senses differing from those which they have in other languages, namely g for denoting voice, and ŋ for denoting nasalization (not a separate nasal consonant).

It is therefore doubtful whether in these circumstances the introduction of new symbols for the clicks themselves is feasible.[1]

In Nama, a dialect of Hottentot, other symbols for clicks have been used for some time. These are:

    / for the dental click;
    ≠ for the alveolar click;
    /̣ for the retroflex click;
    // for the lateral click.

As Nama is a language of little importance and somewhat removed from the other languages in which clicks occur, it will no doubt be best not to alter the existing spelling.

(x) *Labialization.* In the new alphabet for the Shona dialects the letters ş and ʐ have been adopted to represent labialized s and z.

A symbol seems desirable for 'front labialization' which plays an important part in the grammar of the languages of the Suto-Chwana group. Tucker has suggested ɥ for this purpose (see *Suggestions for the Spelling of Transvaal Sesuto*, pp. 15–18).

Vowels.

3. The vowel letters a, e, i, o, u shall have the so-called 'Italian' values. In cases where it is necessary to distinguish between a 'close' e and an 'open' e,[2] the letter e shall represent the close vowel and the special letter ɛ shall be used for the open vowel. And when it is necessary to distinguish between a 'close' o and an 'open' o[3], the letter o shall represent the close vowel and the special letter ɔ shall be used for the open vowel.

4. When a language contains a 'middle' o in addition to a close o and an open o, as in Ibo, the letter ɵ is recommended to represent the 'middle' o.

5. *Central Vowels.* There exist vowels of a 'neutral' or intermediate character, which are neither 'front' (like i, e) nor 'back' (like u, o). Such a sound is the first vowel in the English words *about, along.* There are numerous varieties of central vowels: some have lip-rounding and others

---

[1] In writing Zulu and Xosa, if x is retained to represent the lateral click, it has been suggested that χ be used to denote the 'velar fricative' (the Scotch *loch*-sound).

[2] As between the French *é* and *è*.

[3] As between the French vowels in *Beaune* and *bonne*.

have not; some are nearer to the front series and are therefore more e-like, while others are nearer to the back series and are more o-like.

6. When a language contains only one central vowel and this is e-like, the letter ə is recommended for representing it. The letter o with the diacritic mark ˙˙ , thus ö, is recommended for the representation of an o-like central vowel. When in any language there are several central vowels which must be distinguished, it is difficult to avoid the use of diacritic marks. For example, in Nuer besides o, ə, and a there are three central vowels which cannot well be represented otherwise than by ö, ɔ̈, and ä.

Diphthongs.

7. It is recommended that diphthongs be represented by groups of letters, e.g. ai, ɛi, ei, au, əi. Ya and wa might also be regarded as diphthongs and could be written ia, ua, &c. But as the spellings ya and wa are in common use, their retention is recommended.

Nasalization.

8. It is recommended that nasalized vowels be represented by the sign ˜ placed over the vowel-letter.

9. It is not necessary in every case to indicate the nasalization of a vowel, particularly when a nasal consonant (m, n, ny, ŋ) precedes or follows it. Even in some cases where no nasal consonant is present the nasal sign can be omitted. For example, in Mende the word for 'in' is pronounced hũ, but as no other word occurs in the language in any way resembling it—i.e. there is no hu—there can be no doubt about the meaning. For this reason, and because the word is such a common one, it has been decided to leave out the nasalization mark in this word.

10. Good illustrations as to when and how far the use of nasalization marks can be omitted will be found in the *New Ga Primer, Teachers' Handbook*, by C. P. Moir, Chapter I, Notes on the new Ga Script (London, 1929).

11. The use hitherto made in certain languages of the letter n to indicate nasalization is not to be recommended, as it undoubtedly leads to mis-understanding.

Length.

12. It is recommended that long or doubled sounds be represented by doubling the letter. This applies to both consonants and vowels. Examples: Luganda **siga** (sow (verb)), **sigga** (scorpion); Akan **əmã** (he gives), **əmmã** (he does not give); Ewe **godo** (yonder), **godoo** (around), **fa** (to be cool), **faa** (freely).

13. In some cases, especially where the lengthening of a vowel can be used for expressing two different meanings, the mark   following the letter may be used to denote length.

14. Vowel-length, like nasalization, need not always be marked. It will suffice to mark it in those cases where vowel-length is the only method of distinguishing words otherwise alike in all respects, but which differ in meaning or in grammatical usage.

Tones.

15. In books for Africans, tones, generally speaking, need only be marked when they have a grammatical function, or when they serve to distinguish words alike in every other respect; and even then they may be sometimes omitted when the context makes it quite clear which word is intended. As a rule, it will suffice to mark the high or the low tone only.

16. For marking tones an accent above the vowel is recommended: thus high tone á, low tone à. Rising and falling tones may be represented, if necessary, by ǎ and â respectively, and mid tone by ā̇. Examples: Ewe mí (we), mi (you, pl.); lé (seize), le (be), Efik mî (me), mí (here), mi (my), efé (shed), efe (flying squirrel), éfě (which (interrog.)), éfě (it flies). (The syllables here unmarked have low tones.)

17. Professor D. Jones recommends the following more comprehensive system of tone marks: ā for a high-level tone, a̱ for a low-level tone, á for a high-rising tone, a̱ for a low-rising tone, à for a high-falling tone, a̱ for a low-falling tone, â for a rise-fall, and ǎ for a fall-rise.

18. This system may be recommended for those languages in which a more precise method of tone-marking is necessary, and for scientific purposes. In certain languages, e.g. the Kru-group, even these tone-marks are not sufficient to show the whole tonal system of the language. It should be stated once more, however, that this Memorandum is concerned with the representation of tones only in so far as their marking is necessary for the understanding of the African.

Table of Sounds.

19. The letters recommended by the Institute are classified and set out systematically in the Sound Chart on p. 15.

GENERAL PRINCIPLES
DEFINITIONS
1. Phonemes.

20. It often happens that two distinct sounds occur in a language, but the Native is not aware that they are different, or at most regards one of them as an unimportant variety of the other. This happens where one of the sounds occurs only in certain positions in connected speech, while the other never occurs in those positions.

21. Thus in English the k's in *keep* and *collar* are different sounds, but the use of these sounds is determined by the following vowel. Hence we regard

	Bi-labial	Labio-dental	Dental and Alveolar	Post-alveolar	Retroflex (Cerebral)	Palatal	Velar	Laryngal
CONSONANTS								
Explosive	p b		t d		ʈ ɖ	ty dy ky gy	k g	ʼ
Implosive	ɓ		ɗ					
Affricate	pf bv		ts dz	tʃ dʒ (= c j)			kx	
Nasal	m		n			ny	ŋ	
Lateral — Explosive			tl dl					
Lateral — Fricative			ɬ ɮ					
Lateral — Frictionless			l			ly		
Rolled and Flapped			r					
Fricative	f ʋ	f v	s z	ʃ ʒ		sy zy	x ɣ	h
Semi-vowel	w					y	(w)	
VOWELS								
Close	(u)					i	ʉ u	
Half-close	(o)					e	o	
Half-open	(ə)					ɛ	e	
Open							a	

them as two varieties of **k**. The same applies to the **k**'s in the French *qui*, *quoi*, and the German *Kiel*, *Kuh*.

22. Again, there are languages in which the sound **ŋ** occurs only in the groups **ŋk, ŋg, ŋw, ŋh** but not in any other circumstances. In such a language the **ŋ** may be regarded as a variety of **n**, and these combinations can be written **nk, ng, nw, nh**. For instance, the *n* in the Italian *banca*, *lungo* has the sound **ŋ**; but since **ŋ** does not occur in Italian as an independent sound (e. g. before a vowel), it may be regarded as a variety of **n**. On the contrary, in English and German, **ŋ** is not a variety of **n**, because both occur in identical positions; compare English *sin, sing* (phonetically **sin, siŋ**), German *sinnen, singen* (phonetically **zinən, ziŋən**).

23. There exist languages and dialectal variants of languages showing a tendency to give the velar pronunciation to every final nasal consonant, i. e. to substitute **ŋ** for every final **m** or **n**. If the pronunciation with **m** and **n** exists and **ŋ** is not found as a separate phoneme, it is better to write **m** and **n** and ignore the velar pronunciation.

24. If, on the other hand, **ŋ** is found in a language as a separate phoneme, it is recommended that the sound should be written **ŋ** wherever it occurs, that is to say not only before vowels but also before **k, g,** &c.

25. In Zulu there exist a 'close' **e** and an 'open' **e**. These sounds are, however, used in accordance with a certain principle of vowel harmony. Therefore they may for practical purposes be regarded as one speech-unit in Zulu, and may be written with the single letter **e**. In the Akan language of West Africa the **w** in **wu, wo,** and **wɔ** is quite a distinct sound from the **w** in **wi, we,** and **wɛ**, but as the use of the two sounds is determined by the following vowel, they may be considered for practical purposes as one. In Kikuyu the sound **g** only occurs in the group **ŋg**, but the related sound **ɣ** occurs in other positions though never after **ŋ**; **g** and **ɣ** may, therefore, be treated as a single entity in Kikuyu. In Chwana a **d**-like variety of **l** is used before **i** and **u**, but an ordinary **l** is used before all other vowels. The distinction is negligible from the point of view of the Natives.

26. The term *Phoneme* is used to denote any small family of sounds which may be regarded as a single entity for reasons such as those applying to the above examples.

27. In very many cases phonemes consist of only one sound. Thus *phoneme* and *sound* are identical in the case of English **f, m, n, v**, since the pronunciation of these sounds is not appreciably affected by neighbouring sounds in the sentence.

28. It is phonemes that serve to distinguish one word from another in every language. Thus the phonemes **n** and **ŋ** distinguish words in English and German, as mentioned above. Close and open **e** and **o** (i. e. **e** and **ɛ**, **o** and **ɔ**) distinguish words in French, most West African languages, Chwana,

Suto, and many other languages in other parts of Africa; they are separate phonemes in those languages.

2. *Diaphones.*

29. Very often different speakers of the same language pronounce the same word in somewhat different ways. For instance, the value of the *a* in *bad* is different in different parts of England. In French and in German *r* is sounded by some with the tip of the tongue and by others with the uvula.

30. The term *Diaphone* is used to denote a normal sound together with the variants of it heard from different speakers of the same language.

PRINCIPLES OF ORTHOGRAPHY

31. The following general principles should be observed in fixing the orthography of any particular language:

(1) The orthography of a given language should be based on the principle of one letter for each phoneme of that language. This means that whenever two words are distinguished in sound they must also be distinguished in orthography.

(2) The existence of diaphones must be recognized and allowed for. Thus Fante speakers of Akan pronounce the syllable **di** as **dzi** and **ti** as **tsi**; but the orthography **di, ti** is adequate for covering both pronunciations. Again, the Hausa **f** is pronounced in some dialects as labio-dental **f** and in others as bi-labial **ƒ** and in others as **p**; but the letter **f** can be used in orthography with the necessary conventions as to dialectal pronunciations.

(3) It may sometimes be convenient to depart from a strictly phonetic system, in order to avoid writing a word in more than one way. Thus it is better to write in Luganda **soka oleke** (wait a bit), although the pronunciation is **sok oleke**. Similarly, it is better to write in Akan **ɔ hwɛ no** (he saw him), although in many districts the final **o** is not pronounced. Again, it is preferable to write always the same form of the Akan word **hwɛ**, in spite of the fact that it is actually pronounced **hwe** when followed by a syllable containing **i** or **u** (as in **ɔ hwɛ mu**).

Similar considerations hold good for numerous other cases of vowel harmony in Akan and in other languages.

It must, however, be very definitely stated that the rules governing vowel harmony and assimilation in Akan and other languages are often numerous and complicated. It is not possible to formulate them once for all by means of a simple rule. The extent to which these phenomena should be reflected in current spelling must depend upon the special phonetic and grammatical usages of each particular language.

(4) As a concession to existing usage an ordinary Roman letter may sometimes be used in place of one of the special new letters, when the
sound denoted by the Roman letter does not occur in the language.
Thus f may be used instead of ſ in writing Sechwana, because the
labio-dental f does not occur in that language. Similarly, s may be
used instead of ſ in writing Oshikuanyama because an ordinary s
doés not occur in that language. Again, if every t in a language is
retroflex, the letter t can be used to represent it; it is not necessary
to employ the special symbol for the retroflex sound. In Hausa
there exists a **ts** combined with glottal stop (**ts'**); this sound is
replaced in some dialects by **s'** and in others by **t'**. As, however,
the language has no **ts** *without* glottal stop, it is recommended that
the sound be written simply **ts** without marking the glottal stop.

CAPITAL LETTERS AND WRITTEN FORMS

32. A table is subjoined showing the printed capital forms of the most
important of the special letters, also the handwriting forms of both small
and capital letters. Information as to the precise forms of other letters may
be had on application to the Institute.

Roman.	Italic.	Written Forms.	Roman.	Italic.	Written Forms.
a A	a A	a a	l L	l L	l L
b B	b B	b B	m M	m M	m M
ɓ Ɓ	ɓ Ɓ	ɓ ɦ	n N	n N	n n
c C	c C	c C	ŋ Ŋ	ŋ Ŋ	ŋ ŋ
d D	d D	d D	o O	o O	o O
ɗ Đ	ɗ Đ	ɗ or d Đ	ɔ Ɔ	ɔ Ɔ	ɔ ɔ
e E	e E	e e	p P	p P	p p
ɛ Ɛ	ɛ Ɛ	ɛ ɛ	r R	r R	r or ɾ R
ə Ə	ə ə	ə ə	s S	s S	s or ſ ſ
f F	f F	f f	ſ Σ	ſ Σ	ſ ſ
ſ Ƒ	ſ Ƒ	ſ ſ	t T	t T	t T
g G	g G	g g	u U	u U	u u
ɣ Ɣ	ɣ Ɣ	ɣ ɣ	v V	v V	v V or ʋ Ʋ
h H	h H	h H	ʋ Ʋ	ʋ Ʋ	ʋ ʋ or ʋ Ʋ
x X	x X	x X	w W	w W	w W
i I	i I	i i	y Y	y Y	y y
j J	j J	j j	z Z	z Z	z Z
k K	k K	k K	ʒ Ʒ	ʒ Ʒ	ʒ ʒ

ALPHABETICAL ORDER OF THE LETTERS

The following is recommended as the alphabetical order of the principal letters:

a b ɓ c d ɗ e ɛ ə f ƒ ɡ ɣ h x i j k l m n ŋ o ɔ p r s ʃ t u v ʋ w y z ʒ '

Nasal vowels should follow ordinary vowels, and central vowels should follow nasal vowels, thus: o õ ö. Other new letters should follow those from which they are derived: thus ɗ should follow d, and ş should follow s. If special letters are introduced to represent clicks, it is suggested that they be placed at the end of the alphabet.

It is recommended that in vocabularies and dictionaries words beginning with digraphs (dy, dz, dʒ, kp, ts, tʃ, &c.) be placed in separate groups following all the words beginning with simple d, k, t, &c.

Names of the Consonant Letters.

b	ɓ	c	d	ɗ	f	ƒ	ɡ	ɣ	h	x	j	k	l	m	n
be	ɓa	ce	de	ɗa	ef	if	ga	ɣe	ha	ex	je	ke	el	em	en
		(tʃe)									(dʒe)				

ŋ	p	r	s	ʃ	t	v	ʋ	w	y	z	ʒ	'
iŋ	pe	ra	es	iʃ	te	ve	ʋi	wa	ya	ze	ʒi	a'a

SPECIMENS OF THE RECOMMENDED ORTHOGRAPHY

(The specimens illustrating the languages marked * are taken from books in which the new orthography is employed.)

Akan.*

Ɔdɔ dwo ne ani, ne yam ye, ɔdɔ nyɛ ahõɔyaw, ɔdɔ nyɛ ahoahoa, ɛŋhoraŋ, ɛnyɛ nehõ sɛnea ɛmfata, ɛŋhwehwɛ nea ɛyɛ ne aŋkasa de, ne bo ŋhaw no, ɛmfa bone ŋhyɛ ne yam, ne ani nye nea ɛntɛ̃ɛ hõ, na ɛne nokware ani gye, etie a ade nnyina, egye ade nnyina di, enya ade nnyina mu anidaso. Ɔdɔ to ntwa da. Na afei gyidi, ɔdɔ, anidaso na etrã hɔ, na ɔdɔ na ɛne mu kɛse.

(From 'Ɛha amanne kwaŋ so aware Ɛso Ɗhyira', p. 7).

Bambara.

Kŋo sogo bee yi i nyogõ la dye k u be dlo dõ u ko sogo o sogo bee ka na ni nyo more more ye. Sogo bee nana n ata ye. Suruku ba e o me mi ŋke a y ala muru ba ta, a bina a da la dia la.

Chwana.

Tlhaloxanyɔ ya tlou xoŋwe yane ekete ke ya motho. Betʃwana ba boxolo-xolo bare tlou ekile ya foloxɛla mo nokeŋ ya Sampisi, ya fitlha ya nwa.

Erile e santse e nwa, ya utlwa kwena e e kapa ka selɔpɔ, ere e e xɔxɛla mo metsiŋ. Kefa tlou e inola kwena, e e tʃholetsa ka selɔpɔ, e e kakamara, e e isa ko naxeŋ, kxakalakxakala le noka. Erile e fitlha ko likakeŋ ya baya kwena fa fatshe, yare: 'kana orile oa m polaya? Sala jalo hɛ, ke bɔnɛ xore a o tla tshela kwa ntlɛ xa metse!'

Duala.

Ngɔkɔlɔ na dibobɛ ba ta dikɔm, ba yenga babɔ babanɛ ponda yɛsɛ. Nde ba ta ba ja o ekwali bunya bɔɔ, nde na ngɔkɔlɔ e kwalanɛ dibobɛ na : A dikɔm lam la ndolo, na malangwea nde oa na mbalɛ, bato ba si masenga, be ndɔki.

(From a text in *Africa*, vol. ii, p. 72, Jan. 1929.)

Efik.

Tiŋ enyin tim se uŋwana oro, neŋere tiene enye; ke ntre ke afo edikut inua-otop oro; tuak, ndien mɔ eyeteme fi se afo edinamde. Ndien ŋkokut ke ndap mi nte owo oro otibide itɔk efege. Ekem enye ika-ikaha kaŋa anyan usuŋ ikpɔŋ ufɔk esie; ndien kadaŋemi ŋwan esie ye nditɔ esie ekutde, mɔ etɔŋɔ ndifiori ŋkot enye, ete afiak edi; edi enye esin nuenubɔk ke utɔŋ, efege itɔk, ete, 'Uwem! uwem! nsi-nsi uwem!'

Ewe.*

Asime. Asi ɖina le tefe geɖewo le ŋkeke ene sia ŋkeke ene megbe. Ame geɖewo va foa ʃu ɖe afima. Wotsɔa bli, te, mɔli, agbeli, fofoŋ, fetri, agbitsa, atadi kple kutsetse bubu geɖewo, ɖetifu, de, nɛfi, amidzẽ, nɛmi, yɔkumi kple nu bubu geɖewo va dzrana. Ga si woxɔna la, wotsɔnɛ ʃlea avɔ, ɖeti, atama, sukli, kple ŋudowɔnu siwo wohiã. Ðeviwo lɔ̃a asimedede.

(From 'Eʋegbegbalẽxɛxlẽ na Gɔmedzelawo', p. 64.)

Ga.*

Dʒata ko hi ʃi yɛ dʒeŋ a·hu. Agbɛnɛ egbɔ hewɔ lɛ enyẽẽ emomo hewalɛ na· doŋŋ. Enɛ hewɔ lɛ eyakã ʃi yɛ ebu lɛ mli akɛ ehe mi· ye. Koloi lɛ ba· eŋo ekome-kome ni amɛbasra· lɛ yɛ ebu lɛ mli. Osɔ le enɛ fẽ hewɔ lɛ ete koni eyasra dʒata helatʃɛ nɛ. Beni ete lɛ ebotee bu lɛ mli. Edamɔ sɛ ʃoŋŋ ni ebi dʒata lɛ akɛ, 'Helatʃɛ! te oyɔ teŋŋ?'

(From the *New Ga Primer*, by C. P. Moir, Part 2, p. 24.)

Ila.

Uʃesu udi kwizɛulu, nadiile iʒina dyako, nabuzize buɔneki bwako, nalu- tʃitwe luzando lwako anʃi ano ubudi kwizeuḷu. Σidyo nʃi tubula utupe bwasunu. Utulekelɛle milandu, bubɔna mbu tubalekelɛle kale obadi milandu kudi uswɛ. Utatuenʒa mu kutepaulwa, utuʋune ku bubiabe. Ukuti buɔneki mbu bwako, iinsana, obulɛmu, ʃikwense o ʃikwense.

Kikuyu.

Idɛ wito we igoro, reetwa reaku nereamorɔɔ. Odamaki waku ookɛ. Ɔ orea wɛndɛtɛ wɛ, newekagwɔ goko de, ɔ ta orea wekagwɔ kou igoro. Tohɛ omode iriɔ ciito cia gotoigana. Na otorɛkɛrɛ madire maito, ɔ ta orea idue torɛkagera area mare na madire maito. Na ndogatotwarɛ magɛriɔ-ine, nɔ kohɔnɔkia otohɔnɔkagiɛ ooru-ine.

Lokele.

Bowase atolimba ɔnɔkɔ.
Mbuu esoofeta.
Bosokola ngwa nda liulu, inde koicakae anyo.
Itɔɔ kwa ʃa ombolo wa koba.
Loo loca okuki, angowa ae kosinga.

Mende.*

Mu gɔnɛi gbe, ngi mayomboi manyɛingɔ, tɛli lɔ hu kɛ kolei.
Ngi yamɛisia gbe kea ta vo dão.
A kulɔlɔ a foloi kɛ kpindii.
Ta hani manɛma tɛnga nyina mia.
Ta hei kpɛ, ngi wolii mia a sɛsia.
Ngi longɔ i ye hanii hou ngi lenga va.
(From 'Koyɛima kaa Golɔisia', Yehalayɛi, p. 25.)

Nyanja.

Mphepo yakumpoto ndidzua zinali kumenyana, imodzi yaizo inati ine ndiri wamphamvu kupambana iwe, ndipo inzace inati iai ine ndiri wamphamvu kupambana iwe. Koma zinaona mlendo mmodzi alikupita anabvala ntsaru yorimba ndithu, zinapaŋgana ndani abvule ntsaru yamlendo uyu adzaitanidwa wamkulu kupambana mnzace. Mphepo yakumpoto inaomba kwambiri koma iŋgakhale inaomba ndithu, mlendo uja anagwiritsa ntsaru yace. Ndipo mphepo yakumpoto inalephera kumbvula ntsaru, ndipo dzua linaturuka ndikutentha ndithu. Mlendo anamasula ntsaru yace ndikucotsa yontse, ndipo mphɛpo yakumpoto inati wanditha ndiwe mfumu.

Pedi.

Moleta ŋwedi o leta lefsifsi.
Moruswana xe o tshela lefao o eletʃa o moŋ.
Pshiu tʃa tlou xa di pataxanywe.
Mpʃa e tala e bolaya ka xo tsoxɛla.
A e tswhe dibza.
Mokxola morithi xa se modudi wa ɔna.

Xa o tʃhaba pula o tʃhabe modumɔ; xa o tʃhaba marotholodi a pula, ea xonɛla. (Mma, tʃaka xe diapɥa se ʃetʃe; ke pɥhapɥha diatla, ka lesa tʃampholoxa ka maxetla.)[1]

*Shilluk.**

Ya yito ki gin dɔc. Agin? Ya yiti riŋo. Dɔc, kani yuk othal wa. Riŋo mi awany ki kɛli lum. Kani loth o yiejo nak. Yanythenho anaki yiec ma gir. Kɛtho wak dway yuk. Ya yito ki tɔŋ mia ma dɔc. Ya dwato bɛth ki loth anan. Gin cam athal? Ŋɛ! Dɛ wa bɛ cam. Wa ocamo anan.
(From 'Wanyo Kipa Tiiŋ Gwɛt' No. 1, p. 11.)

Shona (Zezuru Dialect).

Ruŋgano rwaTsuro naHamba. Ʋakafurirana kundocera tsime. Ȝino Tsuro akaramba. Hamba wakaenda kundotʂaga ʋanaΣumba. Ȝino ʋanaΣumba ʋakacera tsime. Ȝino Tsuro wakauya kuzoβa mvura. Akauya namadʼende ake. Akawana Hamba aripo. Akamuwona, akatiza.
Rimŋe zuʋa akawana Hamba akahwanda mumvura. Ȝino akadʼa kucera mvura. Hamba akaβata ruwoko rwaTsuro. Ȝino Tsuro akati, 'Rega kundiβata.' Tsuro akati, 'Rega, ndinokutʂagira huci.' Hamba waregera Tsuro. Ȝino Tsuro wakapa huci kunaΣumba. Tsuro wakati, 'Rega, nditaŋge ndakusuŋga sekuru'. Ȝino Tsuro wakayisa mabge muhuci. Akayisa mabge mukanwa maΣumba. Ȝino Tsuro wakasimuka oroʋa Σumba.

Shona (Karanga Dialect).

Σuro icinyeŋgere-ʃumba.
Rimŋe zuʋa ʃuro yakaʃoŋgana neʃumba, ikati, 'Sekuru munotʂakei?' Σumba ikati, 'Ndinovima.' Σuro ikati, 'Cihendei kugomo, muŋgondoʋata makaita majadʼa pamukwara wemhuka, ini ndigondodziŋge-mhuka mugomo, imi makagaridzira.' Nambera ʃuro inonyeŋgerɛ-ʃumba, kuti ʃumba igotakwa nebge rinokuŋguruswa mugomo neʃuro. Ȝino ʃumba yakandoʋatapo, ndokuhwa hurumatanda dziciʋirima dzicibvo-mugomo. Σumba ndokuʋata padʼiʋi, mabge aya ndokupfuʋura. Σumba ndokudzokera paya payasiyiwa neʃuro, ndokuʋata ʒe yakaita manedʼe. Ȝino ʃuro ndokuʋaŋga, ndokuti, 'Ndakaŋguʋa ndarubvira rwokuʋuraye-ʃumba!' Ȝino ikati icitore-βaŋga rokuʋuraye-ʃumba, ʃumba ndokuβate-ʃuro, mambaʋa ndokuwadzuka, ʃuro ndokutiza icidziŋgana neʃumba. Σuro ndokupinda mugwiriŋgwindi, ʃumba ndokuβato-mŋise weʃuro. Σuro ikati, 'Mandikoniwa maβato-mudzi!' Σumba ndokuregedza. Σuro ikati, 'Ohii, hamuzandikoniwa!' Ndokugara mumŋena kuʂika ʃumba yainda.

---

[1] In this sentence the symbol ɥ suggested by Tucker for 'front-labialization' is used provisionally (see Section 2 (x), p. 12).

Soso.

Woŋ fafe, naxaŋ na ariana, i xili xa sɛniyeŋ. I yamanɛ xa fa. I sago xa niŋa dunia ma, alɔ a niŋaxi ariana kɛnaxai. Woŋ ki to woŋma lɔxɔ o lɔxɔ doŋse ra. Anuŋ ixa woŋma fekobi kafari, alɔ woŋtaŋ nee kafarima kɛnaxai naxaŋ fekobi niŋa woŋ ra. Anuŋ i nama woŋ raso fekobi maniŋa. Kɔnɔ i xa woŋ rakisi fekobi ma. Katugu itaŋ naŋ gbe yamanɛ ra, anuŋ sɛmbɛ anuŋ yigi ra abada anuŋ abada.

Swahili.

Akanena yule mtume: 'Ee Muungu wangu, aliyecukua feza mtu mgine, na aliyeuawa mgine, amezulumiwa yule.' Mwenyiezi Muungu akamʃuʃia walii akamwambia: 'Wewe tazama ibada yako, na ukitaka mambo haya, si kazi yako.' Akamwambia: 'Baba yake yule wa kwanza alimnyaŋanya dinar alf katika mali za babae yule kijana, hamleta yule kijana kuja twaa mali ya babae. Na yule mcanja kuni alimua babae yule wa kwanza hamleta kijana kuja kutoa kisasi tya babae.' [1]

Temne.*

Hawa ɔ yi ro rɔ su.
A lɔkɔ o lɔkɔ ɔ ti kɔ ro karaŋde.
Hawa ɔ ti karaŋ akafa kɔtɔtɔkɔ kaake.
Ɔ karaŋ mump mɔfinɔ ɔ yema ŋa.
Anfɔm ŋa Hawa ɔ bɔnɛ ŋa tɔk karaŋ ka ɔwan kaŋaŋ.
Hawa ɔ karaŋ akafa ka ɔkas kɔŋ yi ɔya kɔŋ.
Aŋ yema yi ɔbana.

(From 'Atafa Takaraŋ ta Koyɛima', Kɔtɔtɔkɔ, p. 13).

Xosa.

Kwathi xa umoya wase zantsi wauphikisana ne laŋga ukußa ŋguwuphina onamanⱬa kußo ßoßaßini, kwa fika umhambi ambethe iŋgußo efudumeleyo. Ɓavumelana ukußa oŋgaqala a mendze umhambi ukußa alaɬe iŋgußo yakhe woßa woyisile. Utheke umoya wase zantsi wavuthuza ŋgawo oŋke amanⱬa awo, kwathi okukhona uvuthuzayo kwaßa kokukhona umhambi ayisonde-zayo iŋgußo yakhe. Ekupheleni umoya wase zantsi wancama. Laza ke lona ilaŋga la khanya ŋgokuʃuʃu, waza umhambi wayilaɬa iŋgußo. Wavumake umoya wase zantsi ukußa lilaŋga elinamanⱬa.

---

[1] In view of the fact that there are not many Swahili words containing ŋ imme-diately followed by a vowel, it is suggested that the sound-group ŋg be represented by the spelling **ng**. It would be more consistent, from the point of view of the native, to write it ŋg, but the use of **ng** has the advantage of involving less change from the orthography hitherto used.

Yoruba.

Ida li akɔ. Aroko tu ilɛ. Ɔmɔbirĩ wɛ ɔwɔ rɛ. Onile ra iʃu. Ki ɛ duro de wa nihĩyi titi awa o fi lɔ si ɔhũ. Ɖwɔ su adi. Apɔ̃ da ɛkɔ̃. Aŋwɔ aroko ro oko. Ɛ nyĩ fa kɛkɛ. Awa bɛ nyi. Alase se onjɛ. Σile mɛta ni yi. Mo ri ɛgbɔ̃. Ewurɛ jɛ koriko. Ɔrɔ otitɔ li o ŋsɔ. Ɖwɔ ŋlu agogo ile-ɛkɔ wa.

Zulu.

Aɓelungu ɓahamba ngemikhumbi, ɓayizingele. Ɓaphatha imikhonto eminingi emikhulu, enezintlenɠa, nezintambo nemiphongolo emingi. Ɓathi qedi ɓafike elwanɠe umkhomo uɓonakale, ɓasondela kaɫe ɓathekelezele intambo emkhontweni ɓawugwaze.

(Adapted from the version in Doke's *Phonetics of Zulu*, p. 279.)